The Responsibility of a Constitution for the Future

Rainer Arnold · Toni Fickentscher
Editors

The Responsibility of a Constitution for the Future

Contributions to the World Congress of the International Association of Constitutional Law in Johannesburg

Springer

Editors
Rainer Arnold
University of Regensburg
Regensburg, Germany

Toni Fickentscher
Amberg, Germany

ISBN 978-3-031-65295-0 ISBN 978-3-031-65296-7 (eBook)
https://doi.org/10.1007/978-3-031-65296-7

This Springer imprint is published by the registered company Springer Nature Switzerland AG
The registered company address is: Gewerbestrasse 11, 6330 Cham, Switzerland

Foreword

The decision of the World Congress of Constitutional Law to hold its December 2022 conference in Johannesburg was inspired, at least from a South African point of view. Not only did it underscore the twenty-fifth anniversary of the adoption of the country's liberatory Constitution, but the focus on "Constitutional Transformations" resonated with the aspirational dream articulated in its Preamble to:

- Heal the divisions of the past and establish a society based on democratic values, social justice, and fundamental human rights;
- Lay the foundations for a democratic and open society in which government is based on the will of the people and every citizen is equally protected by law;
- Improve the quality of life of all citizens and free the potential of each person; and
- Build a united and democratic South Africa able to take its rightful place as a sovereign state in the family of nations.

The privilege of hosting a prestigious body of jurisprudents who met to confer on pertinent issues of constitutional principle occasioned a sense of déjà vu in those of us who had been party to the great national adventure that saw South Africa segue from the edge of civil war into a negotiated constitutional democracy. During the 1980s the conventional wisdom was that mounting tension between the increasingly repressive apartheid regime and the increasingly belligerent liberation movements was destined to end in a bloody racial conflagration.

But when wiser counsel prevailed and the political leadership gathered around the negotiating table, the law stepped in to play the vital task it has performed since time immemorial—to speak reason even in the clamor of war, to reconcile opposing interests, and to afford to each what is due. While the political dynamics provided the main thrust, the teams of skilled and dedicated legal advisers gave crucial direction in the negotiations, isolating and resolving sticking points and maintaining the momentum of the process. Throughout, the facilitating context was multilateral adherence to the Rule of Law.

Likewise, when the popularly elected Constitutional Assembly settled down to build the structure of the new state, the Rule of Law was both the foundation and the leitmotif. As importantly, a crucial feature of the grand pact forged in the negotiations was that the integrity of the draft constitution would be determined by a specially created body, the Constitutional Court of South Africa. That was a judicial body, its members were lawyers, and their discipline was the law. It was accordingly fitting—and poignantly moving for me, a former member of that Court—that a quarter of a century later the World Congress of Constitutional Law made time in its overbusy schedule to honor Constitution Hill, the home of the Constitutional Court, with a visit.

It is in my respectful opinion also particularly important for us South Africans that the substance of the conference and its consolidated wisdom are to be perpetuated in book form. Even for those who were able to attend on each day, it was possible to participate in only a fraction of the proceedings. The opportunity to have to hand and to study the whole corpus of the learning exchanged during deliberations is invaluable. I am confident that this will make a significant contribution to a vitally important field of knowledge.

I welcome this opportunity to express thanks, not only my own but also those of constitutional lawyers generally, to all whose efforts have made this publication possible. Its appearance is timely when even in some so-called "mature democracies," democracy is encountering a headwind. Indeed, constitutionalism is under challenge worldwide, more particularly in younger democracies where disenchantment and cynicism are on the rise. May this publication prove a ringing endorsement of the values free people hold dear.

Johannesburg, South Africa
February 2023

Johann Kriegler

Introduction

The constitution is the permanent basic order of a state, which establishes institutions and determines the basic values of the constitutional order. As a rule, constitutions are intended to apply for an indefinite period of time and remain effective throughout their existence. They are "living instruments" that must take into account the changes in social reality that take place over time. The constitution has an inherent dynamic that ensures that the functional goal of a constitutional norm is maintained through adequate adaptation to the changing reality, i.e., to the changing object of the norm. The constitution is the normative framework for policy and thus for legislation throughout the entire period of the state community's existence. The policy that concretizes the constitution only implements good governance if it takes the future into account in the necessary way when shaping the present, i.e., if it considers the effects on the future and the predictable needs of the future. Politics is obliged to consider the well-being of the community from an overall perspective, not just from the present. Looking into the future is obviously associated with uncertainties and requires a forecast that is as well-founded as possible.

These statements relating to politics also apply to the constitution, which forms the basis and framework for politics. The constitutional structural provisions of a state (democracy, the rule of law, welfare state, etc.) are not only relevant for the present but are also clearly designed for the future. Particularly where the protection of important goods that must also be preserved in the future is concerned, the constitution's obligation to take adequate account of future generations is especially clear. As an example, Article 20a of the German Basic Law provides a paradigmatic statement according to which the foundations of human life, including those of future generations, are entrusted to the special protection of the constitution. But even without the existence of written guarantees for the future in a constitution, this responsibility for the future exists normatively.

This responsibility of a constitution for the future, for future generations, is a current internationally discussed issue of fundamental importance in constitutional law.

So far, this issue has been addressed from time and time again but has not yet received sufficient scientific attention. The current climate protection jurisprudence of the German Federal Constitutional Court has again given special impetus to the discussion of this issue. The conference in Johannesburg, the World Congress of the International Association for Constitutional Law (IACL), dealt with this issue in a comparative constitutional way in workshop number 26 (chairs: Rainer Arnold/Toni Fickentscher) and brought in the perspective of 13 authors from 10 countries (Europe North and Latin America as well as Central Asia).

This book comprises 13 contributions by internationally renowned constitutional lawyers, professors, presidents, and current or former judges of constitutional courts and supreme courts of the various countries.

The book is divided into two parts: the first examines basic general questions about the responsibility of the constitution for the future, mostly based on the example of one country. The second part includes contributions that deal with specific questions within the framework of the topic.

Prefaced by a foreword by Johann Kriegler, one of South Africa's best-known legal scholars, a former confidant of Nelson Mandela, Chairman of the Independent Electoral Commission of the First Democratic Elections in South Africa, and an early member of the Constitutional Court. He has played a major role in shaping South African legal thought. His foreword has given the workshop an internationally acclaimed flavor and is also significant for the appreciation of the book in South Africa and also in other countries.

The first contribution in the general section, written by the Vice-President of the Portuguese Constitutional Court, Prof. Gonçalo de Almeida Ribeiro, an internationally recognized legal theorist, analyzes and evaluates the conceptual foundations of the future responsibility of a constitution and is therefore particularly important as an introductory contribution.

The second contribution, written by Prof. Alan Bronfman-Vargas, Valparaiso/Chile, a former constitutional judge, clarifies further dogmatic foundations of the intergenerational relationship in constitutional law, with specific comparative reference to fundamental rights.

The third contribution by Prof. Andrzej Jackiewicz, Poland, examines the question of a constitution's responsibility for the future from the perspective of the constitutional normative structure, choosing the constitution of Poland as an example.

The fourth contribution, by Prof. Mirosław Granat, Cardinal Stefan Wyszynski University of Warsaw and former Polish constitutional judge, deals with the essential future orientation of constitutionalism from several angles regarding state obligations in the field of human rights, the concept of common good as expressed in Art. 1 of the Polish Constitution and the importance of liberal constitutionalism.

In the fifth contribution, the President of the Supreme Court of Estonia Villu Kõve and his coauthors Berit Aaviksoo and Mait Laaring address the constitutional protection of future generations in the field of fundamental rights, with reference to the Preamble of the Constitution of Estonia and its interpretation, especially with regard to the concept of "intergenerational solidarity."

The sixth contribution by Prof. Anna Rytel-Warzocha, University of Gdansk, Poland, deals with the constitutional rights of future generations and their judicial protection, using Poland as an example.

In the seventh contribution, Amanda L. Tyler, University of California, Berkeley School of Law, takes up the question, which has been discussed particularly vehemently in the United States, of whether the Constitution should be interpreted in the light of the time of its creation or the time of its current interpretation. Originalism stands here in contrast to contextualism, which views the Constitution as a living instrument. Only this second methodological position can adequately explain the future orientation of a constitution. Reference is made to the developments in U.S. constitutional law.

The eighth contribution by Prof. Tudorel Toader and Prof. Marieta Safta makes the future orientation of the constitution clear and, with comparative legal references focusing on Romanian constitutional law, points to the tension between the constitution's striving for stability and preservation on the one hand and the need for flexibility and adaptation on the other.

The second part of the book (articles 9–13) presents reflections on specific aspects that contribute to an understanding of the overall topic.

In the ninth article, the President of the Constitutional Court of Georgia, Prof. Merab Turava, and his coauthor George Lomtadze, examine the extent to which Georgia's constitutional jurisprudence is able to assert itself against the ordinary judiciary and thus ensure the uniform validity of Georgian constitutional law, an important aspect of the durability of a constitution for the future as well.

Ms. Vice-President Meergul Bobukeeva, Constitutional Court of the Kyrgyz Republic, contributes the tenth article, which deals with the formation and development of constitutional law in the Kyrgyz Republic. The future orientation of a concrete constitution becomes clear only from its historical development. Therefore, this historical insight into the development of the constitution in a young independent society is quite revealing.

The eleventh contribution was authored by Prof. Jörn Axel Kämmerer, Bucerius Law School, President of SIPE (Societas Iuris Publici Europaei), an expert in financial and capital market issues. His study deals with the role of central banks, which contribute significantly to shaping the future of a state, and this with repercussions on its constitutional order.

Ass. Prof. Dr. Ekaterini Iliadou, University of Athens, is the author of the twelfth contribution on the problems of climate protection and energy transition from the perspective of the European Union. This topic is essentially future-oriented and is determined by ordinary legislation conform to constitutional and EU law. The future orientation of the constitution which is realized to be an important part of these two areas is linked to the implementation by ordinary law in accordance with the supranational legal order. It can be seen that the future orientation of a constitution is also embedded in the precepts of international and supranational law.

The thirteenth contribution deals with social security law, also one of the central future areas of policy, which must be shaped in accordance with constitutional law and its responsibility for the future. Dr. Toni Fickentscher examines this with regard to German constitutional law.

The book, with the 13 contributions of Workshop 26 at the World Congress of the International Association for Constitutional Law (IACL) in Johannesburg, South Africa, provides insights into the intensively discussed problem of the responsibility of a constitution for the future from the perspective of authors from different countries, on dogmatic and area-related aspects of the topic.

Rainer Arnold
Toni Fickentscher

Contents

Specific Studies

General Reflections

General Reflections

General Reflections

Between a Rock and a Hard Place: Constitutional Theory and Intergenerational Equity

Gonçalo de Almeida Ribeiro

Abstract Constitutional theory may approach the subject of intergenerational equity from two main and quite different directions. The first is the so-called intergenerational paradox of constitutionalism, which concerns the authority of a constitution-making generation to bind future generations to its political choices through a combination of justiciable constitutional provisions and a relatively rigid procedure of constitutional amendment. The second is a plea to use constitutional law to protect the rights of future generational cohorts or to secure the commitment to sustainable development, given the diagnosed short-termist bias of ordinary processes of collective decision-making. Alas, these two are on an ever-recurring collision course: while the most promising way to dissolve or at least manage the intergenerational paradox is to limit the scope of constitutional choices, particularly when it comes to substantive matters of rights and policy that are deeply divisive in a pluralist society, the short-termist bias of democratic arrangements implies that intergenerational equity can only be realized through robust constitutional safeguards. In a nutshell, addressing one of the sides of the problem increases the size of the other. I shall argue that the only way out of this dilemma is to think of future generations as an endangered minority for the purposes of judicial review of majoritarian legislation and to conceive an architecture of decision-making that enables the correction of generational externalities.

This paper was previously published in E-Pública: Public Law Journal, vol. 9, Issue 3, 2022, 4–25. Sections 2, 4, and 5 draw on what I wrote in Gonçalo de Almeida Ribeiro, "A Constitutional Theory of Intergenerational Equity", in Luís Brites Pereira, Maria Eugénia Mata & Miguel Rocha de Sousa (org.), Economic Globalization and Governance: Essays in Honor of Jorge Braga de Macedo, Springer, 2020, pp. 281–301.

G. de Almeida Ribeiro (✉)
Catholic University of Portugal, Lisbon, Portugal
e-mail: gmvaribeiro@gmail.com

R. Arnold and T. Fickentscher (eds.), *The Responsibility of a Constitution for the Future*, https://doi.org/10.1007/978-3-031-65296-7_1

1 Introduction

Constitutional theory may approach the subject of intergenerational equity from two main and quite different directions. The first is the so-called intergenerational paradox of constitutionalism, which concerns the authority of a constitution-making generation to bind future generations to its political choices through a combination of justiciable constitutional provisions and a relatively rigid procedure of constitutional amendment. The second is a plea to use constitutional law to protect the rights of future generational cohorts or secure the commitment to sustainable development, given the diagnosed short-termist bias of ordinary processes of collective decision-making in representative democracies. Alas, these two are on an ever-recurring collision course: while the most promising way to dissolve or at least manage the intergenerational paradox is to limit the scope of constitutional choices, particularly when it comes to substantive matters of rights and policy that are deeply divisive in a pluralist society, the short-termist bias of democratic arrangements implies that intergenerational equity can only be realized through robust constitutional safeguards. In a nutshell, addressing one of the sides of the problem increases the size of the other.

It seems almost pedantic to stress that these worries, in spite of their grand theoretical appearance, are of obvious interest to any serious engagement with climate change from a constitutional perspective. Indeed, climate policy is in many ways the paradigm issue of intergenerational equity, for addressing it implies a trade-off between, on the one hand, the present-day interest in maintaining a carbon-dependent lifestyle or avoiding the undoubtedly heavy costs of speeding towards a carbon–neutral economy and, on the other hand, the longer-term—although not by any means all that far-removed in time anymore—consequences of letting things run their course, imposing on future generations the astronomic burden of drastic changes in lifestyle and of coping with the predictably catastrophic effects of a substantially warmer climate. In a recent landmark ruling to which I shall return in the concluding section of this paper, the Federal Constitutional Court of Germany remarks that "(…) environmental protection is elevated to a matter of constitutional significance because the democratic political process is organized along more short-term lines based on election cycles, placing it at a structural risk of being less responsive to tackling the ecological issues that need to be pursued over the long term. It is also because future generations—those who will be most affected—naturally have no voice of their own in shaping the current political agenda" (BVerfG 2021 § 206). The underlying issue—addressed in the ruling under various guises—is how to reconcile, in the vast and intricate domain of climate policy, the rightful worry about the short-termist bias of the political process with democratic legitimacy over time.

The rest of this paper is organized as follows. In Sect. 2, I briefly characterize the short-termist bias of ordinary political arrangements and the associated claim that these create negative generational externalities. In Sect. 3, I turn to the intergenerational paradox of constitutional safeguards and the associated claim that the latter demote the political self-determination of future generations. In Sect. 4, I will explain the dilemma at the heart of my inquiry: one horn of the dilemma is that the more politically open or inclusive a constitution is, the less it will encroach upon the political rights of future citizens; the other horn is that the less constitutional law redresses the short-termist bias of ordinary democratic arrangements, the more it will compromise the freedom and welfare of future individuals. In Sect. 5, I sketch a way out of the dilemma: to think of future generations as an endangered minority for the purposes of judicial review of majoritarian legislation and to imagine an architecture of decision-making that enables the correction of generational externalities. In Sect. 6, I take by way of conclusion the recent ruling of the *Bundesverfassungsgericht* on climate change policy as a paradigm of proper constitutional management of intergenerational equity.

2 The Short-Termist Bias of Democratic Politics

What does the *constitutional* protection of future generations bring to the table of intergenerational equity? The usual assumption underlying the elevation of an individual right or a policy choice to the constitutional level is that constitutions are endowed with extraordinary normative force: *normative* here in the sense that their prescriptions, to the extent that they are justiciable, are not proclamations serving a rhetorical or expressive function, but standards against which the validity of ordinary laws and other decisions of public authority is measured; *extraordinary* in the sense that constitutional laws cannot be changed through the ordinary legislative process, but only through a qualified procedure of constitutional amendment, typically comprising the requirement of a supermajority (see generally García de Enterría 1994). It follows that the constitutional elevation of a particular decision—say, a public debt ceiling—limits the political freedom of ordinary law-making agencies empowered by the electorate. The constitution plays an *inhibiting* or *constraining* role (see Holmes 1995: 134–77).

That suggests an immediate analogy with individual *precommitment*.[1] The classical paradigm is the episode in Book XII of the *Odyssey* in which Ulysses, knowing the siren's chant to be irresistible, has the sailors bind him tightly to the ship's mast (Homer; Wilson, translator, 2018: 301–15). Everyday life furnishes many examples. Take the case of the gambler who asks to be put on a list of individuals barred from entering casinos. Consider as well the glutton on a weight loss regimen who eats a light and healthy meal before a dinner party. These situations seem to embody a paradox: a free and rational individual—an *agent*—deliberately limits her freedom of choice. But the paradox is only apparent. For the agent is aware that she is afflicted by the deliberative pathology classically labelled *akrasia*—incontinence or weakness of the will—whose effect is to prevent action upon grounds that the agent herself acknowledges as reasonable or adequate (Aristotle; Ross, translator 2001: 1036–1058). Precommitment is hence a *warrant* of freedom because it enables *self*-control, the ability of the agent to affirm reason against passions, impulses, inclinations, and

[1] On the rationality of precommitment, see Elster 1984: 36–110.

the like. Indeed, that is an indispensable precaution in those typically akratic states—such as intoxication, addiction, lust, hysteria, laziness, depression, and jealousy—in which rationality loses its way. In spite of its inhibiting or constraining nature, then, precommitment turns out to be an assurance of *autonomy*.

Here is how the *constitutional* appropriation of individual *precommitment* looks like. Taking stock of the multiple prejudices and distortions that *may* pollute popular deliberation in the ordinary political process—such as racism, misogyny, homophobia, xenophobia, fundamentalism, populism, and alarmism—we must acknowledge the wisdom of the people binding itself to the mast of constitutional precommitments endowed with extraordinary normative force. Hence, there is a good reason to raise a decision to the constitutional level—say, proscribing discrimination on grounds of race and gender, requiring just compensation for takings of property or protecting the freedom to worship of religious minorities—if a solid case can be made that ordinary democratic deliberation is pathological in that regard. The particular deliberative pathology that vindicates the constitutional protection of future generations is what we may call *short-termism*—the predisposition of the current generation, which controls the ordinary political process, to *disregard* the impact of its decisions on future generations (MacKenzie 2016: 24–45).

Cultural factors may go a long way into explaining the short-termism of contemporary politics. Maybe in our societies dominated by individualism and materialism—as opposed to notions of personal excellence and the common good—there is no room for any serious concern with the future (McIntyre 2007). If that is all there is to say, the honorable thing to do is to enlist in the old-fashioned but surprisingly ever-renewed jeremiad about the moral bankruptcy and apocalyptic fate of modernity, liberalism, and capitalism.

Yet there is quite a bit more to be said. For short-termism is built into the *structure* of representative democracy as we know it—it is a pervasive *institutional bias* of our regimes. It stems from four characteristic features (Silva 2015: 418–21). The first is *representativeness*: since future individuals cannot participate in current elections, they are not represented in any meaningful electoral sense by elected officials. The second is *accountability*: since they cannot vote, future individuals cannot hold current officials accountable for any decisions that have a negative impact on them. The third is *majoritarianism*: the *intra*generational legitimating force of majority rule, which is based on political equality, does not hold *inter*generationally, as a majority of the current generation could very well turn out to be a minority in a hypothetical intergenerational vote. The fourth is *temporality*: there are no intergenerational surrogates for the mechanisms that mitigate the power of temporary majorities—such as periodic renewal of mandates, limits on renewability, and lame duck restrictions—for the obvious reason that it falls necessarily on the current generation to rule.

Therefore, skepticism about the ability of the ordinary political process to dispense fair treatment to future generations seems to be vindicated by an analysis of the structure of representative democracy. Moreover, this a priori judgment—a priori because it is based on conceptual analysis—resonates with the casual observation of many democratic systems, afflicted by chronic fiscal imbalances, excessive consumption of non-renewable energy sources, high levels of carbon dioxide emissions, unsustainable social security systems, and policies that hurt the long-term competitiveness of the economy.

It seems to follow that our constitutional arrangements ought to incorporate clauses of environmental protection, financial sustainability, fiscal moderation, and the like (Häberle 2006: 215–29). Some already explicitly do so at least to some extent (consider Article 20a of the German Basic Law on the protection of the natural foundations of life and animals, which gets off with the assertion "mindful of its responsibility towards future generations…"; or paragraph *e)* of Article 66–2 of the Portuguese Constitution, which, following the dramatic and pioneering entrenchment of a fundamental right to the environment and quality of life, prescribes a rational use of resources and ecological stability with "respect for the principle of intergenerational solidarity"). Such provisions should hence be construed quite liberally. Other constitutional documents that are silent on the issue should be updated through a combination of reform and creative interpretation. More importantly, constitutions should go beyond majestic generalities and programmatic language in this domain. They should contain explicit, detailed, effective safeguards against short-termism. That is the argument from short-termism to constitutionalism.

3 The Generational Paradox of Constitutional Democracy

Let me turn now to *the generational paradox*.[2] How can it be that a constitution-making generation binds future generations to its political choices? Thomas Jefferson wrote that "no society can make a perpetual constitution, or even a perpetual law. The earth belongs always to the living generation" (Thomas Jefferson 1958: 392–8). History teaches us that, while constitutions are most certainly not perpetual, their drafters invariably aspire them to give them a very long life. In the debate over the draft of what would eventually become the French Constitution of 1791, a member of the National Assembly, Monsieur Thouret, declared passionately that "a fundamentally good constitution" (*une constitution fondamentalement bonne*) would have to be amended only with respect to "minutia" (*détails*) because it would be "founded upon the immutable bases of justice and the eternal principles of reason" (*fondée sur les bases immuables de la justice et les principes eternelles de la raisón*).[3] His optimism turned out to be misguided: France had a baffling sixteen constitutions in the period of sixty nine years following the French Revolution. Jefferson's own suggestion was that constitutions should expire after 19 years (Thomas Jefferson 1958). But that is at once a very rough index of generational cohorting in constitutional matters and a source of the very political instability that constitutional arrangements are expected to thwart.

---

[2] I elaborate on this theme in Almeida Ribeiro 2022.

[3] *Reimpression de Ancien Moniteur Tome Neuvième:* 575.

It is undoubtedly true that constitutions can be repealed. As Jefferson noticed, however, that is hardly the same as each generation having an equal chance to adopt its own constitution. In his words: "the power of repeal is not an equivalent. It might be indeed if every form of government were so perfectly contrived that the will of the majority could always be obtained fairly and without impediment. But this is true of no form. The people cannot assemble themselves. Their representation is unequal and vicious. (…) [A]nd other impediments arise so as to prove to every practical man that a law of limited duration is much more manageable than one which needs a repeal" (Thomas Jefferson 1958).

The generational paradox is closely associated with what might called the *democratic paradox*. How can it be that a minority favorable to a political choice entrenched in the constitution prevails over the majority? Imagine a constitutional provision that reads "no person shall be obliged to pay retroactive taxes", interpreted as a categorical prohibition, as opposed to a principle that merely operates as a *prima facie* prohibition or a *pro tanto* reason to be balanced against countervailing considerations relevant in the circumstances. The Portuguese Constitution contains such a provision, and the case law tends to conceive it as a categorical prohibition of so-called genuine retroactivity or retroactivity in the narrow sense.[4]

The adoption of such a rule expresses the choice of the constitutional lawmaker. But once the constitution is enacted, the constitutional lawmaker is no more—all we are left with are the branches of government, including the legislative body.[5] Now imagine the majority in the legislature wishes to get rid of the constitutional rule, arguing that while retroactive taxes are in principle unfair, since they frustrate the legitimate expectations of the taxpayers, they may be justifiable, all-things-considered, in outrageous cases of tax avoidance or in sovereign debt crises. One may or may not agree with this position, but it is undoubtedly reasonable. Yet, so long as there is a minority in a position to veto an amendment to the constitution, the rule will stand. From a *diachronic* perspective, that reveals the generational paradox—the dead ruling over the living. From a *synchronic* perspective, it reveals the democratic paradox—the few ruling over the many.

You may tell me at this point that nothing prevents the current majority from amending or reforming the inherited constitution. Surely that puts the matter to rest? Well, I do not think it does. For when we consider any regime of amendment carefully, we encounter two more paradoxes—close relatives, as it were, of

---

[4] As opposed to mere retrospectivity. A tax law is said to have a genuinely retroactive effect when it applies to circumstances that have taken place before the law came into force, such as an increase in the personal income tax rates referring to the previous year. Conversely, a tax law is merely retrospective when it applies to a stream of events that began before the law came into force but continues afterwards, such as an increase in the personal income tax rates referring to the current year. See, e.g., Acórdãos n.os 128/2009, 85/2010, 399/2010, 617/2012, 85/2013, and 751/2020. For the dissenting view that the prohibition against retroactive taxes is both wide reaching and merely *prima facie*, see Acórdão n.º 171/2017. These rulings are available at https://acordaosv22.tribunalconstitucional.pt/.

[5] As Thayer JB, 1893: 5, puts it: "The sovereign himself, having written these expressions of will, had retired into the clouds…".

the generational paradox. First, there is *the amendment paradox*. How can it be that a constitution may be enacted by a simple majority while requiring a qualified procedure to be amended? Constitutions may be adopted in a variety of ways documented in political history: monarchical concession, popular referendums, foreign imposition, corporatist bargaining, among others. Nevertheless, the most democratic procedure is usually taken to involve a constitutional assembly elected specifically for that purpose. When that is the case, the constitution is usually enacted by a simple majority—half of the votes plus one in the constitutional body. It may be, of course, that the proposed draft is supported by more than half of the members; from a legal standpoint though, half plus one is all that is required for the adoption of the constitution. Moreover, a possibly broad consensus on the constitution as a whole does not necessarily extend to each of its parts—it may be that a general vote yielded robust support for the constitution while a particular provision made it to the final version with the support of a simple majority.

That generates the paradox of amendment. The procedure to amend the constitution is typically more stringent than the procedure for its adoption. Even in the simplest case, that of a constitution that can be amended solely by a qualified majority in a single chamber, it is typically harder to change than to make a constitution. A simple majority is all that is required to entrench a political choice that can never be repealed by a simple majority. That discredits the notion that, from a procedural standpoint, the constitution-making power is democratically superior to ordinary legislative power.[6] It also puts a question mark over the claimed authority of the constitutional lawmaker to demand a qualified procedure for constitutional amendment (see Schmitt 2012: 38–57).

You may tell me that the practical response to the amendment paradox is to make the constitution amendable by a simple majority in the legislature or any other procedure that mimics that which led to the adoption of the constitution itself. That, however, is tantamount to making the constitution *flexible*—and procedural rigidity is precisely one of the two principal mechanisms, the other being judicial review

[6] Schmitt 1993: 20–28 asserts that making and changing a constitution are *qualitatively* different powers and draws a fundamental distinction between *the constitution*—a sovereign decision over the form and type of political unity of the people—and *constitutional law*—an instrumental decision that presupposes the constitution and is by nature amendable. The opposite view is epitomized by the jurisprudence of Hans Kelsen. The constitution is, according to the strictures of the *Reine Rechtslehre*, "the rule that determines the genesis of statutes, of the general norms whose execution constitutes the activity of the organs of state, namely of the courts and administrative agencies". That is "the essential, original, and narrow concept of constitution'. Moreover, 'nothing stands in the way of using this form also for norms that do not fall under the concept of constitution in the narrow sense…". It follows that "[i]f one wants to distinguish (…) between the material and the formal unconstitutionality of a statute, one should be mindful that this is permissible only with the qualification that (…) a statute that, by virtue of its content, comes into conflict with the relevant provisions contained in the constitution will lose the defect of unconstitutionality once it is enacted as a constitutional statute" (Kelsen 2010: 1485–531).

of ordinary state action, put in place to protect the constitutional order.[7] Thus, the paradox of amendment cannot so easily be set aside.

To make things worse, we also face the reverse problem. This is where what I like to call *the identity paradox* enters the picture. The point of enabling constitutional amendments is to prevent the constitution from wearing down. Yet nothing prevents the amendment power, so long as the procedural requirements are met, from subverting the very constitutional order that it was instituted to safeguard (see Schmitt 2012: 16–20, 25–26). Over time, a whole new substantive constitution may be established in this way, its only continuing element being the regime of amendment.[8] If we use all the stones of the Milan Cathedral, one by one, to build a massive wall to keep migrants at bay, is it still the Milan Cathedral? If the amendment power is used to turn a liberal democratic regime into a fascist dictatorship or a dictatorship of the proletariat, is it still the same constitution? Of course, some constitutional texts contain clauses setting substantive limits to the power to amend. But these clauses are themselves paradoxical. For either the limits are regarded as absolute, in which case they exacerbate the paradox of amendment, or they are regarded as disguised procedural limits, in the sense that the amendment power may be used to change the provision that establishes the limitation clause, clearing the way for the subversion of the constitutional order. One way or another, the aporia is seemingly inevitable.

The bottom line in all of this, I think, is that by writing a constitution and protecting it from ordinary politics, the drafting generation limits considerably the political freedom of future generations. It sets the ruling of the dead over the living, of the few over the many, and of form over substance.

4 Between a Rock and a Hard Place

This leads us into the dilemma or conundrum of the constitutionalization of intergenerational policies. The idea of precommitment—whether individual or collective—is premised on the contrast between two first-person agents: "The Rational I" and "The Akratic I". The former knows what is best and has the will to do it. The latter might or might not know what is best, but, in any case, lacks the will to do it. Rational-Ulysses knows that it is best not to respond to the chant of the sirens, and wills to avoid it.

---

[7] The classic treatment of the distinction between flexible and rigid constitutions is by Dicey 1982: 65–72, 317–25.

[8] Not everyone sees a problem here. Thoma 2000: 163, writing about the Weimar Constitution, cavalierly advocates the contrary view: "The opinion that the double *pouvoir constituent* regulated by Article 76 [concerning the amendment of the Weimar Constitution] cannot be without limits (…) fails to appreciate the idea—daring, perhaps, but sublime in its consistency—of free, democratic self-determination. Certainly this freedom can be demagogically misused. But how would it be freedom otherwise? However, from the standpoint of democracy and liberalism (…) it would be impossible to evaluate what the resolute and undoubted majority of the people wills and decides in a legal way as a coup d'état or rebellion, even if it subverts the basic pillars of the present Constitution!".

The problem he faces, in that thoughtful moment, is how to secure the right course of action in akratic circumstances in which freedom of choice is likely to produce bad outcomes. This problem is *technical* or *instrumental* in nature: it concerns the selection of the means suitable to keep the effects of akrasia under control.

The problem is quite different and more complex if instead of a conflict *between* "The Rational I" and "The Akratic I" the agent experiences a conflict *within* the former—not a conflict between reason and inclination but within reason itself. Take the following example. Imagine a scholar named Carl who decides to write a book on the issue of whether generational cohorts can have rights. Following a great many hours of careful research and study, he is torn between the view that only identifiable subjects—such as natural persons, non-human animals, artificial entities, and verifiable groups—can have rights and the view that anything can be a bearer of rights—an estate following the death of the deceased, an endangered species, a language nearing extinction, and generational cohorts—so long as there are good reasons to grant them rights.[9]

Consumed by the flames of doubt and pressed by the publisher's deadline, our man Carl commits to the positive view, according to which generational cohorts can have rights. To seal the commitment, he informs his publisher about the central thesis of the book. The reasons to do so are intelligible and compelling. Yet they have nothing to do with a conflict between Rational-Carl and Akratic-Carl—that is to say, with limiting the possibility of irrational choices. On the contrary, the whole point of Carl's precommitment is to *inhibit* the continuing exercise of his rational powers, because the more he delves into the problem the more aware of its complexity he becomes, making it even harder for him to take a stance on it (Waldron 1999: 269–70). In other words, he takes steps to control the rational affluence, as opposed to the indigence, of his future self. That is the only way of making sure that his book will see the light of day.

Now, with respect to a broad range of issues, as Jeremy Waldron has forcefully argued (Cruft 2019: 266–75) the people in a constitutional moment finds itself in a situation at least as close to that of Carl as that of Ulysses. That is so because of the *reasonable pluralism* characteristic of our liberal and democratic societies. People disagree reasonably and obdurately not only about religious, metaphysical, and ethical issues that modern social arrangements largely confine to the private realm but also about matters of unavoidably public concern, such as the scope of basic liberties, the demands of social justice, the direction of economic policy, the design of collective institutions, and the like. Library bookshelves, academic seminars, public debates, social networks, and other *fora* of discussion provide eloquent testimony to the loud and interminable cacophony. The disagreement comes in all shapes and sizes, from more or less articulated conceptions of justice to the relatively mundane realm of public policy in areas such as taxation, health, education, culture, social security, and environmental protection. Moreover, the diversity of views is headquartered everywhere in civil society, from the dinner table to the lecture room, such that it cannot be explained away as a symptom of thoughtlessness. It is, in the famous

[9] See the distinction between natural rights and conventional rights in Cruft 2019: 71–79.

words of John Rawls, the "normal result of the exercise of human reason within the framework of the free institutions of a constitutional democratic regime" (Rawls 2005: xvi).

In the constitutional realm, reasonable pluralism manifests itself in the following way: there is a broad consensus over a small set of basic principles—equal protection, due process, legal certainty, the separation of powers, and a few others—and over human rights—civil and political rights, surely, but to a large extent over so-called second and third generation rights as well—accompanied by persistent controversy over the concrete implications of those principles and the scope and relative weight of these rights. In other words, a shared core of foundational platitudes supports a wildly diverse repertoire of rival political agendas more or less explicitly informed by disputed moral, economic, psychological, and historical assumptions. To give but a few examples, consider the controversies over the legalization of surrogate motherhood, the criminalization of abortion, the role of the market in the provision of social goods such as health and education, the correct macroeconomic policies in the wake of a sovereign debt crisis, the sustainability of pay-as-you-go social security in aging societies, the magnitude, consequences and policy implications of climate change, and affirmative action in access to higher education, the labor market, and public office (see Ribeiro GA, 2020: 11–12).

In these vast and convoluted matters, the people in a thoughtful moment is no agent confident about the right course of action; it is a deeply conflicted soul. Bringing one of the views in contention to the constitutional level is hence not simply a technique to inhibit the akratic degeneration of the political process—i.e., an effective means against collective irrationality—but a way of foreclosing the democratic management of our political differences, an alienation of the reasonable pluralism characteristic of an open society. Just as Carl commits to a particular thesis not out of conviction but out of expedience, suspending along the way the exercise of his intellectual powers, the people in its constitution-making capacity ties the whole of society—including, of course, future generations—to the mast of a controversial decision, preventing its revocation as a result of public debate and democratic deliberation.

Here is our dilemma then. On the one hand, we are right to think that representative democracy has a systematic short-termist bias that leads to collective choices that disregard or at least underestimate the interests of future generations affected by them. On the other hand, intergenerational equity is a controversial subject, reasonably dividing public opinion, which makes it an appropriate object for democratic deliberation. In other words, we have good reasons both to accept and to reject the democratic management of intergenerational problems. The challenge when it comes to the constitution of intergenerational equity is thus how to address the worry of short-termism without squashing the political rights of future generations.

5 A Way Out: Heightened Scrutiny and Beyond

Let me introduce here an important distinction for constitutional theorists—that between rules and principles (see, generally, Dworkin R, 1977: 22–31, 71–80; Alexy E, 2018: 71–157; Sieckmann J-R, 1990: 52–87; Atienza M, Manero JR, 2007: 23–50). Leaving aside the many subtleties that have become commonplace in the enormous literature on the subject, the distinction comes to the following. If a norm is a *rule*, it applies mechanically or in an all-or-nothing fashion; so long as the conditions that are specified in the antecedent clause of the rule obtain, it provides a definitive outcome to the case at hand. If a norm is a *principle*, it is a consideration to be balanced in proportion to its strength; so long as it is applicable to the case at hand, a principle furnishes a *pro tanto* reason to be weighed against countervailing reasons before an all-things-considered judgment is reached. As an illustration of the distinction in the domain of the constitutional protection of future generations, consider two *interpretations* of a constitutional provision to the effect that 'the public deficit on the government budget cannot exceed 3 p.p. of the GDP'. According to one possible interpretation, the provision simply rules out a public deficit higher than 3 p.p. of the GDP; according to an alternative interpretation, whether a deficit above that threshold is tolerated in a given context depends on the strength of the underlying reasons. The same distinction applies to a constitutional provision setting the goal of carbon-neutrality by a specified year—say, 2050. It may be read as a rule, in which case no departure from the goal can be constitutionally justified; or as a principle, in which case it sets a reason to be balanced contextually against constitution-sensitive countervailing considerations.

The distinction should not be overstated. On the one hand, notwithstanding their categorical semblance, rules are *not absolute*, even if their scope of application is not explicitly limited by exceptions (See Ribeiro GA, 2017: 226–32). In abnormal circumstances, when the reasons not to apply a rule are evident and massive, so as to make its application self-defeating or plainly absurd, it may be cast aside; the provisions against an excessive deficit and setting the goal of carbon.neutrality, for instance, could presumably be cast aside in the event of a public calamity. On the other hand, principles are not symbolic or programmatic expressions, but genuine reasons binding on their addressees, such that they ought to be observed, subject to a *balancing constraint*, to all cases that fall within their scope of application. The principle that carbon-neutrality should be achieved by 2050 and kept from then on places the government under a duty to honour it unless it can offer a plausible argument that countervailing reasons justify discarding it—and even then the sacrifice ought to be kept at the minimum required by such reasons.

In spite of these relativizing remarks, there is an obvious affinity between rules and mechanical arrangements, on the one hand, and principles and fiduciary arrangements, on the other. Within a model of rules, the constitutional lawmaker decides on certain issues in advance. The people in its presumably thoughtful constitutional moment makes decisions that cannot be revoked in the akratic circumstances of the ordinary political process, decisions that are to be mechanically enforced by an institution such as a constitutional court. Within a model of principles, the constitutional lawmaker entrusts the decision to a third-party—typically a constitutional court. The people in its presumably thoughtful constitutional moment delegates on an institution insulated from the akratic circumstances that tarnish the ordinary political process the authority to balance the competing reasons at stake and to issue a final all-things-considered decision.

The pros and cons of rules and principles are fairly obvious: rules have the advantage of preventing errors and abuses carried out by the guardian of the constitution; principles have the advantage of flexibility, preventing outcomes that are unreasonable in the actual circumstances. This distinction furnishes a promising starting point to work ourselves out of the dilemma between collective akrasia and democratic illegitimacy. Indeed, the democratic objection against the constitutional protection of future generations is on a much stronger footing when it takes the form of rules. That is so because principles may be balanced in different ways by ordinary lawmakers, reflecting their divergent political judgments, perhaps even the skeptical judgment that future generations are only worthy of protection as long as we are talking about already existing individuals, notably persons under voting age. In fact, it is plausible to argue that the constitutional entrenchment of *intergenerational principles*—say, a principle of sustainability—is justified along the exact same lines of other constitutional principles: consent only breaks down once we move from the principle to its application. Insofar as it remains a *matter of principle*, then, the constitutional protection of future generations is seemingly unproblematic.

The application of principles is subject to a balancing proviso. The technical expression of that notion is the *doctrine of proportionality* in the broad sense of the term, also known as the "prohibition of excess" (*Übermaßverbot*).[10] It establishes that the sacrifice of a principle cannot be *excessive*. When the principle embodies a reason to act instead of a limitation to action—a positive instead of a negative duty—, proportionality takes the form of a "prohibition of deficit" (*Untermaßverbot*), meaning that the legislature cannot fall below a threshold of *sufficient* protection or promotion of the principle at stake That translates into the requirement that any law that infringes upon a principle fulfills *four conditions*. The first condition is *legitimacy*: the goal pursued must be some other principle to which the legislature is bound, such that the sacrifice may be justified. The second condition is *suitability*: the sacrifice must be a suitable means to promote a legitimate goal, or it would be incurred in vain. The third condition is *necessity*: the sacrifice must be the least costly of the means suitable to attain the goal, or it would be wasteful. The fourth condition is the balancing test properly so called, *proportionality* in the narrow sense of the term: the sacrifice must be worth having in light of the goals or reasons underlying the law, that is to say, the overall benefits must outweigh the costs.

Now with respect to each of these conditions, and particularly the last two, there is a question concerning the proper degree of *judicial scrutiny* of legislative choices.

[10] The jurisprudential literature on proportionality is enormous. Considering only the last decade, see, e.g., Schlink 2012: 718–737; Barack 2012; Klatt and Meister 2012; Canas 2019.

Judicial scrutiny is a variable, ranging from a perfunctory "rational basis" test on the lower end of the spectrum, which merely determines whether the law subject to review is not manifestly disproportional, to full-blown judicial second-guessing of the legislature on the higher end of the spectrum (see Ribeiro GA, 2020: 86–87).

If we are serious about democratic rule, we must be supportive of the notion that judicial scrutiny should remain as close as possible to the lower end of the spectrum, and repudiate any suggestion that the normal procedure to settle political disagreements is to subject the matter to voting by a handful of nonelected and unaccountable judges. A democracy is a self-governing community of equals, meaning that the decisions by public authorities should ultimately be traced back to the authorship of the very people to whom they are addressed. On the many issues of principle that divide the citizenry, that translates into a requirement that each citizen's opinion, either about the issue itself or about who should decide it, be given the exact same weight as that of any other. Hence, the political branches representative of and directly accountable before the electorate enjoy a presumption of legitimacy when they take a side in the ongoing dispute within society about matters of common concern (see Ribeiro GA 2017: 77–86).

Thus, special circumstances must obtain for the opinion of a majority of judges to prevail over that of a majority of elected officials—circumstances that evince a failure of the political process. Indeed, courts may only deploy *heightened scrutiny* when reviewing laws that draw on suspect classifications of race, gender, sexual orientation, age, and others that may serve to oppress political minorities or disenfranchised social groups (see Ely 1980: 135–80); the discrimination against future generations is another instance where tighter control is warranted. This is all the truer when it comes to environmental policy, for what is at stake is not only the welfare of future generations considered holistically, but even more dramatically that of poor people who lack the means to adapt to a warmer climate and often have little voice in the political process. Both categories—future and poverty—are robust proxies for discrimination. In this domain of collective akrasia, therefore, a public authority that is electorally unaccountable, yet bound to offer arguments for its decisions, such as a constitutional court, is more representative of reasonable pluralism than the rule of little more than "Aye!" and "Nye"; it embodies a form of "argumentative representation" (Alexy 2005: 578–81), a virtuous synthesis of pluralism and thoughtfulness. How plural and thoughtful that type of representation actually is depends on the particular features of judicial arrangements in a society—for instance, one might argue that a specialized constitutional court staffed by judges appointed by a robust parliamentary majority or by a mix of political institutions for a non-renewable term in office offers better assurances of pluralism than an ordinary supreme court staffed by judges appointed for life (Kumm 2017: 55–56). In any case, these institutional worries should not distract us from the basic point that under conditions of collective akrasia strict judicial review of legislative choices serves the vital task of preventing democratic government from degenerating into a tyranny of the many—the rule of majority *deliberation* from decaying into the rule of majority *prejudice* (see Ribeiro 2017: 86).

Let me wrap my argument up. The citizens of a liberal democracy may entrust intergenerational equity to the few among them who serve as judges because judicial deliberation is a more trustworthy method of securing a fair treatment of future generations than casting ballots in general elections and voting in the parliamentary process of legislation. Following some twists and turns, the way out of the dilemma between collective akrasia and democratic illegitimacy seems finally straightforward: protect future generations under the form of constitutional principles and subject the laws that infringe upon them to strict judicial scrutiny within the framework of proportionality analysis. Since the composition of a high court changes over time and purportedly reflects the reasonable pluralism proper to each generation, robust judicial review appears to reconcile the two horns of the dilemma—justice and legitimacy.

Alas, it is not as simple as that. The problems of intergenerational equity implicate quite a bit more than the balancing of rights and interests that is the bread and butter of constitutional justice. They involve complex empirical prognoses and technical judgments regarding the future impact of current decisions. Judges are not cut out for these tasks. Imagine a constitutional court scrutinizing, on account of the principle of sustainability, the macroeconomic assumptions of the overall state budget or the accuracy of competing accounts of the impact of greenhouse gases in climate change. We would not just have a variety of constitutional philosophies represented at the apex of the judicial system but also a variety of half-baked economic ideas and scientific theories. That sounds crazy. The same applies to decisions in areas such as social security, the labour market, and energy policy. It seems highly unlikely that pushing the courts into the thick of the woods of public policy will create much added value in collective deliberation. Indeed, things usually take a turn for the worse when the agent selected to execute a fiduciary arrangement is incompetent to decide in the relevant domain. Judges know this all too well. Therefore, we should not be surprised that in most cases intergenerational constitutional clauses are dead parchment.

These worries reintroduce and reshape our dilemma. On the one hand, short-termism debases the democratic authority of ordinary political actors in areas where their decisions have a significant impact on the future. On the other hand, the traditional checks and balances of constitutional democracies are ill-suited to adequately protect future generations. There is only a way out as I see it: even if we commit to the judiciary—particularly constitutional judges—the task of enforcing intergenerational equity, we need the sort of advisory and expert institutions that belong in the so-called novel fourth branch of government to produce the knowledge indispensable to the wise fulfillment of that task (see, generally, Tushnet 2021). That recommends the careful study of the experience with institutional innovations in this domain that took place in some countries—e.g., the Hungarian Parliamentary Commissioner for Future Generations or Israel's Commission for Future Generations—and a greater focus on the activity of transnational expert bodies that report the state-of-the-art among experts in a particular area, enabling the design and review of evidence-based policies—the Intergovernmental Panel on Climate Change being perhaps the most prominent example in this category. Relying on the information generated by these institutions, judges—particularly those sitting in constitutional courts—can go a long way into assessing the credibility of the empirical assumptions of legislative packages with significant intergenerational effects and detect potential blind spots or cynic silences in them. The combination of scientific knowledge supplied by these institutions with the deliberative virtues of a properly fashioned system of judicial review might be the only hope of reconciling our deep-seated commitment to democratic legitimacy with the imperative of protecting the freedom and welfare of those who lack a political voice proportionate to the stakes they have in current policy choices.

6 A Landmark Ruling on Intergenerational Equity

In a recent judgment, the Federal Constitutional Court of Germany (FCC) ruled on a number of complaints issued, among others, by German residents of young age and individuals residing in Bangladesh and Nepal against provisions of the Federal Climate Change Act setting a schedule for reducing greenhouse gases emissions by 2030 as part of a prior commitment undertaken by the Federal Republic of Germany in the Climate Action Plan for achieving carbon-neutrality by 2050, in line with the goal of limiting the increase in average global temperature to well below 2°C and preferably to 1.5° established by the Paris Agreement.[11] In a nutshell, at stake were the issues of whether the state created a legal framework sufficiently robust to achieve the set target—required to fulfill constitutional duties to protect life and health, as well as the environment—and whether the emissions scheduled until 2030 consume a disproportionate fraction of the CO^2 budget consistent with the aim of achieving carbon-neutrality by 2050, thus offloading a heavy burden on people of young age, who would later on be bound to make an urgent and tragic choice between undertaking drastic measures to reduce emissions swiftly or abandoning the set target with all its deleterious consequences (BVerfG 2021, §§ 1–15).

The FCC relied on the assessment reports and special reports published by the Intergovernmental Panel on Climate Change (IPCC) to paint a grim picture of reality. The IPCC is an intergovernmental committee established by the United Nations Environment Programme and the World Meteorological Organization in 1988, and endorsed by the United Nations General Assembly. Its task is to report the state of scientific research on climate change, summarizing the key findings in the literature and assessing their implications. The ruling draws from such reports the governing notion that "[a]ccording to virtually unanimous scientific opinion, the rapid acceleration of global warming that is currently observable in comparison with historical levels is essentially due to the change in the material balance of the atmosphere caused by anthropogenic emissions. The increase in CO^2 concentrations is deemed to play a particularly significant role here" (BVerfG 2021, at § 18). Indeed, "human-induced increases in concentrations of greenhouse gases in the atmosphere change the Earth's radiation balance and thus lead to global warming" (BVerfG 2021, at §

[11] For an excellent analysis of the intergenerational dimensions of the judgment, see Winter 2022: 209–221.

19). This, in turn, has “a wide range of impacts on the environment and the Earth’s climate”, notably rising sea levels and disruptions of tipping point elements, meaning those “components of the Earth system that have special significance for the global climate and which, when placed under increasing stress, undergo abrupt and often irreversible change”, such as “the Siberian and North American permafrost, the ice masses in the polar zones, the Amazonian rainforest, and major wind and current systems” (BVerfG 2021, at §§ 20–22).

The consequences of global warming for human beings are widely believed to be dire. “If the global temperature rises by more than 3 ºC by 2100—the judgment asserts—, which is considered likely unless additional measures to combat climate change are taken, the consequences of global warming and climate change are expected to be drastic” (BVerfG 2021, at § 22). Among these are shortages of food and water, damage to infrastructure, proliferation of infectious diseases and respiratory ailments, displacement of entire populations, submersion of coastal settlements, long periods of drought, and impairments to agricultural production (BVerfG 2021, at §§ 22–30). The only way to significantly slow-down climate change is by reducing CO^2 emissions, a greenhouse gas that does not naturally leave the atmosphere within a relevant period of time. Although in theory there are other strategies to cope with anthropogenic climate change, such as carbon removal technologies and social adaptation to a warmer climate, their present-day limited effectiveness and exorbitant cost determine that it is only by reducing carbon-intensive activities, namely those which involve the burning of fossil fuels, that climate change can be adequately tackled (BVerfG 2021, at §§ 31–37). It follows that, “[i]n order to achieve climate neutrality in our current way of life—including activities as common and mundane as the construction and utilization of new buildings or the wearing of clothes—fundamental changes and restrictions are needed in patterns of production, consumption and everyday activity” (BVerfG 2021, at § 37).

Once again on the basis of the scientific evidence amassed and presented by the IPCC, the FCC asserts that there is an “almost linear correlation” between the concentration of CO^2 in the atmosphere and the global average temperature. Since the current volume of concentrated CO^2 is approximately known, “it is possible to determine roughly how much CO^2 can still be released into the Earth’s atmosphere and remain there permanently without causing the desired temperature to be exceeded. If the (currently small) amounts of negative CO^2 emissions (i.e. emissions that never reach the atmosphere or are subsequently removed) are also factored in, the result is the total (global) amount of CO^2 that can still be emitted if the resultant warming of the Earth is not to exceed the temperature limit. Within the climate policy and climate science discourse, this amounts to as the ‘carbon budget’ or ‘CO^2 budget’” (BVerfG 2021, at § 36). The constitutional issues raised by the contested provisions of the Climate Change Act largely revolved around the carbon budget—both as to whether the legislative framework was sufficiently robust to meet the ultimate target of carbon-neutrality by 2050 and whether the schedule of emissions up to 2030 embodied a fair distribution of the burden of CO^2 emissions over time. The former issue concerns the duties of the state to protect life, health, and property, as well as the duties arising from the environmental and intergenerational clause contained in

Article 20a of the German Basic Law. The latter could be framed either as a matter of proportionality or of equality—balancing the freedom of individuals over time or distributing the burden evenly among generational cohorts; the ruling opted for the first course of reasoning.

Apart from the decision on the merits, the judgment is of great importance for what it says about the procedural standing of two groups of complainants. In relation to the residents in Nepal and Bangladesh, the FCC acknowledged their standing on the basis that "it cannot be ruled out from the outset that the fundamental rights of the Basic Law also oblige the German state to protect them against the impacts of global climate change" (BVerfG 2021, at § 90). Although it does not take a definitive position as to whether "duties of protection arising from fundamental rights also place the German state under an obligation vis-à-vis the complainants living in Bangladesh and Nepal to take action against impairments caused by global climate change", the Court states that "it is conceivable in principle", adding that "the complainants are particularly exposed to the consequences of global warming caused by global greenhouse emissions" and the Basic Law "does not explicitly restrict [the] binding effect [of fundamental rights] to German territory" (BVerfG 2021, at §§ 173–81). With respect to the complainants of young age, who based their claims on fundamental rights to life, health, property, and others, the Court was careful to note that "[t]he complainants are not asserting the rights of unborn persons or even of entire future generations, neither of whom enjoy subjective fundamental rights" but "their own fundamental rights". Moreover, "[t]he possibility of a violation of the Constitution cannot be negated here by arguing that a risk of future harm does not represent a current harm and therefore does not amount to a violation of fundamental rights", for "[e]ven provisions that only begin posing significant risks to fundamental rights over the course of their subsequent implementation can fall into conflict with the Basic Law" (BVerfG 2021, at §§ 108–09). Nevertheless, the judgment speaks of an "objective duty" to protect the life and health of future generations—including unborn people—, particularly "where irreversible processes are at stake" (BVerfG 2021, at § 146). This is a very bold assertion indeed, even if it is ingeniously wrapped in the language of caution and modesty (BVerfG 2021, at § 151).

When it comes to the merits, the judgment addresses first the issue of whether the challenged provisions fall short of the constitutionally required level of protection of the fundamental rights imperiled by climate change, notably the rights to life, health, and property. The Court concluded somewhat ambiguously that "[i]t is not presently ascertainable that the duty of protection arising from fundamental rights has been violated", an assertion that opens to door to a fresh assessment in the future if more information is available. The judges faced the challenge of finding a delicate balance between the duty to deploy heightened scrutiny of policies potentially polluted by a short-termist bias and the duty to defer to the legislature in a domain where epistemic and structural discretion loom large. They concede that "[t]he question of whether sufficient measures have been taken to fulfill duties of protection arising from fundamental rights can only be reviewed by the Federal Constitutional Court to a limited extent (…)", for "duties of protection are essentially unspecified", leaving it "for the legislator to decide how risks should be tackled, to draw up protection strategies and to implement those strategies through legislation" (BVerfG 2021, at § 152). The Court "will find a violation of a duty of protection is no precautionary measures whatsoever have been taken, or if the adopted provisions and measures prove manifestly unsuitable or completely inadequate for achieving the required protection goal, or if the provisions and measures fall significantly short of the protection goal" (BVerfG 2021, at § 152). Put briefly, that would only be the case if the legislator allowed climate change to run its course, if the adopted policy disregarded the precautionary principle, if it did not aim for climate neutrality, if no adaptation measures to climate change were available, or if the framework ruled out future adjustments required by further developments in knowledge or reality (BVerfG 2021, at §§ 154–81).

Much the same reasoning is used by the Court to dismiss the challenge grounded in the environmental and intergenerational clause of Article 20a of the Basic Law. In spite of acknowledging that the clause would be deprived of normative force if "[its] material content (…) were fully determined by the day-to-day political process with its more short-term approach and its orientation towards directly expressible interests" and that "Article 20a GG may not be drained of substance as an obligation to take clime action", the judgment insists that the constitutional provision "does leave the legislator considerable leeway to design" an appropriate policy course, such that "[i]t is not, in principle, for the courts to translate the wording (…) into quantifiable global warming limits and corresponding emission amounts or reduction targets" (BVerfG 2021, at §§ 206–07). Reviewing the legislative framework under the light afforded by the scientific evidence contained in the IPCC reports, the judges conclude that "the legislator has set the fundamental course of national climate change law in a direction that gives the German state an opportunity to effectively fulfil its constitutional mandate to take climate action through its own efforts embedded within an international framework" (BVerfG 2021, at § 210).

These were the arguments given in the judgment to reject the claim made by the complainants that the challenged provisions of the Climate Change Act were not sufficiently robust to meet the ultimate target of carbon-neutrality by 2050. Yet the Court did decide that the schedule of emissions up to 2030 imposed a disproportionate burden on younger generations. In a critical passage of a very long and laborious ruling, one reads that "[since] the emission amounts until 2030 (…) significantly narrow the emission possibilities available after 2030, the legislator must take sufficient precautionary measures to ensure that freedom is respected when making the transition to climate neutrality. (…) As intertemporal guarantees of freedom, fundamental rights afford the complainants protection against the greenhouse gas reduction burdens imposed by Article 20a GG being unilaterally offloaded onto the future" (BVerfG 2021, at § 183). Indeed, "[w]hen Article 20a GG obliges the state to protect the natural foundations of life—partly out of responsibility towards future generations—it is aimed first and foremost at preserving the natural foundations of life for future generations. But at the same time, it also concerns how environmental burdens are spread out between different generations. (…) [That] encompasses the necessity to treat the natural foundations of life with such care and to leave them in such condition that future generations who wish to carry on preserving these foundations are not forced to engage in radical abstinence" (BVerfG 2021, at § 193).

I cannot think of a better illustration of the role that my account of intergenerational equity ascribes to constitutional adjudication than this landmark ruling of the *Bundesverfassungsgericht*. It is exemplary of the delicate balance between democracy, expertise, and justice that any conscientious engagement by a judge with the enormous complexity of climate policy requires. The judgment repudiates both the conservative impulse to fall back on some vague notion of institutional incapacity to give the legislature free ride to tackle climate change as it sees fit and the activist temptation to invoke the failures of the democratic process to turn the judiciary into the compassionate savior of the species and herald of distributive justice. One hopes that, styles of judgment and procedural variations apart, this measured approach takes root in other jurisdictions facing similar challenges, all the more so as climate change is a matter of global significance that can only be addressed by the coordinated efforts of many national governments. Perhaps even more ambitiously, the same approach can be taken, with the necessary adaptations, in other areas of policymaking where intergenerational equity ought to be a major concern. In so doing, constitutional judges would not be usurping political power, but acting as stewards of self-government; the government of the people, by the people, and for the people—the old and the young, the born and the unborn—that constitutes the essence of modern democracy.

References

Alexy R (2005) Balancing, Constitutional Review, and Representation. Int J Const Law 3

Alexy R (2018) Theorie der Grundrechte. Suhrkamp

Aristotle (2001) Ethica Nichomachea. Ross WD, translator. In McKeon R, editor. The Basic Works of Aristotle. New York: The Modern Library

Atienza M, Manero JR (2007) Las Piezas del Derecho: Teoría de los Enunciados Jurídicos. Ariel, Barcelona

Barack A (2012) Proportionality—Constitutional Rights and Their Limitations. Cambridge University Press, Cambridge

BVerfG, Beschluss des Ersten Senats vom 24. März 2021, available at https://www.bundesverfassungsgericht.de

Canas V. O (2019) Princípio da Proibição do Excesso na Conformação e no Controlo de Atos Legislativos. Almedina

Cruft R (2019) Human Rights, Ownership, and the Individual. Oxford University Press, Oxford

Dicey AV (1982) Introduction to the Study of the Law of the Constitution. 8th edn. Liberty Fund

Dworkin R (1977) Taking Rights Seriously. Oxford University Press, Oxford

Elster J (1984) Ulysses and the Syrens: Studies in Rationality and Irrationality. Cambridge University Press, Cambridge

Ely JH (1980) Democracy and Distrust: A Theory of Judicial Review, Cambridge. Harvard University Press, Mass.

García de Enterría E. (1994) La Constitución Como Norma Y El Tribunal Constitucional. 3ª Edición. Madrid: Civitas

Häberle P (2006) A constitutional law for future generations—The 'Other' form of the social contract: The generational contract. In: Tremmel J (ed). Handbook of Intergenerational Justice. Cheltenham: Edward Elgar

Holmes S (1995) Passions and Constraint—On the Theory of Liberal Democracy. The University of Chicago Press, Chicago and London

Homer (2018) The Odyssey. Wilson E (ed). New York and London: W. W. Norton & Company

Jefferson T (1958) Letter to James Madison. In: MacClure JP (ed) The Papers of Thomas Jefferson Vol 15: 27 March 1789 to 30 November 1789. Princeton University Press. Available at <https://jeffersonpapers.princeton.edu/selected-documents/thomas-jefferson-james-madison#notes27b>. Accessed October 3 2020

Kelsen H (2010) Wesen und Entwicklung der Staatsgerichtbarkeit. In: Kletatsky HR, Marcic R, Schambeck H (eds). Die Wiener rechtstheoretische Schule—Schriften von Hans Kelsen, Adolf Merkl, Anfred Verdross. Vol. II. Vienna. pp. 1485–531

Klatt M, Moritz M (2012) The Constitutional Structure of Proportionality. Oxford University Press, Oxford

Kumm M (2017) Constitutional Courts and Legislatures: Institutional Terms of Engagement. Católica Law Review 1

MacKenzie M (2016) Institutional Design and Sources of Short-Termism. In: González-Ricoy I, Gosseries A (eds) Institutions for Future Generations. Oxford: Oxford University Press; 2016.

McIntyre A (2007) After Virtue: A Study in Moral Theory. University of Notre Dame Press, Notre Dame

Rawls J (2005) Political Liberalism. Columbia University Press, New York, p xvi

Reimpression de Ancien Moniteur Tome Neuvième: Mai 1789—Novembre 1799 (Paris Bureau Central 1842).

Ribeiro G (2020) Almeida. controlo judicial das restrições aos direitos sociais. E-Pública: Rev Electrónica Direito Público 7(3)

Ribeiro G (2017) Almeida. Is Judicial Restraint a Matter of Bright Lines or of Democratic Deference? E-Pública: Rev Electrónica Direito Público 4(1)

Ribeiro G. Almeida (2020) O Conceito Pós-Moderno de Constituição. In: Ana Gouveia Martins et al, organizers. O Poder Judicial: Revisitar o Passado e Pensar o Futuro, Actas do XII Encontro de Professores de Direito Público. Available at https://drive.google.com/file/d/1BEJbEvUM-sKDfV3nPlb9I-ar8nTlwBq5/view

Ribeiro G. Almeida (2017) The Effects of Fundamental Rights in Private Disputes. In: Collins H, organizer. European Contract Law and the Charter of Fundamental Rights. Cambridge: Intersentia

Almeida RG (2022) What Is Constitutional Interpretation? In Int J Const Law 20(3):1130–1161

Schlink B (2012) Proportionality (1). In: Rosenfeld M, Sajó A (eds). The Oxford Handbook of Comparative Constitutional Law, Oxford: Oxford University Press

Schmitt C (2012) Legalität und Legitimität. 8th edition. Duncker & Humblot

Schmitt C (1993) Verfassungslehre. 11th edn. Duncker & Humblot

Sieckmann J-R (1990) Regelmodelle und Prinzipienmodelle des Rechtssystems. Nomos Verlag, Baden-Baden

Silva J (2015) Pereira da. Universidade Católica Editora, Deveres do Estado de Protecção de Direitos Fundamentais. Lisboa

Thayer JB (1893) The Origin and Scope of the American Doctrine of Constitutional Law. Little, Brown, and Company

Thoma R (2000) The Reich as a democracy. In: Jacobson A, Schlink B (eds) Weimar: A Jurisprudence of Crisis. University of California Press

Tushnet M (2021) The New Fourth Branch—Institutions for Protecting Constitutional Democracy. Cambridge University Press, Cambridge

Waldron J (1999) Law and Disagreement. Oxford University Press, Oxford

Winter G (2022) The Intergenerational Effects of Fundamental Rights: A Contribution of the German federal Constitutional Court to Climate Protection. J Environ Law 34(1)

Intergenerational Constitutional Regulation

Alan Bronfman-Vargas

Abstract The article reviews the constitutional problems that arise from the recognition of fundamental rights of people that do not yet exist. Given the need to impose limits on activity that threatens the future of the environment, it explores the protection that environmental preservation bodies endowed with constitutional autonomy can offer. Finally, it examines the minimum requirements for these bodies to fulfill their future protection function.

1 Introduction

All constitutions have the ambition to create a stable political order that will ensure peaceful coexistence in the future. To accomplish this goal, constitutions establish a set of procedures and substantive rules concerning how relations should operate between the state and the population and between the members of the community. Constitutionalism is particularly ambitious when it comes to setting up procedures and rules that will govern people who have not had any say in the development and approval of the constitution used to govern them. To be successful in governing the future of the political community, a constitution must build and establish a proper avenue for democratic life, as well as institutions that defend and promote it, while also setting reasonable and effective boundaries for exercising government power.

The history of constitutionalism shows some differences when it comes to the capacity to impact the future. Institutional arrangements, procedural rules, and precise regulations allow for only limited room for adaptation to a changing society. When circumstances create no possibility for adaptation, a constitution can be subject to formal reform or mutation.

Regarding fundamental rights, future needs can be well served by the use of broad language that offers elasticity to the interpreter. Much of the protection provided by the fundamental rights of freedom originates from judges' abilities to adapt the application of those rights to the needs of contemporary society. In practice, fundamental

A. Bronfman-Vargas (✉)
Faculty of Law, Pontificia Universidad Católica de Valparaíso, Valparaíso, Chile
e-mail: alan.bronfman@pucv.cl

R. Arnold and T. Fickentscher (eds.), *The Responsibility of a Constitution for the Future*, https://doi.org/10.1007/978-3-031-65296-7_2

rights can be protected by a judge in the case of deprivation or future harm that affects the free and full exercise of such rights by a person. In this sense, even when the interest protected by a fundamental right has a permanent and universal character, making it reasonable to expect that the right will also protect unborn generations, it is not easy to grant the judge tutelage powers without individuals being affected. We cannot know the will of unborn rights holders or those who may be their proper representatives. Nevertheless in recent cases of intergenerational litigation in national and international Courts, the right holders were considered persons (Sacchi v. Argentina, 2021; Billy et al. v. Australia, 2022; Duarte Agostinho et al. v. Portugal, 2020; Urgenda, 2015; Lozano Barragán, 2018; Shresta v. Office of the Prime Minister of Nepal, 2017; Gloucester Resources Ltd. v. Minister for Planning, 2017; D. G. Khan Cement Company v. Government of Punjab, 2021; Juliana v. United States, 2020; Neubauer et al. v. Germany, 2021). Despite the decisions' references to plaintiffs' children or unborn generations, the impact on individuals of the current generation remains a key issue in all cases.[1] Future generations have no way of selecting representatives or validating their work, which is a problem inherent in trying to represent those who are unable to speak for themselves.[2]

The weighing of costs and benefits by the judge regarding rights protection depends on the ability to predict the consequences of current activities in the future, and such a prediction is not always possible or only minimally accurate. As long as it is possible, the judge can prevent future harm (or affectation) that threatens rights. Predicting the future is usually more precise in determining the consequences of human actions on the environment (e.g., climate change forever altering the natural scenery). Nevertheless, it is difficult "to asses if the benefits outweigh the cost with such faraway horizons".[3]

A third problem is the tension between the rights of future generations and the rights and duties of current generations. The problem is related to "[t]he opaque scope and content of intergenerational rights".[4]

The situation is different in the case of fundamental rights, whose title holders are the community or society, compared with environmental or cultural rights.[5] Article 19 Number 8 of the Chilean Constitution (hereafter called the Constitution or CPR), for example, protects the right to live in an environment free of pollution and is a fundamental right whose proper holder is the entire community, not an individual (although it has been invoked in some lawsuits as a classic individual right). The same constitutional provision establishes the state's duty to ensure "*this right is not*

---

[1] Bertram (2022), 9–19.

[2] Karnein (2016), 84.

[3] Zuber (2016), 66.

[4] Bertram (2022), 19. We also have "uncertainty about the very existence of people in the future", González-Ricoy and Gosseries (2016), 5. We cannot know whether there will be minorities whose rights are affected (future generations may be composed of a plurality of different persons with dissimilar interests). Karnein (2016), 87.

[5] Bertram, "Intergenerational Equity," 19. Litigation against climate change is the commonplace and older ground of the rising constitutional protection of future generations. Araújo and Koessler (2021), 12–14, 44.

jeopardized" and to promote "*the preservation of nature*". Likewise, the Constitution explicitly authorizes the law to establish specific restrictions on the exercise of certain rights and freedoms to protect the environment.[6] The formulation of this fundamental right allows judges, fulfilling the assumptions of the second paragraph of Article 20 CPR ("*unlawful act or omission attributable to a specific authority or person*"), to adopt protective measures, even in cases where there are no persons directly affected by a polluting activity given the state's duty to "*protect the preservation of nature*". Although the judicial decisions handed down in this warranty did not invoke consequences for future generations, the preservation of nature has a clear benefit for the human beings who will inhabit the Earth in the future. In the case of Palza Corvacho (Num. 19.824, 19.12.1985), the Chilean Supreme Court ruled on the extraction of water of Lake Chungará. Even though this case has consequences for the constitutional rights of the applicants, the Court's decision was made on the basis of the environmental consequences of the exploitation of those waters, which included damage to the flora and fauna of the area due to a five-meter decrease in the water level. There is no reference to future generations, although the purpose of guaranteeing the "better development of life" stated in the decision precisely refers to the lives of subsequent generations.[7]

Additionally, nothing hinders the design of rights that are specifically aimed at protecting the fundamental interests of holders that are expected to exist in the future. In a design of this type, both the holders of the right and the available remedies should be specifically regulated. Declarative decisions of the courts alone invite non-invasive action on the executive and legislative branches (e.g., an Ombudsman for Future Generation's proposal). Judicial injunctions may encroach upon the domain of democratic politics. Redressability of the action refers to a task that is properly judicial.[8]

2 Constitution and Freedom

The Constitution holds a key position in the democratic political system as a result of its purpose and function. The purpose of the Constitution is to protect people's freedom. To the extent that it reasonably offers this protection, the Constitution serves the key function of legitimizing the democratic political system. If the Constitution does not effectively protect present freedom, it does not contribute to the legitimacy of the political system, and if the Constitution does not contribute to the legitimacy of this system, it loses its key position.

---

[6] Otherwise the idea of "environmental heritage" was described as part of the social function of property (Article 19, Num. 24) in the case Palza Corvacho, which reinforces the power of the law to regulate without indemnity.

[7] In the same way is the global leading case Horvath v. Comisión Nacional de Medio Ambiente (Num. 2.732, 19.3.1997). González-Ricoy (2016), 170.

[8] Beckman and Uggla (2016), 141.

The key role of the Constitution also depends on other elements that are essential for its proper functioning and legitimacy. Elements such as recent historical experiences that validate it, the visibility and capabilities of public servants, the qualifications and working aptitude of the population, the tradition of judges' independence, and the regulation and practices of public administration or the court system can be of equal or greater importance for a proper democratic system.

To contribute to democracy, the Constitution must be effective at protecting freedom. The effectiveness of the Constitution relies, in part, on its implementation of the separation of powers and the effective protection of constitutional rights. The separation of powers requires the existence of political interests that make checks and balances operational, and the protection of rights requires a powerful jurisdiction endowed with effective guardianship powers. Outside these areas, compliance with constitutional mandates is not ensured, and there are long lists of good intentions outlined in the Constitution, which are systematically irrelevant for present and future generations.

From another perspective, the Constitution offers lawyers the possibility to impose rules, principles, and values on legislatures that promote their political ideologies. This factor gives citizens the dream of freedom: liberation from an oppressive ruler and their interests through replacement by a limited government where everyone can grow and prosper freely. A constitution's success depends, in part, on its ability to accommodate the future within the constitutional project and each individual's desire for freedom. By its nature, the Constitution may threaten the sovereignty of future generations by imposing upon them provisions adopted by a previous generation. Current, fixed, and future-oriented clauses are even more limiting of the sovereignty of future generations.[9]

The success of the Constitution and its elasticity indicates how other political projects not directed toward the protection of freedom are incorporated into constitutionalism, dismissing state abstentionism to promote the duty of state action in favor of common interest and well-being. Setting aside the debate on the legitimacy of these added goals, it can be argued that such goals do not always fit well within the design and functionality of the instruments of historical constitutionalism. The separation of powers is useful in restraining and controlling power by counteracting opposing political, social, cultural, economic, or territorial interests. However, the same separation of powers can be an obstacle to advancing social goals when such goals are understood to represent a threat or harm by political forces with parliamentary representation. The same applies to the protection of fundamental rights that impose limits on government action in service of collective interests.

One way to overcome the negative outcome of pursuing (constitutional) goals that could diminish an individual's current freedom is to design "future-focused institutions", which are specialized institutions that have the promotion of future-oriented

---

[9] However, as an instrument, the Constitution "is necessary to the pursuit of valuable public and personal endeavours", setting the conditions of self- government and the pursuit of future-oriented projects. Muñiz-Fraticelli (2009), 407.

policies as their main or exclusive aim.[10] The Constitution must specify the goals that the future- focused institution ought to pursue (protection of the environment, sustainability of energy sources, etc., the policy domain, the degree of discretion in the exercise of its assigned powers, and the nature of the powers entrusted). The law must set the means for the functions of such an institution.

This type of institution enables the pursuit of a variety of political and legal objectives through the Constitution, providing the law with the possibility to collaborate in the achievement of objectives in accordance with the democratic will. It is not reasonable to prevent the legislator from regulating within the policy domain in which the institution operates to protect the rights of those who do not yet exist by granting open competencies to political and judicial bodies (as open as hypothetical protection). The law not only complements the Constitution but also allows for the creation of a political and social consensus that is adapted to the present conditions and acts as a legitimate tool to steer public consent for the benefit of the current common welfare.

3 New Social Needs and New Demands for Constitutional Regulation

It is possible to recognize a set of evils or problems in the present that could seriously harm the political community in the future. Good governance involves attending to present-day needs, as well as identifying evils and taking actions to mitigate or eliminate them. Political parties have strong incentives to promote policies that will have obvious net benefits over a small number of electoral cycles and strong incentives "to avoid policies that have near-term costs and longer term benefits".[11] Future benefits are less credible than near-term ones. Examples of these problems include the current budget imbalance that prevents the retention of sufficient fiscal resources for the future, the unsustainability of the pension system due to demographic changes, the cumulative negative impact of environmental pollution, insecurity in the energy supply, the development of technologies that are incompatible with the protection of private life, and health insecurity resulting from uncontrolled experimentation. Law and policy have already provided some answers to these challenges involving future governance, including balanced budget clauses that politically and legally make it difficult to approve budget deficits, special tax savings provisions designed

[10] González-Ricoy and Gosseries (2016), 6. This institution is different from institutions in which farsightedness is not part of their core business but can contribute to the implementation of future-oriented policies (future-beneficial institutions).

[11] MacKenzie (2016), 27.

to guarantee funding to pensions, the environmental precautionary principle, policies on development and energy sustainability[12] controls over the data traffic and its treatment, and the adoption of standards and health coordination policies.

With respect to balanced budget in 2006 Chile adopted Law No. 20.128 on fiscal responsibility. Constitutional rules regulate the distribution of budget power between the President of the Republic and the National Congress (notwithstanding the fact that some believe the Constitution demands a balanced budget). This law is a response to President Lagos announcing the implementation of a structural budget surplus rule in 2000, renouncing part of the presidential power on the matter to increase economic agents' confidence. This law sets explicit goals based on structural income and creates two sovereign funds to manage the resources generated by fiscal discipline. This new law respects the recommendations of the IMF, WB, IDB, and the OECD and was used as a reference for other countries. Nonetheless, from a legal point of view, these regulations are weak since the Executive Power retains discretionary power to intervene in relevant variables of the process.[13]

In regards to guarantee funding to pensions the Pension Reserve Fund (Article 5, Law No. 20.128) complements existing fiscal obligations regarding pensions (basic solidary old-age and disability pension and Solidarity Old-Age and Disability Retirement Contribution). This fund seeks to transfer resources between generations, thereby reducing the impact of commitments made by the state in the context of the right to social security recognized by the Constitution (Article 19, No. 17). Nonetheless, the Chilean pension system is based on an individual capitalization scheme, and thus, the role of the state is subsidiary.

As regards the environmental precautionary principle it was considered in some decisions of the Supreme Court. According to doctrine, this principle is handled in Article 15 of the 1992 Rio Declaration. It could also derive from general principles of administrative law (Article 32 of Law No. 19.880).[14]

The rule is that these and similar responses were implemented through laws—in the best cases—and regulations and resolutions, although some of them have components in constitutional regulation.

The key role of the indicated matters and others in the future of the political community suggests their importance as constitutional issues. This situation would require broad consensus on the actions or policies that will be promoted. This consensus must be based on knowledge established and accepted by the relevant scientific communities and would depend on the viability of setting a rule to guide the state's actions over a long period. The stability and permanence of the Constitution recommend that such a rule would be unquestionably useful for the attainment of the intended social good. The absence of consensus or the impossibility of establishing a fixed end (the basis of a constitutional obligation) dismisses the hope of useful constitutional regulations.

---

[12] The Executive Decree No. 148/2016 of the Ministry of Energy mandates this ministry to "lead the implementation of the National Energy Policy". The policy horizon is the year 2050.

[13] Gallegos (2018), 612–614.

[14] Costa Cordella (2014), 168–170.

4 New Constitutional Ends and Constitutional Responsibility

The question of the best protection for the rights of future generations does not have a clear and single answer. Giving fundamental rights to future people has practical and legal problems that are difficult to overcome. Nevertheless, the deficiencies in contemporary democratic government suggest that strengthening the constitutional jurisdiction would be a good idea.

One possible answer is to include a particular end within the Constitution and transfer the duty of developing the means of ensuring that goal into either an institution or a law. The constitutional regulation of such a goal can give direction, content, and strength to present-day and relevant political and social interests for the future and, if necessary or appropriate, can be supplemented with rules for effectiveness. In any case, the inclusion of new goals in the Constitution must be adapted to this document's essential characteristics as the paramount legal and political tool of the democratic regime. If the aims do not adjust to the Constitution's role as a legal and political tool, its constitutional recognition will be unfruitful.

The ends may place obligations on individuals, the state itself, or both. Imposing ends on individuals has the disadvantage of enforceability and creates the danger of colliding with freedoms and rights already protected by the Constitution. Setting an end goal as a state duty is less burdensome for the ideals of liberal constitutionalism.

The setting of a constitutional end (e.g., the preservation of nature) and an associated state duty (e.g., ensuring the protection of environmental heritage) enables a constitutional responsibility for the fulfillment of the new obligations created. This responsibility could be subject to both ordinary and extraordinary check-and-balance mechanisms, as well as judicial review. The choice between one or the other should depend upon legal institutional development and the power that tradition and conventions reserve for independent judiciaries. The specific end will determine the degree of politics and law that the institutional design must include in the relevant mechanisms and institutions. Clearly, a governing body can set the regime of responsibility of a constitution that it deems appropriate. Responsibility based on general obligations is usually controlled by political bodies and only exceptionally by the courts. Courts can demand responsibilities established by law in accordance with the rules and principles of due process.

This constitutional design can be found in the mandates that regulate autonomous institutions that are responsible for pursuing specific objectives. The Central Bank provides a good example of this type of institution and the related constitutional goals: to promote a secure and efficient payments system (Sweden),[15] protect the value of the currency in the interest of balanced and sustainable economic growth (South Africa),[16] attain stability for the purchasing power of the national currency,

[15] Instrument of Government, Chap. 8, Part 4, Article 13.

[16] Article 224 of the Constitution.

strengthen the guiding role of the state regarding national development (Mexico),[17] assure price stability (Germany, Czech Republic),[18] and maintain the purchasing power of the currency (Colombia).[19]

Experience suggests that this design can be useful in addressing serious and dangerous problems for the effective enforcement of fundamental rights for future generations. I review this possibility in the next section.

5 Constitutional Autonomy as a Response to Future Challenges

Uncertainty about the future does not prevent the Constitution from guaranteeing appropriate protection for elements that are relevant to the development of the lives of both present and future generations. In the example given in the previous section, the stable value of the currency has been regarded as a goal that deserves sustained protection over time and should, to some extent, remain independent of the current political parties' interests. Therefore, an autonomous body was created with specific objectives and competencies that can take any decisions deemed necessary to ensure this value now and in the future. This same model could be extended to other pressing political and social interests, such as the environment, energy supply, water supply, and pensions.[20]

The constitutional regulation of the autonomous Central Bank allows for several conclusions. First, subjects (currency, environment, and energy) cannot be completely removed from the domain of democratic politics, e.g., the domain of law and government decisions, even if political powers and agents (political parties) may not appear to be adopting correct decisions. Second, the constitutional purpose must be precisely established to secure adequate political and legal control and prevent autonomous entities from extending the powers of the Constitution out of bounds. Duties that are extensive and poorly defined can hardly be enforced outside of a political institution (as only representative bodies can take actions that hold people accountable). Constitutional duties, such as those derived from the protection of social rights, are difficult to enforce through judicial competencies. The possibility of establishing a judicial review must be associated with the generation of a regulation that is dense enough to set or deduce appropriate standards for the deployment of a judicial function.[21] The accuracy of constitutional duty can be obtained through

---

[17] The Constitution of Mexico, Article 28.

[18] Constitution of Germany, Article 88; Constitution of Czech Republic, Article 62.

[19] The Constitution of Colombia, Article 373.

[20] Current independent authorities tend to focus on matters in which political parties' influence leads to a poor outcome. Such matters include bodies for overseeing or auditing the public administration, anti-corruption entities, electoral offices, boards of the judiciary, human rights commissions, ombudsmen, and transparency agencies.

[21] González-Ricoy and Gosseries (2016), 12.

a combination of general and specific duties, each of which can have suitable mechanisms to secure effective enforcement. This mechanism represents a common technique in social rights: a general state obligation ("right to education") from which a set of specific obligations stem (free education clauses, availability of secular education, parents' freedom to choose their children's education, etc.).

The proper functioning of entities endowed with constitutional autonomy also requires respect for the values of constitutional democracy: impartiality, responsibility, transparency, and deliberation.[22]

Impartiality

Impartiality demands that the authorities in charge of the autonomous agency not exercise their competencies to advance their self-interest but instead to promote the public good.

The law can be influenced by partisan, social, or economically dominant interests, preventing legislation from adequately facing current and urgent problems with well-known outcomes in the future. By setting clear constitutional duties with objective reference standards, decisions can be entrusted to autonomous entities that are free, or partially free, from the influence of dominant interests. Nonetheless, this freedom must be exercised on a disciplinary basis to justify a departure from democratic principles.

The impartiality required of an independent body depends on at least four key aspects: the appointment and removal of authorities, governance and responsibilities, the autonomy of subjects, and relationships with political authority.

For appointments, it is not viable to exclude political powers from the designation of executives of the autonomous entity, as it is also evident that their intervention increases the risk of absorption or pressure from political parties. In the operation of the entity, autonomy should not be completely disconnected from political parties since an institution that lacks any support in democratic representation is usually weak. Several clauses decrease the political parties' pressure and influence over the entity: the requirement of high technical qualifications to access the board of the institution,[23] the participation of legislative and executive powers in the appointment of the chair or board,[24] mandates that exceed those of the authority that appoints them, and systems of regulated removal.[25]

---

[22] Vermeule (2007), 4.

[23] Good disciplinary training and extensive professional experience.

[24] In the designation of counselors of the Central Bank, the President and the Congress are involved in Uruguay, Chile, Mexico, and Brazil. In Colombia and the Czech Republic, only the President appoints counselors, and in Finland and Sweden, only the Congress or Parliament elect can make such appointments. In Uruguay and Chile, a special quorum is required for appointment.

[25] For example, the Uruguay Constitution demands that the Senate's ratification be based on the "personal, functional, and technical qualifications" of the candidate proposed by the President and the Council of Ministers. In Mexico, the Constitution delegates the regulation of the election of

Another basic issue to promote the impartiality of an entity is internal organization.

Although it may be chaired by one magistrate, it is more difficult to harmonize with political parties' interests and soft choices over those of an institution. A board or collegiate direction allows for different affinities, types of education, and partisan sympathies, diluting the appetite for absorption. The institution also requires administrative and financial autonomy granted by the Constitution or the law.

The scope of autonomous competencies must be defined by the Constitution and the law. This scope excludes the exercise of powers by other state entities. Some Constitutions explicitly prohibit interfering with the competencies of the Central Bank (such as the Swedish Constitution). The South African Constitution states that the Reserve Bank must exercise its competencies independently and without fear.

The definition of autonomy's scope can also be reduced in specific matters that are excluded from the prerogatives of the institution. In the case of central banks, the prohibition of granting loans to the government or buying debt from government institutions can be found in several constitutions (Brazil, Chile, Colombia, and Mexico). The constitution may, however, include exceptions to these prohibitions. The Chilean Constitution allows the Central Bank to guarantee or acquire state debt instruments in exceptional circumstances to preserve the normal functioning of internal and external payments. It can also finance expenses or loans in the case of a war or external threat. This type of exclusion or prohibition can be useful in preventing the entity from becoming involved in matters that should be resolved by the political system.

To maintain impartiality, it is recommended to establish the entity's relationship with the government and oversee the system's complete regulation.

Accountability

Constitutional democracy requires that political authorities be held accountable for the decisions they adopt and implement. One of the problems with excluding political entities from decisions on matters assigned to autonomous entities is that the traditional mechanisms of democratic accountability cannot operate in the sphere of autonomy.

Protection against the influence of political parties requires other means of holding members of autonomous entities accountable. Special constitutional and legal accountability arrangements must, therefore, be established. Constitutional responsibility can be established through causes of removal based on abuse or negligence under the competencies of the legislative or judicial authorities. If congress has the power to dismiss authorities, some safeguards can be taken to prevent a simple majority from interfering with the autonomy of the authority.

---

counselors to the law, as well as the duration of their tenure, but requires that the law regulate both topics in the most appropriate manner for the autonomous exercise of its functions. The Constitution also provides for their removal through impeachment in serious cases.

The law can provide instruments (e.g., regular reports) to scrutinize the performance of an autonomous body in the exercise of its competencies. The public monitoring techniques of agencies experience natural endogenous development. They are not necessarily fixed and can improve with the development of the autonomous agency's competencies.[26] Accountability is linked to transparency and requires full intelligibility of what comprises the constitutional work reserved for the autonomous body.

Accountability can also be associated with internal procedures. The exercise of powers should be linked to reinforced internal quorums or, when necessary, unanimity. Acting as a unit (and not with the fragmentation of interests expressed in minority votes) constitutes the autonomous entity's contribution to constitutional duty and the political system as such.

Finally, the political responsibility of the legislative power does not cease with the transfer of a constitutional duty, along with the competencies to fulfill it, to an autonomous entity. The legislative body remains responsible for the constitutional and legal provisions that support the operation of a special regime.

Transparency

Transparency increases public control in the democratic constitutional regime and should be considered in the operation of autonomous entities that assume the responsibility of satisfying the interests of future generations. Transparency promotes impartiality and makes it difficult for authorities to act in their interest. Nonetheless, transparency can have negative effects when it calls upon particular interested groups to inappropriately interfere in a decision in the public interest. Special interest groups can influence a transparent board to win concessions that distribute costs to others.[27] In collective decision-making processes, transparency (for example, streaming a session of the board of the autonomous entity) can strengthen the quality of the debate because of the advantages of exhibiting political positions toward groups promoting the defense of their interests.[28]

Those with critical views of the dominant positions in public debate can also be silenced and remain unwilling to accept the costs of a minority negative vote that has limited influence on the final decision. In both cases, incorporating transparency into the internal debate reduces the deliberative reserve and decreases the quality of the discussion.

In the case of autonomous entities, transparency has the main function of communicating to citizens the reasons behind the decisions of an entity that are not under the direct control of the political powers. To fulfill this function, as mentioned before,

[26] Vermeule (2007), 80.

[27] MacKenzie (2016), 27.

[28] Fenster adds risks to national security and higher tax costs. Fenster (2006), 906–908.

it is fundamental to ensure the intelligibility of the information flow that the institution generates. At this point, the creation of indicators and the regular issuing of reports by the autonomous entity provides evidence to the community that the entity is fulfilling its constitutional duty. Access to technical debate is of little use if there is no knowledge or minimal understanding of the topic; information that does not make sense to the public does not contribute to transparency.[29]

Deliberation

In a constitutional democratic regime, deliberation is the standard procedure before making collective decisions and, therefore, cannot be absent from the procedures of an autonomous entity. Deliberation promotes the exchange of relevant information and the evaluation of actionable alternatives to achieve a consensual outcome. Although deliberation is not fully open to evidence and good reasoning, an autonomous entity directed by qualified experts who neither serve nor represent political parties can help to reduce the scope of decision- making discretion to a list of viable options based on scientific knowledge. For future generations, this reduction at least offers scientific knowledge to act in the face of the unknown.

6 Conclusion

In successful democracies, the constitution is not an instrument that fulfills countless tasks of current and future political and social interest, nor is it a tool that guarantees good outcomes in all dimensions. The constitution works reasonably well in some areas and political systems by setting a few general rules that allow for the challenges of the contemporary government to be addressed.

It is not an easy task to defend the fundamental rights, freedoms, and interests of future generations. In democracies, there are certainly urgent demands for anticipatory state action based on available knowledge, thereby giving the political community some certainty about its future life.

Under these circumstances, it is not viable to remove democratic representation from crucial medium- and long-term decisions regarding the future of the political community. Among other reasons, democratic representation cannot be removed because this type of exclusion weakens democracy itself, which then experiences a reduction in its decision-making scope that strains the political system and undermines the legitimacy of the constitution.

We understand that under the current level of constitutional development, the best way to manage topics of special relevance for the future is to establish precise and consensual state goals supported by an autonomous, responsible, and qualified body

[29] Fenster (2006), 924–925.

that is responsible for pursuing those goals. The constitutional and legal technique used to create a central bank or reserve aimed at ensuring good management of predetermined economic variables is a model that, although imperfect, deserves more in-depth study.

In the end, the Constitution is an instrument that aims to protect freedom. To move away from this goal, even to address pressing social and political interests, undermines the success and legitimacy of the Constitution, closing off alternatives to the freedom that determines who we are collectively and as individuals.

References

Araújo R, Koessler L (2021) The rise of the constitutional protection of future generations. In: Legal Priorities Project Working Paper 7

Beckman L, Uggla F (2016) An Ombudsman for Future Generations Legitimate and Effective? In: González-Ricoy I, Gosseries A (eds) Institutions for Future Generations. Oxford University Press, Oxford, pp 117–134

Bertram D (2022) 'For you will (Still) be here tomorrow': The many lives of intergenerational equity. Transnatl Environ Law 1–29. https://doi.org/10.1017/S2047102522000395

Costa E (2014) Principio de Precaución y Regulación Ambiental en Chile: Operando sin instrucciones, pero operando. R Justicia Ambiental 6(6):159–179

Fenster M (2006) The opacity of transparency. Iowa L Rev 91:885–949

Gallegos J (2018) Análisis normativo crítico de la regla fiscal en Chile. R Ch De Derecho 45(3):597–619

González-Ricoy I, Gosseries A (2016) Designing Institutions for Future Generations: An Introduction. In: González-Ricoy I, Gosseries A (eds) Institutions for Future Generations. Oxford University Press, Oxford, pp 3–23

González-Ricoy I (2016) Constitutionalizing Intergenerational Provisions. In: González-Ricoy I, Gosseries A (eds) Institutions for Future Generations. Oxford University Press, Oxford, pp 170–183

MacKenzie MK (2016) Institutional Design and Sources of Short-Termism. In: González-Ricoy I, Gosseries A (eds) Institutions for Future Generations. Oxford University Press, Oxford, pp 24–45

Muñiz-Fraticelli VM (2009) The Problem of a Perpetual Constitution. In: Gosseries A, Meyer LH (eds) Intergenerational Justice. Oxford University Press, Oxford, pp 377–410

Karnein A (2016) Can we Represent Future Generations? In: González-Ricoy I, Gosseries A (eds) Institutions for Future Generations. Oxford University Press, Oxford, pp 83–97

Vermeule A (2007) Mechanism of Democracy. Oxford University Press, Oxford, Institutional Design Writ Small

Zuber S (2016) Measuring Intergenerational Fairness. In: González-Ricoy I, Gosseries A (eds) Institutions for Future Generations. Oxford University Press, Oxford, pp 65–82

Specificity of Constitutional Norms Relating to the Protection of Future Generations on the Example of the Constitution of the Republic of Poland

Andrzej Jackiewicz

Abstract The purpose of the article is to answer the question of how and, in particular, through what legal constructions modern constitutions express the responsibility of the present generation for the future. This question will be answered using the example of the Constitution of the Republic of Poland, adopted on 2 April 1997. The methodology used in the research was to first isolate those provisions of the Constitution that relate to the long-term future and aim to protect future generations, and then to analyze which legal constructions were used in doing so. An analysis of the provisions of this Constitution shows that it refers to future generations in several places and using various legal formulas that aim to have a long-term impact, with an eye to the distant horizon. These solutions include the elevated provisions of the preamble to the Constitution, the constituent elements of constitutional principles, the programmatic norms that set the directions of state activity, human rights, the duties of the individual, as well as provisions relating to discipline in public finance. In conclusion, it should be stated that the problem of protection of future generations in the Polish Constitution has been defined very broadly, using various legal constructions addressed to different addressees. As a result, the intensity of their impact, but also the possibility of their enforcement, varies.

The purpose of the article is to answer the question of how and, in particular, through what legal constructions modern constitutions express the responsibility of the present generation for the future. This question will be answered using the example of the Constitution of the Republic of Poland, adopted on 2 April 1997. First, it should be noted that the Polish Constitution is relatively young, having been enacted in 1997. Its authors already recognized the issue of responsibility to future generations and decided to address it in several places. The analysis of these provisions shows that it has been done in the form of different legal formulas. While

A. Jackiewicz (✉)
Associate Professor, Faculty of Law, University of Białystok, Białystok, Poland
e-mail: jackiewicz@uwb.edu.pl

R. Arnold and T. Fickentscher (eds.), *The Responsibility of a Constitution for the Future*, https://doi.org/10.1007/978-3-031-65296-7_3

reviewing constitutional provisions in order to distinguish those relating to the interests of future generations, it should be also noted that it follows from the essence of the law that their specificity lies in the fact that they concern the future and regulate events that are yet to come. However, the purpose of some of these legal norms is to regulate the future in the short term, while the purpose of others is to have a long-term impact, with a distant time horizon in mind. The methodology used in the research was to first isolate those provisions of the Constitution that relate to the long-term future and aim to protect future generations, and then to analyze which legal constructions were used in doing so.

First of all, future generations are already mentioned in the introduction to the Constitution. It states that "We, the Polish Nation—all citizens of the Republic (…) obligated to pass on to future generations all that is valuable from our heritage of over a thousand years (…) we establish the Constitution". It is therefore an indication of one of the duties imposed on the Nation as sovereign, referring both to the sovereign establishing the Constitution in 1997, but also to the sovereign in the present time, making the Nation obligated to pass on to future generations all that is valuable from the heritage of more than a thousand years, through the principles of so-called "intergenerational solidarity". As Marek Piechowiak points out, the aforementioned obligations only make sense if the interest of future generations is recognized as a constitutional value (Piechowiak 2016a, b, c, p. 141). However, the preamble does not specifically mention what is included in this heritage. There is no doubt that, within the framework of these values, cultural achievements or the environment can be mentioned as examples of extremely important goods that will objectively be of fundamental importance for future generations. It should also be pointed out that the first value indicated in the preamble, as well as the primary purpose served by the Constitution, is "the existence and future of our Homeland", which undoubtedly goes beyond the formula of the state, referring to the concern of the legislator for the future of Poland treated as a community of its citizens (Piechowiak 2016a, b, c, pp. 132–133).

Furthermore, the preamble refers to the principle of social solidarity, which can also be interpreted in a way that is consistent with the aforementioned idea of intergenerational solidarity (Piechowiak 2020, p. 86). Also relevant from the point of view of future generations is the principle of subsidiarity included in the preamble, which prescribes the involvement of the state in those spheres in which citizens and their communities are unable to meet their needs on their own. This becomes even more crucial from the point of view of the protection of constitutional values, such as a clean and healthy environment, for the benefit of future generations who are obviously unable to look after their interests themselves. They should therefore be able to rely on the assistance of a State guided by the principle of subsidiarity in ensuring an adequately preserved environment in the future. Boguslaw Banaszak aptly wrote about the preamble that, on the one hand, it reflects a certain socially accepted system of values and beliefs and, on the other hand, by formulating a programmatic for the future, it embodies certain ideas and seeks to implement them by influencing both the consciousness of society as a whole and its individual members (Banaszak 2009, pp. 4–5). Similarly, Piotr Tuleja points out that the preamble is an important element defining the constitutional identity of the state, which is done both by reference to the past shaping Polish political traditions, to the present and to the future shaping the goals and tasks of the state and society (Tuleja 2019a, b, c, p. 22).

Given the above, it should be pointed out that the first formulations of the constitutionalization of the issue of the protection of future generations are the provisions of the Preamble, which on the one hand testifies to the importance of this problem for the legislator, and on the other hand leads to the discussion, present not only in the Polish science of constitutional law, regarding the normative character of the introduction to the Constitution. The author's reference to the aforementioned provisions of the Preamble, however, requires an important reservation concerning the legal character of the introduction to the Constitution of the Republic of Poland and an answer to the question to what extent the provisions of the Preamble, which do not have the form of legal norms, can be given a normative character. As in other states, also in Poland the problem of the normativity of the Preamble of a normative act has not been resolved either by the doctrine of constitutional law or by the Constitutional Tribunal. As stated, by the latter, this situation results "from the ambiguous understanding of the notion of 'normativity' and different approaches to this issue by representatives of various legal sciences. Nevertheless, three approaches to this issue can be distinguished, namely: (1) those assuming that the Preamble has the same normative character as the following articulatory part of the normative act; (2) those denying the Preamble not only a normative but also a legal character; (3) finally, the most popular one, considering that the Preamble has a binding meaning for the interpretation of the articulatory part of the normative act". Until twenty years ago, none of these views was dominant, and the Constitutional Tribunal in its judgment of 18/04 even stated that legal norms in the strict sense could not be derived from the text of the Preamble. In the Tribunal's view, however, it does provide guidance, based on an authentic statement by the legislator as to the directions of interpretation of the provisions of the normative part of the Constitution that are consistent with its intentions.

In democratic states, however, the prevailing view nowadays is that the Preamble to the Constitution, regardless of its specificity, is normative in nature. Despite many doubts, this view is now becoming widespread also in the Polish legal sciences and judicial jurisprudence. Nevertheless, notwithstanding the indicated difficulties with the general recognition of the normative character of the Preamble *in toto*, it is much easier to refer to its particular expressions. Considering these passages, they provide normative arguments for the recognition of the obligations of both public authorities and individuals towards future generations, not only in terms of environmental protection, but also in the broad sense of a strategic impact on the preservation of the entire heritage for the benefit of future generations (Jackiewicz, Rytel-Warzocha 2022, pp. 44–46). Referring to the jurisprudence of the Polish Constitutional Tribunal, Piotr Tuleja states that the most typical cases in which the normative character of the preamble is revealed are the following situations: the use of the Preamble in determining the normative content of the provisions of the Constitution (Judgment of 16 December 2009, Kp 5/08), referring to the Preamble in the process of interpreting laws in conformity with the Constitution in order to resolve interpretative doubts prejudging the possibility of declaring a given act to be consistent with the Constitution (e.g. reliable and efficient operation of authorities as a control model and a directive determining the manner of operation of public authorities, cf. Judgment of 9 March 2016, K 47/15), making the Preamble a benchmark on the basis of which the unconstitutionality of a normative act or an act of law application can be established (Judgment of 12 March 2007, K 54/05) (Tuleja 2019a, b, c, p. 23–24; see also, inter alia, Piechowiak 2016a, b, c, pp. 153–158, Granat 2009, pp. 68–69).

Secondly, reference to responsibility for the fate of future generations can be found in constitutional principles. In doing so, it should be noted that they are directly addressed primarily to public authorities, but since their high degree of generality requires the translation of their normative content to the statutory level, this means that they also affect individuals through these provisions. Since it is not the purpose of the article to discuss all constitutional provisions relating to future generations, only by way of example selected constitutional principles will be indicated to illustrate the thesis that they constitute another form of legal construction relating to the problem of the protection of future generations. Article 1 of the Polish Constitution may serve as the first example. According to this provision, "The Republic of Poland is the common good of all its citizens". Just as statehood itself is a permanent entity that transcends the framework of a given generation, the right to it as a common good, to which not only the present generation is entitled, should be considered in a universal and timeless dimension to be enjoyed by both present and future generations. In particular, because the provision speaks explicitly of all citizens of the republic and there is no reason to place temporal restrictions in this case, especially since the concepts of nation and republic refer to a permanent, multi-generational historical community, including both ancestors and future generations, to whom, as already mentioned, the Preamble refers. Marek Piechowiak proposes the following definition of the constitutional principle of the common good: The Republic of Poland is the totality of the conditions of social life enabling and facilitating the integral development of all members of the political community and the communities they create (Piechowiak 2016a, b, c, pp. 161–215). This understanding of Article 1 seems to be in line with the view of the Polish Constitutional Tribunal. The common good has been recognized by the Constitutional Tribunal as a concept that also includes the natural environment (Judgment of 9 February 1999, U 4/98, Judgment of 17 of July 2011, L10/09), environmental protection (Judgment of 15 May 2006, P 32/05, Judgment of 16 October 2012, K 4/10, Judgement of 13 January 2015, SK 17/13, Judgment of 15 May 2006, P 32/05), the economic and civilizational development of the country and the life and health of all citizens.

It should also be borne in mind that this principle implies that the constitutional legislator is primarily concerned with recognizing the subordinate role of the state and its organs toward citizens, rather than emphasizing the importance of specific behavior of citizens toward the state (Banaszak 2009, pp. 14–15). Such a perspective is important for understanding any other constitutional formulations, regardless of their construction, which can be referred to the protection of the interests of future generations. Indeed, the Constitution draws attention to the state's obligation to undertake various types of measures for the protection of the common good, the content of which follows directly or indirectly from other provisions of the Constitution (Jackiewicz and Rytel-Warzocha 2022, pp. 46–47).

The protection of future generations is also directly affected by other constitutional principles, including those derived from Article 5 of the Constitution: the principle of protecting freedoms and rights, the duty to preserve national heritage, the duty to ensure protection of the natural environment (Cf. Judgment of 7 July 2021, K 20/00), and the principle of sustainable development, which is extremely important from the point of view of the rights of future generations. This is because the principle of sustainable development implies the necessity to find such technical, organizational, legal, etc. solutions conducive to economic or, more broadly, civilizational development that will protect the natural environment (Dąbrowski and Jackiewicz 2023, pp. 35–38; Banaszak 2009, pp. 54–55; Jackiewicz, Rytel-Warzocha 2022, p. 47–48). The science of law emphasizes that the goal of sustainable development is to preserve the environment in a state that ensures its use by present and future generations "while maintaining the sustainability of the functioning of natural processes and biodiversity covering all levels: gene, species, landscape and ecosystem" (Grabowska 2001, p. 197; Tuleja 2019a, b, c, p. 41; Florczak-Wątor 2016, pp. 279–290; Czech and Kropiewnicka 2012, pp. 186–189; Ignatowicz 2015, pp. 223–236; Rakoczy 2015, pp. 35–44, Kowalewska 2013, pp. 303–311). In the judgment K 23/05, the Constitutional Tribunal noted that environmental protection is one of the elements of "ecological security," but the tasks of the public authorities are broader—they also include activities improving the current state of the environment and programming its further development. The basic method of achieving this goal is—prescribed by Article 5 of the Constitution—to be guided by the principle of sustainable development, which refers to international arrangements, in particular to the 1992 Rio de Janeiro Conference. Within the framework of the principles of sustainable development falls not only the protection of nature or the formation of spatial order but also a due concern for social and civilizational development related to the necessity to build appropriate infrastructure, necessary for—taking into account the civilizational needs—the life of man and individual communities (Jackiewicz and Rytel-Warzocha 2022, p. 47–48).

The importance of other constitutional principles for the protection of future generations can also be indicated. Noteworthy is Article 6 (1) according to which the Republic of Poland shall provide conditions for the people's equal access to the products of a culture that are the source of the Nation's identity, continuity, and development. In this provision, the legislature clearly imposes an obligation on the Polish public authorities to take measures that create conditions for, among other things, the preservation of the country's cultural heritage. In the context of this constitutional principle and the obligations placed on public authorities, attention may also be drawn to Article 73, which provides for, among other things, the freedom to enjoy the cultural property. As Mariusz Jablonski points out, ensuring the realization of this freedom requires public authorities to adequately protect these goods, their restoration and storage, as well as to protect the rights and freedoms of persons and institutions that own them (Jabłoński 2002, p. 565).

On the other hand, demographic issues of importance for the future of both the state and the Nation, which obviously relates to future generations, concern Article 18, according to which marriage, being a union of a man and a woman, as well as family, maternity, and parenthood, shall be placed under the protection and guardianship of the Republic of Poland. As Piotr Tuleja reminds us, this article is the basis for the Constitutional Tribunal's formulation of the right to legal protection of family life, including in particular the adequate protection of marriage, family, maternity, and parenthood as values of particular importance for society (Tuleja 2019a, b, c, p. 83). As Witold Borysiak writes referring to the content of Article 18, in light of the Preamble, it can be considered that marriage and the family—due to their social importance—play a key role in the context of the development of future generations and the possibility of passing on the traditions of the Nation to them. All of the constitutional principles invoked here are clearly linked to other constitutional norms, to which reference will be made in the following parts of this article (Borysiak 2016a, b, c, pp. 465–466).

The above-mentioned articles of the Constitution prove that the second formula in which the Polish legislator refers to the protection of future generations are the constitutional principles. Their very general nature, particularly those defining the goals of the state, makes them require concretization and clarification in further provisions of the Constitution, so that they actually take on a specific form of programmatic norms (Florczak-Wątor 2019, pp. 283–285). However, it is also important that the responsibility for their realization rests primarily with the legislator, who by way of ordinary laws should ensure their accomplishment, and possibly also with the Constitutional Tribunal, whose task in this respect should be to ensure that legal norms inconsistent with these principles do not appear in the legal system (Judgment of 8 May 2006, P 32/05, Judgment of 10 July 2000, K 21/99; Banaszak 2009, pp. 12–13, 121). As Piotr Tuleja writes about Article 5 of the Constitution, the legal nature of this provision is such that no explicit orders or prohibitions of conduct addressed to public authorities result from it. It does, however, have a normative significance both in the process of making and applying the law. Since the legislator and other law-making bodies are obliged to pursue the objectives indicated in Article 5, this provision may serve to resolve doubts that arise in the process of purposive interpretation of the law. In particular, when doubts arise as to the *ratio legis* of a regulation (Tuleja 2019a, b, c, p. 41).

Thirdly, the construction of programmatic norms should be taken into account, which is important given the long-term impact of the Constitution. In this respect, it should be borne in mind that also constitutional principles can adopt programmatic formulations. In this sense, one can treat, for example, the aforementioned Article 5 and the objectives set by the state indicated therein. The peculiarity of programmatic norms, by their very nature, is their long-term, 'strategic' character, and therefore they seem to be extremely important from the point of view of protecting the interests of future generations. Among the programmatic norms, the Constitution of the Republic of Poland therefore refers to several values that seem particularly important precisely from this perspective. Such is the nature of the constitutional provisions contained in Article 74 (1,2,4). According to this provision, public authorities pursue policies ensuring ecological security for present and future generations, environmental protection is the duty of public authorities, and public authorities support the activities of citizens to protect and improve the quality of the environment (Dąbrowski and Jackiewicz 2023, pp. 68–85, 97–105; Jackiewicz and Rytel-Warzocha 2022, pp. 48–49; Górski 2016a, b, pp. 1691–1692, 1695–1701; Florczak-Wątor 2019, p. 247).

The same sphere is addressed by the programmatic norm in Article 68 (4), according to which public authorities shall combat epidemic illnesses and prevent the negative health consequences of environmental degradation (Bosek 2016, p. 1549, Florczak-Wątor 2019, p. 233).

A different area is covered by the programmatic norms contained in Articles 71 (1, sentence 1) and 72, which are of significance primarily for the future and continuity of the Nation. Article 71 (1, sentence 1) contains the obligation of the State to take into account the welfare of the family in its social and economic policy, which refers to the already mentioned constitutional principle of Article 18. As the Constitutional Tribunal pointed out in its judgment P 15/00, the provisions of the Constitution in this regard constitute a clear indication both for the ordinary legislator and for the bodies applying the law (Borysiak 2016a, b, c, pp. 1635–1642). Certainly, a rational constitutional legislator, when enacting the abovementioned norms, was guided by the awareness of the value of the family in social life and the importance of this basic family unit for the existence and functioning of the Nation.

The commitment of The Republic of Poland contained in Article 72 (1, sentence 1) to guarantee the protection of the rights of the child from the point of view of the existence of the Nation should be treated similarly (Borysiak 2016a, b, c, pp. 1659–1663). This sphere is also addressed by the programmatic norm contained in Article 68 (5), according to which public authorities shall support the development of physical culture, particularly among children and young persons. Another programmatic norm that explicitly refers to the future is the obligation of public authorities in Article 68 (3) to ensure special health care to children, pregnant women, people with disabilities and elderly. It should be emphasized that the obligations of public authorities derive from the programmatic norms contained in Article 68 (4) and Article 68 (5), but the beneficiary of the programmatic norms is society as a whole (Bosek 2016, pp. 1549, 1551, 1563–1564).

From the point of view of the legal form used in these provisions, all of them should be classified in the group of programmatic norms, whose characteristic feature is that, instead of determining specific obligations, they indicate the directions and goals that should be achieved by public authorities. Consequently, as in the case of constitutional principles, this also implies the obligation of public authorities to take measures, primarily legislative ones, to implement the relevant state policies in the indicated spheres (Jackiewicz and Rytel-Warzocha 2022, p. 50–52). Importantly from the point of view of the nature of programmatic norms, no individual rights can be derived from their content, although the implementation of the obligations arising from them undoubtedly has an impact on the protection of the values to which they refer, i.e., for example, the environment, the family or the health of children and young people (Banaszak 2009, pp. 354–355). As Monika Florczak-Wątor rightly points out, referring to one of the above-mentioned programmatic norms (Article 74), the state is not obliged to ensure ecological security for future generations, but it is obliged to pursue a policy aiming at this goal (Florczak-Wątor 2019, p. 247).

Another formula to be considered in the context of the protection of future generations is human rights. In the case of the Polish Constitution, this refers in particular to rights related to the sphere of family and maternity and, in the context of the subject of this study, to demography. First and foremost, attention should be drawn here to the right to special assistance from public authorities, which is a form of implementation of the already mentioned Article 18 of the Constitution and which has been granted to Families in a difficult material and social situation—in particular, those with many children or a single parent (Article 71, (1), sentence 2). A similar right to special assistance from public authorities is granted to a mother before and after the birth of her child (Article 71(2)). The Constitution, however, does not specify what this special care consists of, referring in this respect to the relevant law, while it is indisputable that the scope of this assistance should go beyond the ordinary assistance available to persons maintaining children or assistance provided to other persons (Cf. Judgment of 7 December 2005, P 3/05, see also Florczak-Wątor 2019, pp. 238–240). However, these are formulations that take the form of individual rights (Borysiak 2016a, b, c, p. 1628).

The category of constitutional rights of the individual of particular importance for the future includes the rights of children, i.e., inter alia, the right to free education in public schools (Article 70 (2)) and the right of a child deprived of parental care to care and assistance by public authorities (Article 72 (2)) In the context of the right to education, attention should be drawn to the opinion of the Constitutional Tribunal, which in its judgment of 8 November 2000, SK 18/99, indicated that the right to education should be percived both in terms of an individual good and an important, fundamental common good of society. The realization of the right to education is not so much some special privilege of modern man, but is an indispensable condition for the development of society and, at the same time, for the full participation of the individual in society. Universal education has become the most important engine of economic and civilizational development in the modern world (Królikowski and Szczucki 2016, p. 1580).

In the sphere of individual rights, in the field of environmental protection, attention should also be drawn to the constitutional right of every person to information on the state and protection of the environment, provided for in Article 74 (See more Dąbrowski and Jackiewicz 2023, p. 85–97; Jabłoński and Wygoda 2003, p. 129; Górski 2016a, b, pp. 1701–1703).

The possibility of pursuing these rights is not homogeneous and may depend on the content of the enacted legislation, such as the right to special assistance, which, however, does not prevent the violation of this right from becoming the basis for a constitutional complaint (Borysiak 2016a, b, c, pp. 1640, 1646), but they may also be asserted directly on constitutional grounds, such as the right to free education in public schools (Florczak-Wątor 2019, p. 240).

Another, fifth legal construction that we encounter in the Constitution of the Republic of Poland, which deals with the issue of protecting future generations, are the duties imposed on individuals. The first and most important among them is the obligation to care for the common good (Article 82). Thus, the constitutional legislator supplements the previously mentioned principle contained in Article 1 of the Constitution by entrusting responsibility for the Republic and its future to all citizens. As the Constitutional Tribunal stated about this provision, all citizens are obliged to the extent of their ability to sacrifice certain self-interests for the common good (judgment of 12 April 2000, K 8/98). There is no doubt that, in line with the principle of solidarity mentioned in the Preamble, this therefore also implies corresponding concern on the part of citizens to preserve the common good for future generations. Indeed, it is worth noting in this context that the common good is sometimes defined as the totality of the conditions of social life enabling and facilitating the integral development of all members of a given political community and the communities they form (Florczak-Wątor 2019, p. 268). Obviously, the very general wording of this obligation in terms of content means that this provision nevertheless requires statutory clarification, i.e. the indication of specific obligations (orders and prohibitions) imposed on citizens (Piechowiak 2016a, b, c, p. 1872). Another duty directly relating to the protection of the interests of future generations is the obligation, arising from Article 86 of the Constitution, to care for the state of the environment and the principle of responsibility for its degradation caused by the individual, also enshrined in this provision (Dąbrowski, Jackiewicz 2023, pp. 133–152). With regard to the determination of the detailed principles of this responsibility, the Constitution already refers to the law, which is the Act of 27 April 2001 Environmental Protection Law (Journal of Laws 2013, p. 1232), where a special section—Title VI—Responsibility in Environmental Protection—is devoted to these issues. The detailed determination of the content of the obligation indicated in Article 86 must also be decoded from statutory provisions (Florczak-Wątor 2019, p. 280, Górski, 2016a, b, pp. 1898,1900). Also of interest from the point of view of future generations is the obligation imposed by Article 70 (1) of the Constitution to educate until the age of 18. Against the background of other legal constructions analyzed, this is an atypical solution insofar as this obligation is imposed on persons who, in the long run, are at the same time the beneficiaries of the benefits resulting from this obligation in the future, as well as, of course, all the solutions indicated in this article protecting the interests of future generations.

As already mentioned in the introduction of this chapter, the Constitution of the Republic of Poland is relatively young, but we consider it among those constitutions that already contain provisions relating to public finances. An entire Chapter X is devoted to them. In particular, it is important to point to Article 216 (5), according to which no loans may be contracted and no financial guarantees and warranties may be issued, as a result of which the state public debt exceeds 3/5 of the value of the annual gross domestic product (Ofiarski 2016, pp. 1465, 1470, 1478, 1479). This is a rule that is particularly important from the point of view of the economic security of future generations, safeguarding against excessive state indebtedness imposing on future generations financial obligations disastrous from the point of view of future state budgets, slowing down development and investment (Florczak-Wątor 2019, pp. 631–632). The provision of Article 220 (1), according to which the increase in expenditure or decrease in revenue planned by the Council of Ministers may not cause the Sejm to establish a budget deficit greater than that provided for in the draft budget act, should also be understood in this context, which is an evident expression of the legislator's concern for the state of budgetary balance and avoiding the situation of an unplanned increase in the budget deficit and thus an increase in public debt (Radziewicz 2019, pp. 639–640; Dębowska-Romanowska 2016, pp. 1534–1535; see also Judgment 12 April 2000, K 22/99).

Attention may also be drawn in this context to the provisions restricting the government in the conduct of the state's financial policy, which manifests itself primarily in the necessity to take the most important decisions in this regard in the form of laws which, although initiated by the government, are adopted by a parliamentary majority. This applies above all to the state budget, which is enacted in the form of law in accordance with the procedure set out in Articles 219–225. It also applies to other issues in this area. For example, the borrowing of money and the granting of financial guarantees and warranties by the State shall be carried out in accordance with the rules and procedures laid down by law (Article 216 (4)). Similarly, the Act defines the organization of the State Treasury and the manner in which the State Treasury's assets are managed (Article 218). Such provisions also include the parliamentary procedure for the scrutiny of the government's implementation of the state budget provided for in Article 226 of the Constitution.

Undoubtedly, the group of provisions aimed at taking care of future generations in the field of economic security also includes those concerning the National Bank of Poland, which, by virtue of Article 227 of the Constitution, is responsible for the value of Polish currency and to which the Constitution entrusts in this provision the exclusive right to issue money and to determine and implement monetary policy (Florczak-Wątor 2019, p. 648–649). This is all the more important because in the jurisprudence of the Constitutional Tribunal, the task of taking care of the value of Polish money has a clear strategic significance, as it implies the duty to conduct monetary policy in a manner conducive to comprehensive economic development and raising the living standards of citizens (Judgment of 26 February 2003, K 26/03. See also: Góral, Koperkiewicz-Mordel, Górski 2016a, b, p. 1603).

Thus, the indicated constitutional provisions relating to the sphere of public finances create another category, adopting yet another legal construction of the competence and procedure norm, the essence of which is the obligation of public authorities to pursue a prudent and responsible budgetary policy.

In conclusion, it should be stated that the problem of protection of future generations in the Polish Constitution has been defined very broadly, using various legal constructions addressed to different addressees. As a result, the intensity of their impact, but also the possibility of their enforcement, varies.

References

Banaszak B (2009) Konstytucja Rzeczypospolitej Polskiej. Komentarz. C.H. Beck, Warszawa
Borysiak W (2016) Komentarz do article 71. In: Safjan M, Bosek L (eds), Konstytucja RP. Tom I. Komentarz do article 1–86, C.H. Beck, Warszawa, 1626–1648
Borysiak W (2016) Komentarz do article 72. In: Safjan M, Bosek L (eds), Konstytucja RP. Tom I. Komentarz do article 1–86, C.H. Beck, Warszawa, p 1648–1670
Borysiak W (2016) Komentarz do article 18. In: Safjan M, Bosek L (eds), Konstytucja RP. Tom I. Komentarz do article 1–86, C.H. Beck, Warszawa, p 464–495
Bosek L (2016) Komentarz do article 68. In: Safjan M, Bosek L (eds), Konstytucja RP. Tom I. Komentarz do article 1–86, C.H. Beck, Warszawa, p 1523–1565
Czech E, Kropiewnicka M (2012) Międzynarodowa współpraca polskiego samorządu terytorialnego szczebla powiatowego w zakresie ochrony środowiska realizowanej w zgodzie ze zrównoważonym rozwojem. Białostockie Studia Prawnicze 12:186–189
Dąbrowski M, Jackiewicz A (2023) Komentarz do Konstytucji RP. Article. 74, 86. Difin, Warszawa
Dębowska-Romanowska T (2016) Komentarz do article 220. In: Safjan M, Bosek L (eds), Konstytucja RP. Tom II. Komentarz do article 87–243, C.H. Beck, Warszawa, p 1533–1546
Florczak-Wątor M (2016) Komentarz do article 5. In: Safjan M, Bosek L (eds), Konstytucja RP. Tom I. Komentarz do article 1–86, C.H. Beck, Warszawa, p 278–290
Florczak-Wątor M (2019) Komentarz do article 68. In: Tuleja P (ed), Konstytucja Rzeczypospolitej Polskiej. Komentarz, Wolters Kluwer, Warszawa, p 229–233
Florczak-Wątor M (2019) Komentarz do article 70. In: Tuleja P (ed), Konstytucja Rzeczypospolitej Polskiej. Komentarz, Wolters Kluwer, Warszawa, p 235–238
Florczak-Wątor M (2019) Komentarz do article 71. In: Tuleja P (ed), Konstytucja Rzeczypospolitej Polskiej. Komentarz, Wolters Kluwer, Warszawa, p 238–240
Florczak-Wątor M (2019) Komentarz do article 74. In: Tuleja P (ed), Konstytucja Rzeczypospolitej Polskiej. Komentarz, Wolters Kluwer, Warszawa, p 246–248
Florczak-Wątor M (2019) Komentarz do article 82. In: Tuleja P (ed), Konstytucja Rzeczypospolitej Polskiej. Komentarz, Wolters Kluwer, Warszawa, p 267–269
Florczak-Wątor M (2019) Komentarz do article 86. In: Tuleja P (ed), Konstytucja Rzeczypospolitej Polskiej. Komentarz, Wolters Kluwer, Warszawa, p 279–280
Florczak-Wątor M (2019) Komentarz do article 216. In: Tuleja P (ed), Konstytucja Rzeczypospolitej Polskiej. Komentarz, Wolters Kluwer, Warszawa, p 629–632
Florczak-Wątor M (2019) Komentarz do article 227. In: Tuleja P (ed), Konstytucja Rzeczypospolitej Polskiej. Komentarz, Wolters Kluwer, Warszawa, p 647–650
Góral L, Koperkiewicz-Mordel K, Górski M (2016a) Komentarz do article 227. In: Safjan M, Bosek L (eds), Konstytucja RP. Tom II. Komentarz do article 87–243, C.H. Beck, Warszawa, p 1601–1605
Górski M (2016b) Komentarz do article 74. In: Safjan M, Bosek L (eds), Konstytucja RP. Tom I. Komentarz do article 1–86, C.H. Beck, Warszawa, p 1690–1705
Górski M (2016c) Komentarz do article 86. In: Safjan M, Bosek L (eds), Konstytucja RP. Tom I. Komentarz do article 1–86, C.H. Beck, Warszawa, p 1899–1902
Grabowska G (2001), Europejskie prawo środowiska. Wydawnictwa Prawnicze PWN, Warszawa
Ignatowicz G (2015) Realizacja zasady zrównoważonego rozwoju w polityce ekologicznej Polski po konferencjach w Rio de Janeiro w 1992 oraz 2012 roku. Białostockie Studia Prawnicze 18:223–236
Jabłoński M (2002) Konstytucyjne gwarancje wolności z article 73. In: Banaszak B, Preisner A, Prawa i wolności obywatelskie w Konstytucji RP, C.H. Beck, Warszawa, p 565
Jabłoński M, Wygoda K (2003) Konstytucyjne uprawnienia jednostki w sferze informacyjnej, In: Garlicki L, Szmyt A (eds) Sześć lat Konstytucji Rzeczypospolitej Polskiej. Doświadczenia i inspiracje. Warszawa, p 129

Jackiewicz A, Rytel-Warzocha A (2022) Natural environment as a fundamental right of future generations in the light of the Constitution of the Republic of Poland. In: R. Arnold (ed) The protection of the environment and constitutional law. Comparative Law Studies, vol. 15. University of Regensburg, p 43–52

Kowalewska M (2013) Zasada zrównoważonego rozwoju jako dyrektywa działań administracji publicznej. Białostockie Studia Prawnicze 14:303–311

Królikowski M, Szczucki K (2016) Komentarz do article 70 (Nb 1–29). In: Safjan M, Bosek L (eds), Konstytucja RP. Tom I. Komentarz do article 1–86, C.H. Beck, Warszawa, p 1572–1584

Ofiarski Z (2016) Komentarz do article 216. In: Safjan M, Bosek L (eds), Konstytucja RP. Tom II. Komentarz do article 87–243, C.H. Beck, Warszawa, p 1464–1482

Piechowiak M (2016) Komentarz do article 82. In: Safjan M, Bosek L (eds), Konstytucja RP. Tom I. Komentarz do article 1–86, C.H. Beck, Warszawa, p 1863–1874

Piechowiak M (2016) Komentarz do article 1. In: Safjan M, Bosek L (eds), Konstytucja RP. Tom I. Komentarz do article 1–86, C.H. Beck, Warszawa, p 159–215

Piechowiak M (2020) Preambuła Konstytucji Rzeczypospolitej Polskiej z 1997 r. Aksjologiczne podstawy prawa. C.H. Beck, Warszawa

Piechowiak M (2016) Preambuła. In: Safjan M, Bosek L (eds), Konstytucja RP. Tom I. Komentarz do article 1–86, C.H. Beck, Warszawa, p 118–158

Radziewicz P (2019) Komentarz do article 220. In: Tuleja P (ed), Konstytucja Rzeczypospolitej Polskiej. Komentarz, Wolters Kluwer, Warszawa, p 639–640

Rakoczy B (2015) Procesowy wymiar zasady zrównoważonego rozwoju. Białostockie Studia Prawnicze 18:35–44

Tuleja P (2019) Preambuła. In: Tuleja P (ed), Konstytucja Rzeczypospolitej Polskiej. Komentarz, Wolters Kluwer, Warszawa, p 21–24

Tuleja P (2019) Komentarz do article 5. In: Tuleja P (ed), Konstytucja Rzeczypospolitej Polskiej. Komentarz, Wolters Kluwer, Warszawa, p 40–42

Tuleja P (2019) Komentarz do article 18. In: Tuleja P (ed), Konstytucja Rzeczypospolitej Polskiej. Komentarz, Wolters Kluwer, Warszawa, p 80–84

The Responsibility of Constitutionalism for the Future of the State and Society (Selected Issues)

Mirosław Granat

Abstract The responsibility of constitutionalism for the future of the state and society is associated with three problems. They include: the functions fulfilled by the constitution itself, the implementation of basic values of the constitution, and, subsequently, the shape of constitutionalism as such. It is crucial that the state authorities fulfil their positive obligations in the field of individual rights. These obligations vary across generations of human rights. The implementation of human rights is important not only in vertical relations between the government and the individual, but also in horizontal relations (certain constitutional human rights also apply to relationships between private entities). One of the key values (under the Constitution of the Republic of Poland) is the implementation of the principle of common good. The role of this principle is that in the case law of the Constitutional Tribunal it is weighted with other legal principles. In essence, this principle is treated as having primary meaning over other principles. Before the constitutional court, it is thus used to balance other competing principles and values. Finally, the shape of constitutionalism itself is important. For many years, we identified constitutionalism only with liberal constitutionalism. Meanwhile, this trend itself is not homogenous. Moreover, a trend of illiberal constitutionalism has been developing, which may have devastating impact on the position of an individual in the state. These are the "hot spots" around which the future of constitutionalism is taking shape.

When examining the responsibility of constitutionalism for the future of the state and society, several issues must be taken into account. The first one is related to the functions attributed to the basic law. Various functions of the constitution are distinguished in the study of law, based on a number of criteria. It seems that the function which is most important for the future is the protection of human rights. One of the dimensions of this function are the positive obligations imposed by the

This Paper Has Been Prepared As a Result of the Research Project No. 2018/31/B/HS5/02667, financed by the National Science Centre (Poland) within the OPUS-15 Funding Scheme.

M. Granat (✉)
Cardinal Stefan Wyszynski University, Warsaw, Poland
e-mail: m.granat@uksw.edu.pl

R. Arnold and T. Fickentscher (eds.), *The Responsibility of a Constitution for the Future*, https://doi.org/10.1007/978-3-031-65296-7_4

legislator on the government (Section 1). Another circumstance which is important for the future of the state and society is related to the role of the legal principle of the common good (Section 2). The third issue concerns the dispute between liberal and illiberal constitutionalism (and especially populism) which can be seen in Europe as well as globally. Will illiberal constitutionalism gain the upper hand, as is the case in several countries of Central and Eastern Europe, or will liberal, "traditional" constitutionalism we are all accustomed to, defend its position? (Section 3).

The issues of contemporary constitutionalism which I discuss below have not been fully resolved, neither in the study of law nor in judicial decisions, and they will probably remain so. They have a universal dimension (e.g. the issue of the function of the constitution) as well as a domestic (national) one (e.g. the substance of the principle of the common good in the Constitution of Poland). However, the very fact of raising them makes us aware of the responsibility of constitutionalism for the future.

1 The Meaning of State Obligations in the Area of Human Rights

The issue of the functions performed by the constitution influences the understanding of what this act currently is and what its role may be in the future with regard to human rights.

What is crucial for the future of the state and society is the implementation of the positive obligations of the state in terms of individual rights. While the issue of negative obligations is generally clear (they are prohibitions and limitations imposed by the constitution on the government so that it cannot violate the rights of citizens), positive obligations are difficult to determine precisely and then to implement. It is well-known that the fulfilment of the state's obligations towards an individual may not consist solely in the state's passive attitude towards threats to human rights (for example, the government cannot spy on citizens). We cannot restrict our understanding of the protective function of the constitution to a "liberal" approach, as a ban on state interference in the sphere of human rights and freedoms. The state has a constitutional obligation to provide citizens with the conditions to exercise their rights and freedoms. These positive obligations of the state towards an individual are formulated as imperatives for the government to ensure the observance of human rights. The constitution must guarantee rights of individuals (and other entities), not just limit power. In the twenty-first century, we not only say to the legislator "stay out of my life", but we expect it to act in order to protect our rights. For example, it is assumed that the state will prevent the social exclusion of the poor, that it will ensure proper access to healthcare facilities or that it will ensure effective protection of our consumer rights.

The protective function of the constitution, expressed through positive obligations of the government towards individuals and their rights, is now more important in terms of the responsibility for the future of the state and society than ever before. This is because it manifests itself not only in vertical relations (i.e. the government—an individual and vice versa), but also extends to certain relations between private entities themselves. In this sphere, constitutions turn out to be effective as a result of the so-called horizontal application of their provisions. This horizontal application of the constitutional provisions on human rights facilitates the implementation of constitutional values. These days, we even expect the "presence" of the constitution in areas which have been "out of its reach" so far, including the sphere of relations between individuals in private transactions.

Obviously, the obligations of the state in the sphere of human rights are different in successive generations of human rights. For example, in the first generation, the obligations of the state resulted from the demands such as "let me speak " or "let me practise my religion". The second generation is different, as evidenced by the disputes over the scope of rights such as the right to social security, the right to healthcare or the right to education.[1]

The constitutional function of protecting human rights is expanding because of the positive obligations of the state towards an individual. We have seen that this function covers not only the protection of human rights in vertical relations but also extends to certain horizontal relations. It seems that the horizontal application of constitutional provisions will gain significance in the twenty-first century, because such application takes place within the sphere of socio-economic rights. Undoubtedly, their importance is constantly growing and they are instrumental in building civil society.[2]

2 The Importance of Implementation of Basic Principles and Constitutional Values

The common good is one of the basic values and principles of law in the 1997 Constitution of Poland. Why should this provision be of key importance for the future of Polish constitutionalism? It says that "the Republic of Poland shall be the common good of all its citizens". In Polish jurisprudence, this provision has an idiomatic substance. This means that it constitutes a whole which cannot be decomposed into parts. It is somewhat paradoxical that, on the one hand, it is difficult to define "the common good", and on the other hand, this category is crucial for the responsibility of constitutionalism for the future of the state and society. Why is this the case? The special role of this principle can be seen in the fact that it cannot be balanced against other principles and values by the Constitutional Tribunal, as it is treated as primary in relation to other constitutional principles.

[1] They are visible in Polish constitutional law and are present in rich constitutional jurisprudence. Cf. L. Garlicki 2022, Chap. 4.

[2] Barber 2018, Chap. 5.

The common good is a principle of law which balances other values and is "assigned" by the Constitutional Tribunal to the result of this balancing in a particular case. Its peculiarity thus lies in the fact that it is used to balance other colliding values and principles of law. In my opinion, it plays the role of a "pointer" which tips the balance of constitutional values in favour of a particular court decision. The common good therefore usually occurs in the context of other principles. It seems that in balancing colliding values the common good cannot be substituted by any other principle or value. For example, it cannot be the principle of social justice (Article 2) or the principle of legalism (Article 7). I am certain that the principle according to which public bodies function on the basis of, and within the limits of, the law, or the principle of social justice (and even both these principles together) would not be able to bear the burden of resolving conflicts of principles and values before the constitutional court.

The case-law of the Polish constitutional court provides several examples of such a role of the common good. Let me briefly present two different cases.

The first case concerned changes in the electoral law to local government bodies, which allowed for the so-called blocking of electoral lists. The amendment was adopted by the Sejm in a relatively short time before the election day.[3] The Tribunal faced the dilemma where on the one hand changes in the electoral law had been introduced shortly before the elections, and on the other hand it was necessary to hold the elections within the time specified by the law. The Tribunal found that the legislator did not exceed the six-month period of the so-called legislative silence, i.e. the period of time between the adoption of significant changes in the electoral law and the date of the election. The statement of reasons to the judgement in case no. K 31/06 says that the Tribunal "has taken into account the normative circumstances at the time of issuing the judgement" and bears in mind that pursuant to Article 1 of the Constitution, Poland is the common good of all its citizens. The common good requires preserving the continuity of the legal order underlying the system of state bodies and ensuring their functioning in such a way that the elements necessary for their operation are not dismantled.[4] The ruling says that "the respect for the common good and other values justified the result of the balancing of constitutional values carried out by the Tribunal in the present case".[5] The Tribunal issued the judgement 10 days before the elections (they were held on November 13, 2006). It can be assumed that if the court had ruled a year before the elections, the operative part of the judgement could have been different, e.g. inclined towards stating unconstitutionality, given the critical evaluation of the challenged regulation in the statement of reasons. A concrete interpretation of the value of the common good by the Constitutional Tribunal made it possible to hold the local elections within the time limit provided for by the law.

[3] Cf. the judgement of the Constitutional Tribunal of November 3, 2006, K 31/06, OTK ZU 2006, no. 10 A, item 147.

[4] Cf. the statement of reasons to the judgement K 31/06, OTK ZU 2006, no. 10 A, item 147, p. 1545.

[5] Cf. ibidem, p. 1545.

The second case concerned the constitutionality of the provisions of the Aviation Law which permitted shooting down the RENEGADE aircraft, i.e. "a civil aircraft used for unlawful acts, in particular as a means of a terrorist attack from the air".[6] The "life for life" dispute which arose on the basis of Article 122a of the Aviation Law seemed unresolvable. A similar dispute may also concern other regulations, such as determining the order in which a paramedic should provide assistance to victims of a road accident (should he or she make decisions based on his or her preference in assessing the chances of survival of a victim or based on other principles?). Without going into the details of the statement of reasons to the judgement, the Constitutional Tribunal decided that the "life for life" dilemma (and this is how the constitutional problem was posed) cannot be resolved on the basis of the value of human dignity. The value of human life was present on both sides of the conflict: both the lives of the passengers on board of the hijacked aircraft and the lives of the inhabitants of the town affected by the downed aircraft are constitutionally protected. Both the people on board of the plane and the inhabitants of the town have dignity and the right to keep their lives. Human dignity does not divide people into "guilty ones", whose aircraft can be shot down, and "innocent ones", who will be saved by the decision of the commander (who remains both outside the aircraft and outside the potential fire range). In the judgement under discussion, the value of the common good was manifested in the obligation on the part of the legislator to respect every life, including a group of innocent passengers. The conscious destruction of their lives would violate the common good. The common good prevented an "economic" approach to life: if some people are shot down, others will be saved. Human life was not examined in terms of minority-majority or subordinating lives of some people to saving others. The value of the common good can be briefly expressed as follows: one cannot sacrifice the lives of a minority in order to save the lives of the majority. It can be seen that the principle of human dignity must act in conjunction with some other principle, e.g. the principle of the common good. In the case under discussion, the value of the common good was attributed by the constitutional court to human life.[7]

The examples presented above demonstrate that it is impossible to imagine the constitutionalism of the future, including its responsibility for the state and society, without taking into account the value and principle of the common good. The first example shows that the common good plays a role in settling seemingly "technical" disputes, e.g. concerning the electoral law. In my opinion, however, the electoral law is of great importance in terms of human rights and is not merely a technical issue. In turn, the second example shows that the principle of the common good is relevant in great legal disputes which involve human life. In the twenty-first century, there will be numerous issues to solve in which human life will be in the foreground.

---

[6] Cf. the judgement of the Constitutional Tribunal of September 30, 2008, K 44/07, OTK ZU 2008, no. 7 A, item 126. Cf. Granat 2013.

[7] Cf. the statement of reasons to the judgement in case no. K 44/07.

3 Debates on the Shape of Constitutionalism

The final issue which determines the future of the state and society is related to constitutionalism itself. What shape will the constitutionalism of the future take? This is particularly important in the context of the dispute between liberal and illiberal constitutionalism, especially in Central and Eastern European countries.

"Constitutionalism" is understood here as a set of views on the constitution, and more precisely, as a doctrine that defines the conditions which the basic law must meet.[8] Its shape is influenced to a great extent by the understanding of the supremacy of the constitution, the organization of state government and the regulation of human rights. Constitutionalism understood in this way is a living doctrine, sensitive to time and circumstances, which is why it is relevant for the responsibility for the future of the state and society. Although it was created in the Enlightenment, it has gained an interesting dynamics in the twenty-first century.

For many years, the term "constitutionalism" has been synonymous with liberal constitutionalism (which originated in the late eighteenth century), and it is still relevant nowadays. Under this view, the constitution is a legal act which places limitations on the political power by binding it with the rule of law, which serves to protect human freedom. Its original purpose was to define what the government cannot do. Human and civil rights and freedoms play a prominent role here. Great importance is attached not only to human freedom as such, but also to its protection, e.g. to the protection of minority rights. Human dignity is treated as inherent and inalienable. It is a kind of mantle under which every individual and citizen can find shelter. In this type of constitutionalism, an individual takes precedence over the community and he or she has inalienable rights and freedoms, the limitation of which is difficult to carry out.[9]

Nowadays, liberal constitutionalism does not view the constitution merely as a "muzzle" for the government, as it was originally assumed in the Enlightenment. It lays down the principles of governance based on the separation of powers, it creates institutions, it defines the powers of state bodies and it aims at implementing the principles of the rule of law. Hence the characteristic saying of this doctrine: "It is not the people who rule, but the law." Despite all these features (advantages indeed), liberal constitutionalism has been subject to criticism and modification for centuries.

In the twenty-first century, the role of the constitution can no longer be reduced to limiting power and guaranteeing human rights. Its function is also to determine the foundations of economic and social relations in the state. This can be seen, for example, in the programmatic norms in the constitution, which determine the directions of development of social and economic life. The constitution remains a legal act, but it has become deeply immersed in social life. Its provisions are addressed not only to state authorities, but also to citizens and other private entities. For instance, they have become important in running a business. As has been mentioned above (cf.

[8] Cf. Granat 2023.

[9] Cf. Böckenförde 1997.

Section I), constitutional provisions can be applied not only vertically but also horizontally. These regulations are usually guaranteed by various institutions, especially by courts and tribunals.

Within liberal constitutionalism, there is a dispute between "judicial" constitutionalism and "political" constitutionalism. The dispute is especially clear against the backdrop of the crisis of liberal democracy, and its resolution is of great importance for the future of the state and society.

"Judicial" constitutionalism assumes a strong role of the courts in a democratic system. Its quintessence is the judicial review of the hierarchy of norms, whose ultimate goal is to protect human rights. On the other hand, "political" constitutionalism, which is obviously also based on law (it does not go beyond the law), understands the role of the courts in a different manner. In this doctrine, constitutionality is determined by the legislative branch, even if there is a "dialogue" between the parliament, which enacts the law, and the court, which declares the law unconstitutional (e.g. after the court ruling, the law returns to the parliamentary chamber for revision). Its proponents argue that if certain political principles, such as political pluralism or representative government, are observed, judicial review of the constitutionality of the law declines in importance. The role of parliament is to settle grand legal disputes by considering and confronting different points of view. The deliberative character of parliament yields a sort of rationality which results from giving the citizens the right to vote. Parliament is more rational than the courts. This is why citizens and their representatives (and not judges) should have the final say in the field of the constitution. The constitution is rooted in social life and it does not belong to lawyers. Under this approach, the position of judicial review becomes problematic. On the other hand, parliament remains at the heart of democracy. Thus, this type of constitutionalism can be characterized by the eloquent title of M. Tushnet's book, *Taking the Constitution away from the Courts*.[10]

The dispute between "judicial" and "political" constitutionalism is invigorating for constitutional law, and it takes place within the framework of liberal constitutionalism. We have become accustomed to a situation in which there is one type of constitutionalism (*liberal*, *democratic*, *ordinary*). It should be remembered that the term "constitutionalism" is adequate only when the constitution and the state system meet certain requirements. Is it then possible to talk about illiberal constitutionalism? In my opinion, it is possible because this term refers to the political changes that are currently taking place not only in Venezuela, but also in Hungary or Poland. Initially, illiberal constitutionalism seemed to be only a weakening of "ordinary" constitutionalism. However, its solutions have become clear since then (e.g. in the Hungarian Constitution of 2011) and its role is growing.

The axis of division between liberal and illiberal constitutionalism concerns defining the relationship between democracy and the rule of law, as well as between the state and the individual. An illiberal constitution assumes the primacy of the sovereign power of the nation (*pouvoir constitutant*). The nation as the sovereign is therefore primary with regard to the law. The limitations on government are by

[10] Cf. Princeton 2000.

no means determined by constitutional provisions, because the rule of law is being questioned. The fundamental assumptions of this type of constitutionalism can be illustrated with the example of Hungary. One could say that if illiberal constitutionalism exists, it certainly functions in Hungary. Why is it the case? Because that's how the Hungarians themselves refer to it.[11]

One type of illiberal constitutionalism is the so-called constitutional populism. In fact, this approach rejects traditional, liberal constitutionalism. Populism is distinguished by a characteristic view of the nation's position within constitutionalism. Populists claim that the sovereignty of the nation in the liberal approach has become fiction, because legislative power is exercised not by the parliament and the government, but by the elites, which has detrimental consequences for the nation. The concept of political representation where the sovereign speaks through political parties is being questioned. Populists promise to reduce the distance between citizens and state bodies and institutions. They argue for constructing a legal order that promotes the good of the nation, as opposed to particular interests. These assumptions provide a foundation for frequent revisions of the constitution, as the existing order is tainted by the heritage of the past (e.g. the communist one). Populism undermines the rule of law, which is viewed as a tool to promote the interests of minorities (the elites) against the good of the nation. The rule of law is an obstacle to achieving political goals. Populism overcomes the so-called legal impossibilism, i.e. barriers and restrictions which are "illegitimate" from the point of view of the majority rule. The liberal attachment to maintaining the procedures for enacting the law and its rationality weakens the ability to achieve goals. In this respect, the law serves as an instrument. The main slogan of populism can be therefore "the constitution is for the people, not for the elites."

4 Summary

It seems that the protective function of the constitution, the principle of the common good, as well as the dispute over the shape of constitutionalism, are "hot spots" around which the future of constitutionalism is unfolding before our eyes. All these issues seem to be a kind of lens through which the prospects of constitutionalism can be seen.

At the same time, the issues in question are not distant but they are of importance here and now. For example, in Poland there is an on-going discussion on how to overcome the constitutional crisis which resulted from political changes introduced after 2015. There are several visions of constitutionalism, and each of them can be important for the future of the state and society. The awareness of different visions of

[11] V. Orban defined it as follows: *Hungarian nation is not a simple sum of individuals, but a community that needs to be organized, strengthened and developed, and in this sense, the new state that we are building is an illiberal state, a non-liberal state. It does not deny foundational values of liberalism, as freedom,* etc.. *But it does not make this ideology a central element of state organization, but applies a specific, national, particular approach in its stead.* (Blokker 2019.

constitutionalism or of the common good is of key importance now and determines our future.

References

Barber N (2018) *The Principles of Constitutionalism,* Oxford University Press

Böckenförde E-W (1997) *Historyczny rozwój i różne znaczenia pojęcia konstytucji,* [in:] Civitas, issue 1

Blokker P (2019) Populism as a constitutional project. Int J Const Law 17

Garlicki L (2022) *Polskie prawo konstytucyjne. Zarys wykładu,* Warsaw 2022

Granat M (2013) Dobro wspólne w pojmowaniu Trybunału Konstytucyjnego. In: W. Arndt, ks. F. Longchamps de Bérier, K. Szczucki (eds.) Dobro wspólne teoria i praktyka. Warsaw

Granat M (2022) On the Experiences of a Constitutional Court in an Illiberal Democracy. Incapacitated but necessary. In: Castellà Andreu JM, Simonelli MA (eds.) Populism and Contemporary Democracy in Europe. Old Problems and New Challenges, Palgrave Macmillan Cham

Tushnet M (2000) Taking the Constitution away from the Courts, Princeton

“A Pledge to Present and Future Generations”: The Preamble of the Estonian Constitution in the Protection of Fundamental Rights

Villu Kõve, Berit Aaviksoo, and Mait Laaring

Abstract This article sets out to examine how the idea of solidarity between generations is expressed in the Estonian Constitution, and how it has been interpreted in the constitutional practice of the Estonian Supreme Court and beyond. For this purpose, the article first deals with the relevant part of the preamble of the Constitution and then examines its “applications” in social and environmental issues. Finally, the article deals with the empowering of future generation’s right to vote as probably one of the most controversial issues of intergenerational solidarity. The legally binding principle of solidarity between generations is derived from the preamble of the Constitution of the Republic of Estonia. As such, it serves as an aid in the interpretation and implementation of fundamental rights, above all when considering limitations arising from the general interest. However, due to difficulties inherent to such a concept—primarily because it is almost impossible to predict what will be good for future generations—this principle has not proved to be omnipotent. To strike down a law on the grounds that it will cause harm in the distant future, the probability of such harm must be high in the constitutional practice of the Estonian Supreme Court. Among other things, the principle of intergenerational solidarity would probably not be sufficiently powerful and practically applicable to justify giving future generations the right to vote. By allowing the present generations to predict the interests of the future generations, we will most probably end up not having empowered the future generations, but having equipped the members of the present generations with multiple voices, which would run contrary to the principle of “one person, one vote”. It is thus rather difficult to translate the idea of solidarity between generations into the language of fundamental rights. However, this solemn pledge, contained

The article is based on the speech given by Villu Kõve at the 11th World Congress of Constitutional Law “Constitutional transformations”, held in Johannesburg on December 5–9, 2022, at the subpanel titled “The constitutions’ inherent responsibility for the future—dogmatic basis and political practice.”

V. Kõve (✉) · B. Aaviksoo · M. Laaring
Supreme Court of Estonia, Tartu, Estonia
e-mail: Villu.Kove@riigikohus.ee

M. Laaring
e-mail: mait.laaring@riigikohus.ee

R. Arnold and T. Fickentscher (eds.), *The Responsibility of a Constitution for the Future*, https://doi.org/10.1007/978-3-031-65296-7_5

in the preamble of the Constitution, in Estonia, must and does constitute a prism through which each and every constitutional problem has to be seen.

Both the Indians and Oscar Wilde have been credited with the phrase "*We Do Not Inherit the Earth from Our Ancestors; We Borrow It from Our Children*".

In the theory of justice, the same idea is expressed by the concept of intergenerational justice, or the fair sharing of the burden between generations. This concept, usually invoked in connection with environmental and social issues, is mainly concerned with how we can and should relate to those who will live in the future, what obligations we have towards them and what we owe them (Aasa 2022: Comm No 108). Among others, a legal philosopher of Estonian decent, Ilmar Tammelo has emphasized that justice involves not only people living today, but also people living in the future, even in the very distant future (Tammelo 2001: 23).

Quite significantly, the idea that can be related to that of intergenerational justice has been present in all the Constitutions of the Republic of Estonia. The preamble of the first Constitution of Estonia, adopted in the Constituent Assembly on June 15, 1920; the second Constitution, adopted by the National Assembly on July 28, 1937, and the current Constitution of 1992, passed by referendum on June 28, 1992 define as one of the goals of the constitution to create and/or strengthen and develop the state which "is a pledge to present and future generations for their social progress and general welfare" (Constitution of 1992).

Intergenerational justice, responsibility for the future, duty to future generations or the protection of future generations, all these terms in one way or another express the idea of solidarity between generations which, below, shall be used as an umbrella term for the principle in question.

This article sets out to examine how this principle is expressed in the Estonian Constitution, and how it has been interpreted in the constitutional practice of the Supreme Court and beyond. For this purpose, the article first deals with the relevant part of the preamble of the Constitution (Part I), and then examines its "applications" in social and environmental issues (Part II). Finally, the article deals with the empowering of future generations, including the children's right to vote as probably one of the most controversial issues of intergenerational solidarity (Part III).

1 Intergenerational Solidarity as a Constitutional Principle

The Constitution is generally present-centred, not future-centred. The principles of democracy and the rule of law are not very conducive to respecting the rights of future generations. The constitutional principle of democracy is the principle of provisional power, i.e., power that is granted only for a limited period of time, and primarily for the purpose of making decisions that need to be made during the period of power (Kirchhof: 89).

Also, when electing their political representatives, people are often guided by their own short-term goals and are unaware of the long-term implications of their decisions. In other words, people tend to elect populists who promise a lot and quickly. Democracy is also about the possibility of revising decisions that have already been made, if the majority so wishes Therefore, classical democracy is in a sense based on short-term interests and tends to favour short-term goals.

Despite of the foregoing, no one today doubts that the constitutions are the source of the general principle of intergenerational solidarity, at least in certain areas of life (and law), like environment or social sphere. In the terms of constitutional theory, this is usually not, however, about protecting specific subjective rights of future generations, but rather about a principle to be taken into account when settling a constitutional case.

The Constitution of Estonia is probably one of the clearest in terms of obligations towards future generations, as the need to ensure the success (progress) and welfare of future generations is (and—as shown above—always has been) clearly written in the preamble of the Constitution.

Although historically created as a guarantee for the continuation of statehood in Estonia—which is indicated by the construction "to create a state which is a pledge to present and future generations"—, this provision of the preamble has been interpreted both in legal theoretical literature and in the practice of the Supreme Court as a constitutional obligation of present generations towards future generations, which goes beyond the narrowly understood obligation of preserving statehood.

In fact, this provision was interpreted more broadly already in 1935, when the Estonian legal scholar Artur-Tõeleid Kliimann noted that this purpose, stated in the preamble, expressed collective origins alongside liberal democratic elements (Aasa 2022: Comm No 107). Moreover, modern legal scholars point out that the obligation and goal of the Estonian state contained in the preamble—to be a pledge for current and future generations for their social progress and general welfare—is closely connected with the principle of just savings. According to this principle, standing at the heart of John Rawls and his theory of justice, the existing human generation has a duty to the future generations, in addition to the obligation of preserving the benefits of culture and civilization, to save sufficient material capital to preserve fair institutions throughout the ages (Aasa 2022: Comm No 109).

The Supreme Court of the Republic of Estonia as a court of constitutional supervision has also confirmed that from the preamble, according to which the Estonian state is a pledge to current and future generations for their social progress and general welfare, one can deduce the principle of an agreement between generations, which obliges the legislator not to impose unreasonably large financial obligations on future generations to fulfil the basic tasks of the state (*Pension Reform*: Para 59). From these lines echoes the idea of just savings as well as that of the solidarity between generations.

Namely, according to the prevailing position in Estonian legal doctrine, the preamble, like other parts of the constitution, is legally binding by nature and may entail direct obligations for state institutions. Thus, it has been argued that, contrary to those theoreticians who consider the preamble of the Constitution as legally insignificant and a mere artificial addition or its explanatory letter, the preambles of the Estonian constitutions have never been and still not are an artificial appendix to, a decoration of polished wording or a mere introduction to the constitution, but rather its regulatory core integrating the whole constitution (Narits et al. 2020: Comm No 24).

The Estonian Supreme Court has also firmly placed itself among those who recognize the normative character of the preamble (first in *Language requirements*, most recently in *Pension Reform*). More specifically, the Supreme Court has explained that since the preamble of the Constitution is, like other parts of the Constitution, of a legally binding nature, direct obligations of the public power may arise from it. Also, one of the tasks of the Preamble of the Constitution is to determine the main goals of the state, among which are the social progress of current and future generations and their general welfare. According to the Court, the provisions of the preamble must mainly be considered when implementing other provisions and principles of the Constitution (*Pension Reform*: Para 60, 61).

Several basic ideas set out in the preamble of the Constitution of Estonia are concretized, further developed, or guaranteed in the so-called content sections of the Constitution. Among others, also the idea of intergenerational solidarity is reflected in a few other provisions of the Constitution. For example, according to the so-called first commentary on the Estonian Constitution—the final report of the Constitutional Legal Expertise Commission—, which was published in 1996, this goal of the state (to be a pledge to present and future generations for their social progress and general welfare) is closely related to the justice stipulated in the third paragraph of the preamble and the principle of the welfare state provided for in Section 10 of the Constitution (*Final* Report 1996: 7).

According to Section 5 of the Constitution, Estonia's natural resources are a national treasure that must be used sustainably, and according to Section 53 of the Constitution, everyone is obliged to preserve the living and natural environment. Section 27 of the Constitution protects the family as the basis for the survival and growth of the nation and of society. According to Section 28(2) of the Constitution, every Estonian citizen has the right to state assistance in the event of old age, incapacity for work, loss of breadwinner and deprivation. Section 32(2) of the Constitution prohibits the use of property against the public interest. The right of everyone to education, provided for in Section 37(1) of the Constitution, is also oriented towards the future.

2 Applications of the Principle of Intergenerational Solidarity

Burdening future generations takes two forms: first, taking resources away from them, i.e., unfairly redistributing environmental or heritage values, money, or other social or educational benefits to the current generation; second, imposing unfair burdens on future generations at the expense of the present, e.g., bailing out or creating an unsustainable social system. In the first case, the resources have already been taken from them, in the second case, they are under obligation to give them up. From the constitutional point of view, there is no difference between the two.

Both ways of creating intergenerational injustice have come to the attention of the Estonian Supreme Court, which has concretized the principle of solidarity between generations in a few cases, mainly related to social and environmental issues.

Pension Reform at the Expense of Future Generations?

Certainly, the most famous case in which the Supreme Court has operated with the principle of intergenerational solidarity, is the so-called Pension Reform case. In this case, decided in 2021, the President of the Republic, in her function of carrying out a preliminary review of constitutionality, applied to the Supreme Court to declare unconstitutional the law which gave working-age people the opportunity to withdraw money from the mandatory pension fund, and pensioners the right to terminate the pension contract concluded before 2021, and demand a one-time payment. In his request, the President of the Republic relied, among other things, on the agreement between generations resulting from the preamble of the Constitution, which obliges the legislator not to impose unreasonably large financial obligations on future generations to fulfil the core functions of the state (*Pension reform*: Para 7.1.2).

The Supreme Court *en banc* disagreed with the President, finding that although the law interfered with the fundamental right to property of those unitholders of the mandatory pension fund not wishing to leave the fund, the freedom of enterprise of insurers, as well as treated unequally those who had joined and those who had not joined the second pension pillar, no violation of the Constitution could be concluded with sufficient certainty in the frame of abstract constitutional review and based on existing forecasts. According to the Supreme Court, the aims of the reform—especially increasing people's freedom of choice—outweighed the ascertained infringements of fundamental rights resulting from it (*Pension reform*: Para 142).

However, the Supreme Court explained in more detail the meaning of the preamble of the Constitution in the context of the state's social obligations. In an earlier case concerning the Treaty establishing the European Stability Mechanism, the Court had already generally noted that in order to achieve the objectives arising from the preamble of the Constitution, the state must create an environment where the state budget revenue is received as planned, which enables the core functions of the state to be fulfilled and the protection of fundamental rights and freedoms ensured (*ESM*: Para 167, 168).

According to the Court, the constitutional obligation to protect the weaker parts of the population, which derives, *inter alia*, from the principle of the social state and human dignity, also means that the state must, when building its social system, take account of the sustainability of that system in the long term. Among other things, such an interpretation is conditioned by the obligation of ensuring social progress and the general welfare of present and future generations, contained in the preamble. From that follows that the state must ensure the sustainable operation of the pension system at least at the level of the constitutional minimum of social protection, by reasonably planning the expenditure and sources of funding necessary for its operation. The rational and economical use of public money also includes ensuring the long-term viability of the pension system, considering the actual possibilities of society (*Pension reform*: Para 61).

However, the Supreme Court *en banc* noted that despite foregoing, and "in view of the level of generalisation of the preamble ", it was not possible to conclude that the legislator has a duty, arising from the preamble or the principle of the social state, to prefer a particular social security system. Nor does the preamble prescribe how the social and economic interests of different generations should be weighed or responsibility shared in bearing the state's future anticipated financial duties—these choices may be made by the legislator (*Pension reform*: Para 62).

Also, the Supreme Court discussed in its decision the complexity, which is intrinsically related to the protection of solidarity between generations through fundamental rights. According to the Supreme Court, even if it is in principle possible to establish the unconstitutionality of a legislative act based on a violation of fundamental rights that may occur only in the future, in such a case, the future violation must be highly probable. In addition, the assessment of the probability of an alleged violation is more complicated the further the future of the alleged violation and the greater the number of different circumstances that must be considered when assessing the probability of a violation are. The Supreme Court concluded that the effects of legislative amendments called into question in the present case were considerably disputable to establish that the minimum level of state assistance guaranteed under that provision would manifestly fall below the constitutionally required level in the future (*Pension reform*: Para 52).

Environment

It is worth noting that the issue of rights related to the environment and their constitutional foundation received exceptionally high attention during the preparatory works for the Estonian Constitution in the body specially convened for this purpose—the Constitutional Assembly. The future generations were directly and repeatedly mentioned in the respective debates in connection with the task of not to letting our environment get significantly worse, but to keep it also for the next generations (Peep 1997: 538). Although not directly, the idea of borrowing the Earth from the next generations thus resounded in these discussions.

The obligation to preserve the environment for future generations is concretized in Section 5 of the Constitution, according to which Estonia's natural resources are national wealth, which must be used sparingly, and Section 53, according to which everyone is obliged to save the living and natural environment and to compensate for the damage they have caused to the environment. Although the proposal presented in the Constitutional Assembly—to expand the list of national wealth to include economic, social, spiritual, and fundamental resources—did not pass, it illustrates the connection and interweaving of the sustainability of natural, social, economic, and other resources (Aasa 2022: Comm No 112).

Interpreting these sections, the Supreme Court found—in a case where ownership restrictions at a protection site of the lesser spotted eagle were at issue—, although without directly referring to the preamble, that in addition to being the state's task, the protection of the environment is also everyone's duty. The Court added that, since the natural environment was constantly changing, and the measures necessary to protect nature might also change, the entire responsibility for the property restrictions accompanying these measures could not be placed on the state (*RoheInvest*: Para 41). Thus, saving and protecting nature and the environment is everyone's responsibility, for the benefit of future generations.

The same applies to the protection of cultural heritage. For example, in a matter concerning the distribution of competences between the state and local government in the protection of historical natural sacred places in Estonia, including the so-called "cross forests", the Supreme Court's Constitutional Review Chamber found that natural objects of cultural heritage are also part of the living and natural environment, the preservation of which is imposed on everyone by Section 53 the Constitution (*Protection of cross forests*: Para 43).

In addition, according to the practice of the Supreme Court, the sustainable use of mineral resources, and hence their preservation for future generations, must also be taken into account when exercising the fundamental rights of the mining company to freedom of enterprise and freedom of use of property (*Mining permit*: Para 29). The interests of future generations in a healthy living environment must also be considered in planning law (*KAHOS*: Para 23).

In conclusion, sustainability should be a guiding principle for the use of the resources of the state, while maintaining a close link with effectiveness—acting for social progress and the common good requires a balanced resolution of the state's numerous collective responsibilities and liberal individualist aspirations (Narits et al. 2020: Para 15).

Attention should also be drawn to the precautionary principle, which, having originated in environmental law, has also spread to other legal areas (for example, it has been used in lower court decisions concerning corona restrictions, in Estonia). The precautionary principle obliges, in the most general terms, to act proactively against risks that may arise in uncertain future and the stakes are high.

3 Empowering Future Generations

One way to achieve intergenerational justice would arguably be empowering future generations, possibly at the expense of present ones. This could be done in different ways, out of which two will be discussed, briefly.

First, one could try to give a voice to future generations in a rather literal way, by allowing them to vote at the elections. Secondly, and more indirectly, one could try to take birth-inducing measures to change the composition of the population in favour of the younger generation, or, put differently, ensure the very existence of future generations.

Right to Vote for Future Generations

Democracy and the rule of law require informed judgement in decision-making, based on facts, life experience and scientific knowledge (Kirchhof: 89). We can only protect future generations on the basis of prediction, and prediction is always uncertain. The further into the future we go, the less we can predict the situation and needs of future generations. We are always defending what we ourselves imagine to be the needs and fair treatment of future generations, but we may not have a very clear or correct understanding of the actual needs of future generations.

Likewise, the theoreticians of intergenerational justice have noted that the main difficulty in owning and evaluating obligations of justice towards future generations is that there is no physical coexistence between human generations of different times and the possibility of dialogue, which is the usual context for resolving social disagreements (Gosseries and Meyer 2009: 3). Developing this idea further, it has been found that the lack of direct dialogue and the asymmetry of power relations between people living now and in the future lead to a situation where the wishes and needs of future generations must be assumed and predicted in the context of intergenerational justice, although situations and conditions may change over time (Aasa: Comm No 108).

All these difficulties related to the achievement of intergenerational justice have been discussed in the dialogue about children's right to vote, which has been considered as one of the solutions to the problem of asymmetry of power relations between generations, in Estonia.

At a public hearing in the Constitutional Committee of the Estonian Parliament (the *Riigikogu*) on June 3, 2014, it was stated—as a justification for raising the issue—that society was getting older and older people had more and more weight in elections, thus also deciding on issues affecting young people. Lowering the voting age would increase the proportion of young people among those who have the right to vote (PÕSK minutes: 5). In the analysis of the effects of lowering the active voting age completed earlier in 2014 at the University of Tallinn at the request of the Ministry of Justice, it had been found that the central goal of lowering the voting age was to involve young people in the basic process of representative democratic governance through elections and thereby give them real responsibility and the right to shape the present and future of the Estonian state (Toots et al. 2014: 60).

As a result of these debates, 41 members of the *Riigikogu* initiated a draft amendment to the Constitution to lower the voting age in local government council elections, which was adopted by two consecutive assemblies of the *Riigikogu* (Section 163(1), subpara 2 of the Constitution provides for the way to amend the corresponding PS), and entered into force before the local government elections of 2016 (Amendment to the Constitution). According to the initiators, compared to the time when the Constitution was drafted (1992) and the voting age fixed, Estonian society had undergone a noticeable development. Alongside with the society, also young people had matured significantly, being better informed about societal issues, while their opportunities to have a say in the shaping of their living environment had been limited (Explanatory letter: 1).

In the debate regarding the possible lowering of the voting age that had started in Estonia already in 2010, two opposing camps had developed. In addition to those who believed that the right to vote is inalienable and must belong to the child from a certain age (16 years old as a result of the amendment to the Constitution), there were also those who believed that the children's votes should be given to their parents until the child turns 18 (the so-called substitute election approach) (Toots et al. 2014: 36).

Interestingly enough, while the idea of lowering the voting age from 18 to 16 and even that only in local government council elections gained the upper hand in the public discussion and turned into a corresponding amendment to the constitution, the competing idea re-emerged five years later. Although in passing, at the concluding panel of the Days of Legal Scholars—a Symposion of Estonian lawyers, held every two years in Tartu—of 2020, the idea of lowering the voting age—theoretically even to zero—was put forward. According to the eminent legal scholar of Estonia, who came up with the proposal, in such a case the parents would either vote instead of the child or represent him during the period when the child is not yet able to vote (Jaanimägi 2021: 314).

Although one could theoretically distinguish these two models, this does not seem to rebut the fact that, whether voting for the child or representing him in the electoral process, both would eventually lead to an additional vote for the parent. This, however, seems to be moving dangerously close to a possible violation of the basic principle of suffrage, that of "one person, one vote".

Similarly, the Supreme Court has—in connection with the right of the voter to change his or her vote in case of voting by electronic means—explained that the principle of uniform elections, being one of the pillars of democratic statehood, means that all voters must have equal possibilities to influence the voting results. In the context of active right to vote, the principle of uniformity means, first of all, that all persons entitled to vote must have an equal number of votes and that all votes must have equal weight upon deciding on the distribution of seats in the representative assembly (*E-Elections*: Para 16).

In the context of this paper, this could mean that the principle of intergenerational solidarity is not all-powerful, at least not in allowing future generations to have a voice. Most probably, it would not have the potential to break the principle of "one person, one vote", to which the principle of uniformity—every vote has equal weight—is connected in Estonian fundamental rights doctrine. It is not difficult to see that the fact that the voice of future generations will not be automatically transmitted to us becomes an obstacle to ensuring solidarity between generations. Any legal construction that gives children's votes to their parents is rather dubious from a constitutional point of view.

It is interesting to note, though, that according to the opinion of the Government of the Republic on the draft amendment to the Constitution to lower the voting age in local elections, age limitation as a limitation of everyone's right to vote must be necessary in a democratic state based on rule of law, and as the awareness of young people increases, the state is obliged to adjust these restrictions according to the changed situation (Opinion of the Government of the Republic).

Ensuring the Existence of Future Generations

Albeit this far only theoretically, one could ask whether the principle of intergenerational justice could also be used to strengthen the argument in favour of birth-enhancing measures taken by the state. For example, in the *Riigikogu* elections of 2023, the main election pledge of at least one political party was to make old age benefits dependent on the number of children.

Thus, just like in the case of giving the so-called extra votes for children, one could wonder whether the same purpose—raising the birth rate and thus ensuring the very existence of future generations—could constitutionally justify the difference of treatment based on the presence or number of children. According to Section 28 (4) of the Estonian Constitution, families with a large number of children enjoy special care of the state.

The Supreme Court has yet not had a possibility to clarify the constitutional limits of birth-enhancing measures. In the first days of 2023, the President of the Republic, who in the Estonian legal system performs a preliminary review of the constitutionality of laws, promulgated the Family Benefits Act, which increased the allowance for the first and second child to 80 euros per month, the allowance for the third and next child to 100 euros per month, and the allowance for a large family (3–6 children) to 650 euros per month; and provided for the indexation of the allowance for a large family.

Previously, the President had refused to promulgate the same law for reasons of legal clarity. In addition to problems with legal clarity, the President noted that it was at least questionable why the adopted law only provided for the indexation of the support of a large family with children, creating a difference between children of large families and the rest. The President implied that although according to the Constitution, families with many children are under the special care of the state, which means that the *Riigikogu* has the right to treat such families more favourably than other families, the unequal treatment must be sufficiently and convincingly justified

(Decision of the President). In the new reading of the bill, the *Riigikogu* corrected the legal ambiguity of the law, and the President promulgated the law. Therefore, this dispute did not reach the Supreme Court in its constitutional review function.

However, it is not excluded that this law will be contested by way of concrete constitutional review, i.e., the constitutionality of the inequality of child benefits might be raised in the course of ordinary (administrative) court proceedings. Under the Estonian Constitution, everyone has the right to request that the legal norm applicable in her case be declared unconstitutional.

4 Conclusion

Thus, it can be said without a doubt that the principle of solidarity between generations is derived from the preamble of the Constitution of the Republic of Estonia. As such, it serves as an aid in the interpretation and implementation of fundamental rights, above all when considering limitations arising from the general interest.

However, due to difficulties inherent to such a concept—primarily because it is almost impossible to predict what will be good for future generations, as well as what the effects of today's decisions will be on tomorrow—this principle has not proved to be omnipotent. To strike down a law on the grounds that it will cause harm in the distant future, the probability of such harm must be highly probable, under the Estonian constitutional doctrine.

Among other things, the principle of intergenerational solidarity would probably not be sufficiently powerful and practically applicable to justify, for example, giving future generations the right to vote. Albeit attractive on the theoretical level, the idea of giving a voice to the future generations would most probably might prove infeasible in practice. By allowing the present generations to predict the interests of the future generations, we will most probably end up not having empowered the future generations, but having equipped the members of the present generations with multiple voices which would run contrary to the principle of one person, one vote.

It is thus rather difficult to translate the idea of solidarity between generations into the language of fundamental rights. However, this solemn pledge, contained in the preamble of the Constitution, which is legally binding, in Estonia, must and does constitute a prism through which each and every constitutional problem has to be seen.

References

Aasa B (2022). PS preambul. – U. Lõhmus (peatoim.). Eesti Vabariigi põhiseaduse kommentaarid. Eesti Teaduste Akadeemia Riigiõiguse Sihtkapital, Tallinn. https://pohiseadus.riigioigus.ee/v1/eesti-vabariigi-pohiseadus/preambul#l6ik-108 [in Estonian]

Amendment to the Constitution = Eesti Vabariigi põhiseaduse muutmise seadus kohaliku omavalitsuse volikogu valimistel valimisea langetamiseks. https://www.riigiteataja.ee/akt/115052015001 [in Estonian]

Constitution of 1992 = Constitution of the Republic of Estonia (1992). – RT 1992, 26, 349. https://www.riigiteataja.ee/en/eli/ee/530122020003/consolide

Decision of the President = Perehüvitiste seaduse ja perekonnaseaduse muutmise seaduse väljakuulutamata jätmine. Vabariigi Presidendi 22.12.2022 a. otsus nr 234. https://president.ee/et/ametitegevus/otsused/54400-234-perehuvitiste-seaduse-ja-perekonnaseaduse-muutmise-seaduse-valjakuulutamata-jatmine [in Estonian]

ESM (12 Jul 2012) Judgement of the Supreme Court *en banc*. https://www.riigikohus.ee/en/constitutional-judgment-3-4-1-6-12

Explanatory letter = Seletuskiri Eesti Vabariigi põhiseaduse muutmise seadus kohaliku omavalitsuse volikogu valimistel valimisea langetamiseks 703 SE juurde. https://www.riigikogu.ee/tegevus/eelnoud/eelnou/b0f58e59-bf36-40e3-bbd7-3aff08428bdf/Eesti%20Vabariigi%20p%c3%b5hiseaduse%20muutmise%20seadus%20kohaliku%20omavalitsuse%20volikogu%20valimistel%20valimisea%20langetamiseks/ [in Estonian]

E-Elections (1 Sep 2005) Judgment of the Constitutional Review Chamber of the Supreme Court. https://www.riigikohus.ee/en/constitutional-judgment-3-4-1-13-05

Final Report (1996) Eesti Vabariigi põhiseaduse juriidilise ekspertiisi komisjoni lõpparuanne. Põhiseaduse preambula. Justiitsministeerium. https://www.just.ee/era-ja-avalik-oigus/pohiseadus-ja-pohioigused/pohiseadus#ii-osa-pohiseaduse- [in Estonian]

Gosseries A, Meyer LH (2009) Introduction—intergenerational justice and its challenges. In: Gosseries A, Meyer LH (ed) Intergenerational justice. Oxford University Press, Oxford

Jaanimägi K (koost) (2021) 36. Eesti õigusteadlaste päevade lõpudiskussioon „Põhiseaduse tulevik: areng muutmise või tõlgendamise teel". – Riigiõiguse aastaraamat. Eesti Teaduste Akadeemia riigiõiguse sihtkapital, Tallinn. [in Estonian]

KAHOS (veebruari 2022) Riigikohtu põhiseaduslikkuse järelevalve kolleegiumi 8. A otsus asjas nr 5-21-18. https://www.riigikohus.ee/et/lahendid?asjaNr=5-21-18/18 [in Estonian]

Kirchhof P (2007) Mitteln staatlichen Handelns, § 99. Isensee J, Kirchhof P (Hg) Handbuch des Staatsrechts der Bundesrepublik Deutschland, V Band. C.F.Müller Verlag, Heidelberg

Language requirements (4 Nov 1998) Judgment of the Constitutional Review Chamber of the Supreme Court. https://www.riigikohus.ee/en/constitutional-judgment-3-4-1-7-98

Mining permit (mai 2020) Riigikohtu põhiseaduslikkuse järelevalve kolleegiumi 26. A otsus asjas nr 5-20-2. https://www.riigikohus.ee/et/lahendid?asjaNr=5-20-2/11 [in Estonian]

Narits R, Kalmo H, Madise L (2020). Preambul. – Ü. Madise (peatoim.). Eesti Vabariigi põhiseaduse kommentaarid. Juura, Tallinn. https://pohiseadus.ee/sisu/3467 [in Estonian]

Olle V, Almann A, Kolk T, Lahesoo K, Liventaal J (2020) PS § 156. – Ü. Madise (peatoim.). Eesti Vabariigi põhiseaduse kommentaarid. Juura, Tallinn. https://pohiseadus.ee/sisu/3641 [in Estonian]

Opinion of the Government of the Republic, Vabariigi Valitsuse arvamus eelnõule 703 SE. https://www.riigikogu.ee/download/689ef7cc-cdc7-4259-be8c-3cf162e86152 [in Estonian]

Peep V (toim) (1997). Põhiseadus ja Põhiseaduse Assamblee. Koguteos. Juura, Tallinn [in Estonian]

Pension Reform (20 Oct 2020) Judgement of the Supreme Court *en banc*. https://www.riigikohus.ee/en/constitutional-judgment-5-20-3

Protection of cross forests (detsembri 2022) Põhiseaduslikkuse järelevalve kolleegiumi 6. A otsus asjas *nr* 5-22-5. https://www.riigikohus.ee/et/lahendid?asjaNr=5-22-5/16 [in Estonian]

PÕSK minutes, Põhiseaduskomisjoni 8.09.2014 protokoll. https://www.riigikogu.ee/tegevus/eelnoud/eelnou/b0f58e59-bf36-40e3-bbd7-3aff08428bdf/eesti-vabariigi-pohiseaduse-muutmise-seadus-kohaliku-omavalitsuse-volikogu-valimistel-valimisea-langetamiseks [in Estonian]

RoheInvest (15 Jun 2021) Judgment of the Constitutional Review Chamber of the Supreme Court. https://www.riigikohus.ee/en/constitutional-judgment-5-21-3

Tammelo I (2001) Õiglus ja hool. Tartu: Ilmamaa [in Estonian]

Toots A, Idnurm T, Saarts T (2014) Aktiivse valimisea langetamise mõjude analüüs: eelhindamine. TLÜ Riigiteaduste Instituut, Tallinn. https://www.just.ee/sites/www.just.ee/files/vote16.pdf [in Estonian]

Judicial Protection of the Rights of Future Generations in the Republic of Poland

Anna Rytel-Warzocha

Abstract The rights of future generations have been recognised in many constitutions around the world and in acts of international law. The 1997 Constitution of the Republic of Poland refers to them in its preamble and in several of its provisions. They can also be derived from more general constitutional principles. However, it is important not only to recognise rights but also to ensure their effective protection. The purpose of this article was to show the role of courts in Poland in protecting the rights of future generations guaranteed by the Constitution. In particular, it seeks to answer the question of whether it is possible to file a lawsuit on behalf of future generations, and if so, on what legal grounds, and what mechanisms have already been successfully used in this regard. The article considers different types of proceedings before the ordinary courts as well as before the Constitutional Court. It also considers the usefulness of the dispersed constitutional review by ordinary courts that has been practised in recent years. The author concludes that Polish law lacks effective mechanisms for both enforcing the state's obligations in this area and protecting future generations' interests.

1 The Rights of Future Generations and Their Legal Recognition

It is widely recognised that a lot of activities and decisions undertaken nowadays can affect not only the current legal situation of a human and a citizen, but to more or less extend they can also determine the rights of future generations. At the same time, the rights of future generations have been increasingly recognised since 1990s in the constitutions of democratic states. It was estimated that in 2021 41% of all democratic

Publication has been prepared as part of a research project funded by the National Science Centre in Poland (competition OPUS 18, decision no. 2019/35/B/HS5/03215).

A. Rytel-Warzocha (✉)
University of Gdansk, Gdansk, Poland
e-mail: anna.rytel@prawo.ug.edu.pl

R. Arnold and T. Fickentscher (eds.), *The Responsibility of a Constitution for the Future*, https://doi.org/10.1007/978-3-031-65296-7_6

constitutions explicitly referenced future generations (Araújo and Koessler 2022). There is also such tendency in the jurisprudence of the court.

The Constitution of the Republic of Poland of 2 April 1997 (Official Journal of Laws "Dziennik Ustaw" 19,997, No. 78, item 483) refers to future generations' rights determining the duty of all citizens "to pass on to future generations all that that is valuable from our heritage of over a thousand year" (preamble). This fragment of the Constitution refers to the idea of intergenerational solidarity and recognize the well-being of future generations as a constitutional value. Therefore, taking benefits here and now at the expense of future generations, like f. ex. conducting the predatory policy of exploiting the natural environment, must be restricted. The rights of future generations are expressly mentioned also in Article 74 p. 1, which provides that "Public authorities shall pursue policies ensuring the ecological security of current and future generations". Nevertheless, the above provision has the character of a program norm indicating the direction and goals that public authorities are to achieve instead of determining specific obligations. The State's obligation to ensure ecological safety are addressed to both the present and future generations, which underlines its long-term and permanent nature. Therefore, the State cannot be guided in its actions by the need to satisfy only the current interests if this could in any way prevent or adversely affect the ability to meet the needs of future generations. This also works the other way round. Legal protection of the interests of future generations cannot disproportionately harm the interests of contemporaries, although in practice the probability of such a situation is certainly much lower. Therefore, the Constitution requires that actions taken by the State to ensure ecological security assume a compromise between the interests of contemporary and future generations. The above obligation should be implemented by public authorities in a systematic and orderly manner through the implementation of an appropriate environmental policy. From the practical side, it rests mainly with the executive authorities, both central and local, in accordance with the constitutional division of powers (Jackiewicz and Rytel-Warzocha 2022, pp. 43–52).

The future generations' rights can be also decoded from other constitutional principles such as social solidarity (preamble), treating the Republic of Poland as a common good of all citizens (Article 1), the state's duty to "ensure the freedoms and rights of persons and citizens", to "safeguard the national heritage" and to "ensure the protection of natural environment pursuant to the principles of sustainable development" (Article 5), the state's duty to "provide conditions for the people's equal access to the products of culture which are the source of the Nation's identity, continuity and development" (Article 6) (Dąbrowski and Jackiewicz 2023). Moreover, further rights can be derived from the rights that are directly expressed in the Constitution. For example, the right to a clean and safe environment has a close impact on other important rights of future generations, such as the right to life and health protection, food, water and sanitation, self-determination, development, housing, education, or meaningful and informed participation. This is because the failure of the state to protect the environment can lead to climate change, which has all these, direct and indirect, implications.

The rights of future generations have already been referred to in various instruments of international law. The Stockholm Declaration of the United Nations Conference on the Human Environment of 14 June 1972 provided for the right of future generations to freedom, equality and appropriate living conditions in an environment that would allow for a decent living in prosperity. The responsibilities of the present generations towards future generations were also pointed out in the Convention for the Protection of the World Cultural and Natural Heritage adopted by the General Conference of UNESCO on 16 November 1972, the United Nations Framework Convention on Climate Change and the Convention on Biological Diversity adopted in Rio de Janeiro on 5 June 1992, the Rio Declaration on Environment and Development adopted by the United Nations Conference on Environment and Development on 14 June 1992, the Vienna Declaration and Programme of Action adopted by the World Conference on Human Rights on 25 June 1993, or the United Nations General Assembly resolutions relating to the protection of the global climate for present and future generations adopted since 1990. Undoubtedly an important document in this respect is also the Declaration on the Responsibilities of the Present Generations Towards Future Generations adopted at the General Conference of the United Nations Educational, Scientific and Cultural Organization, meeting in Paris from 21 October to 12 November 1997 at its 29th session. It identifies a number of important rights of future generations related to perpetuation of humankind, life, environment, culture, heritage, peace, development, education, and non-discrimination, having in mind "that the fate of future generations depends to a great extent on decisions and actions taken today".

2 The Means of Protection of the Rights of Future Generations

Nevertheless, it is not only important to formally recognise the right of future generations in the provisions of law, in particular provisions of the basic laws, but to provide their effective protection. The regulations declaring certain rights of future generations should be accompanied by legal mechanisms for their protection. These mechanisms can take various forms, including specialised commissioners. Such bodies have been such institutions have already been established f. ex. the Future Generations Commissioner for Wales, or the Parliamentary Commissioner for Future Generations in Hungary. The proposal for an International Ombudsperson or High Commissioner for Future Generations is still under consideration (Vincent 2012).

However, as an ombudsman does not have the power to sanction or compel (Beckman and Uggla 2016), it seems that the most important role in ensuring the protection of the rights and freedoms also of future generations should be played by courts, including constitutional courts, which may constitute, above all, the most effective mechanism in this regard. The growing awareness of the importance of providing an effective juridical tools to protect future generations is reflected in the growing cases aimed at protecting the rights of future generations (mainly lawsuits linked to climate changes and their harmful effects). Even if the litigations are not always successful (like in Sharma and others v. Minister for the Environment case, in which the Full Federal Court of Australia delivered a decision on 15 March 2022 Stocker and Hublet 2022; Camenzuli et al. 2022) they contribute to the discussion by invoking the interests of future generations in mass disputes on the planet's future.

At least some should be mentioned here. The first one is the precedent landmark decision of the Philippine Supreme Court in Oposa et al. v. Fulgencio S. Factoran, Jr. et al. case (G.R. No. 101083, 1993), in which the Court recognised the doctrine of intergenerational responsibility. The Court directly admitted the petitioner's personality to sue and act in behalf of the succeeding generations. The Court recognized the equal right of present and future generations to dispose of, use, and manage national forest, mineral, land, water, fish, wildlife, coastal and other natural resources, pointing out that each generation is therefore responsible to the next for their preservation (see more: Gatmaytan-Magno 2007).

Another important example can be the case considered by the Supreme Court of Norway. According to Article 112 of the Norwegian Constitution, "Every person has a right to an environment that is conducive to health and to natural surroundings whose productivity and diversity are preserved. Natural resources should be made use of on the basis of comprehensive long-term considerations whereby this right will be safeguarded for future generations as well". In 2020, both a first-instance District Court and a Court of Appeal ruled that this provision conferred rights on future generations that may be asserted in court. The Supreme Court subsequently determined that it is not merely a declaration of principle, but a provision with a certain legal content (Araújo and Koessler 2022).

Another examples come from Brazil, where in 2020 some of the largest political parties brought claims to the Federal Supreme Court for the recognition and protection of the rights of future generations against the executive's dismantlement of environmental agencies (PSB et al. v Brazil case). The Justice-Rapporteur preliminarily granted some of the plaintiff's claims acknowledging in a direct way the rights of future generations to environment which is combined with the right to a dignified life. The ruling has been paused after another justice requested further information before voting—but it 2022 the Supreme Court follow the Justice-Rapporteur's vote and recognized the Paris Agreement as a human rights treaty. The intergenerational context of the right to an ecologically balanced environment was facilitated by the direct recognition of the duty to defend and preserve the environment for present and future generation provided for in Article 225 of the Brazilian Constitution of 1988 (Garofalo 2022).

Of great importance (if not the most important in the context of future generations' right) was also the decision of the German Federal Constitutional Court of 24 March 2021, in which the Tribunal held that the provisions of the Federal Climate Change Act of 12 December 2019 (Bundes-Klimaschutzgesetz) are incompatible with fundamental rights insofar as they lack sufficient specifications for further emission reductions from 2031 onwards and thereby infringes the rights of future generations. The decision is particularly inspiring in the context of the protection of future generations' rights not only because it raises the exceptionally important and topical issue of climate protection, but also because the Federal Constitutional Tribunal applied the principle of intergenerational justice in a direct way by extending the protection of fundamental rights to potential, probable violations of rights in the future (see more: Theil 2022; Schramm 2022).

3 Role of Courts in the Protection of the Rights of Future Generations on the Example of the Republic of Poland

As it has been already mentioned, the rights of future generations have been also recognised by the Polish Constitution of 1997. Some of them are directly mentioned in its text and some can be derived from other constitutional provisions. Nevertheless, an important question arises as to whether it is possible on the grounds of the Constitution to construct legal protection of the legal interest of future generations. In particular, is it possible to take legal action on behalf of future generations? If so, on what legal bases could this occur and what mechanisms have already been successfully used in this regard?

Firstly, it can be considered if the civil proceedings can be applied to protect the rights of future generations. The general principle of liability for damage is provided for Article 415 of the Civil Code of 1964 (unified text: Official Journal of Laws "Dziennik Ustaw" 2022, item 1360), which states: "Whoever causes damage to another through his fault, is obliged to compensate for it". In order for tort liability to arise, three conditions must all be met: the damage must have occurred, there must have been a culpable event causing the damage and there must have been a causal link between the damage and the event. However, the use of this provision to protect the rights of future generations is not possible because of the need to show that the damage resulting from someone's wrongful act or omission has already occurred. Damage is understood as harm to legally protected goods and interests that has occurred against the will of the injured party, whether of a pecuniary or non-pecuniary nature. In the case of the rights of future generations, the damage may only become apparent after many years, so that it is difficult to determine whether the damage to future generations will occur and if yes, to what extent. Therefore this provision cannot be used to seek the protection of future generations' rights.

Moreover, the Constitution guarantees in Article 77 the right to compensation for any harm done to a person by any action of an organ of public authority contrary to law. The liability of the Polish state has been also provided for by Article 417 of the Civil Code which states that the State Treasury, a territorial self-government unit or another legal person exercising this authority by law is liable for damage caused by an unlawful act or omission in the exercise of public authority. In this situation, the state is liable, for example, for inaction or tardiness of actions that would have prevented environmental pollution and ecological disaster. But again, this provision cannot be used to protect the rights of future generations, as it is necessary to demonstrate concrete damage, which, in the case of future generations, is only potential.

The role of the common courts can also be considered in relation to a specific right guaranteed by the Constitution to future generations—right to a clean and healthy environment. According to Article 86 of the Constitution, everyone shall care for the quality of the environment and shall be held responsible for causing its degradation. Such regulation is the logical consequence of the fact that the main threat to the environment is caused by humans. The obligation to care about the environment is addressed both to physical and legal persons, which is particularly important in the context of those enterprises which, due to the economic activity they carry out, particularly expose the environment to deterioration. The scale of the environmental impact of this category of entities particularly justifies the inclusion of the compensation clause into the constitutional regulation. At the same time, the Law on Environmental Protection of 2001 (Official Journal of Laws "Dziennik Ustaw" 2001, No. 62, item 627) can be also helpful in this regard as it provides in Article 323 that: "(1) Any person who is directly threatened or harmed by an unlawful impact on the environment may demand from the entity responsible for that threat or infringement to restore the lawful state of affairs and to take preventive measures, in particular by installing installations or equipment to prevent the threat or infringement; where this is impossible or excessively difficult, he/she may demand that the activity causing the threat or infringement be discontinued. (2) If the threat or infringement concerns the environment as a common good, the claim referred to in paragraph (1) may be brought by the State Treasury, a local authority or an environmental organisation". Nevertheless, so far these legal provisions have been used only in individual lawsuits against noise pollution. Due to its construction they cannot be applied to future potential harms caused by climate change.

Secondly, it is important to consider whether under the Constitution the effective protection of the rights of future generations can be provided by constitutional judiciary. The constitutional review adopted by the Polish Constitution of 1997 is based on the centralised model developed by H. Kelsen at the beginning of the XX century. The constitutional position of the Constitutional Tribunal as well as its competences have been directly determined in chapter VIII of the Constitution (Article 188–Article 197). The Tribunal can consider the constitutionality of laws both in the mode of abstract and concrete review, so each of them will be analysed separately for potential use in protecting the rights of future generations.

The above-mentioned ruling of the German Federal Constitutional Court was issued as a result of filing constitutional complaints by individual citizens and environmental associations (in the latter case, however, the complaints were found inadmissible). As the Tribunal stated, the challenged provisions violate the rights of the complainants, some of whom are still very young, as they irreversibly offload major emission reduction burdens onto periods after 2030 which will undoubtedly result in much greater restrictions of a wide range of human rights and freedoms (as practically all aspects of human life are associated with the emission of greenhouse gases) in future than before 2030. Thus, it recognized the claim for the protection of the subjective rights of future generations as justified.

Against this background, it may be considered whether a constitutional complaint provided for in Article 79 of the Polish Constitution could be used to protect the subjective right of future generations. The constitutional regulation of a constitutional complaint is quite extensive and it determines its basic features, including the subjective and objective scopes. Article 79 provides that "In accordance with principles specified by statute, everyone whose constitutional freedoms or rights have been infringed, shall have the right to appeal to the Constitutional Tribunal for its judgment on the conformity to the Constitution of a statute or another normative act upon which basis a court or organ of public administration has made a final decision on his freedoms or rights or on his obligations specified in the Constitution".

As a form of a concrete constitutional review, a constitutional complaint must always be closely related to a case pending before a Polish court or administrative body. Unlike the model of a constitutional complaint in Germany, the allegation presented in the complaint can only concern the generally binding act applied to issue a final judgment or administrative decision. In the light of Article 79 of the Constitution, it is clear, therefore, that the allegation formulated in the complaint may only refer to a legal provision in the positive sense, which has not only been enacted by the relevant authority, but has entered into force, has binding force and may therefore be applied by courts and administrative authorities. On the contrary, a literal interpretation of this provision excludes the possibility of formulating in the constitutional complaint an allegation of violation of the Constitution as a result of the legislator's failure to adopt appropriate legal regulations.

Another problem is the question whether a constitutional complaint can be an effective tool to protect the right to environment provided for by Article 74 para 1 of the Constitution as such, and in particular in regard to the interests of more abstract future generations who do not actually exist yet. Since the provision of Article 74 para 1 is a program norm and it does not explicitly provide for a subjective right to the environment it cannot be subject to a constitutional complaint. This does not mean, however, that there is no such right. There is but it derives from the appropriate interpretation of the constitutional provision. Moreover, the constitutional complaint in Poland may be filed by an entity whose constitutional right or freedom has been violated as a result of a final court judgment or a final administrative decision. This means that the breach of the constitutional right must be factual and already existing so it cannot be merely potential. In regard to the rights of future generations as future generation do not have legitimacy to file a complaint. It cannot be a party to the proceedings so it is impossible to issue a final judgment or final decision infringing its rights or freedoms.

The situation is different with regard to the possibility of protecting the rights of future generations by means of the abstract mode of review. It may potentially happen that if the legislator passes an act that is inconsistent with the constitutional provisions from which the rights of future generations may be derived, the authorized entity, such as the Commissioner for Human Rights, will submit an application for the constitutional review of that act as to its compliance with the Constitution. In such a situation, the constitutional norm that is the source of the future generations' right will become a point of reference, and the entity initiating such proceedings will de facto become the spokesman of the future generations. Similarly, a court may refer a question of law to the Constitutional Tribunal if it has doubts during the examination of the case as to whether the provision to be applied is compatible with certain constitutional norms or not. Thus, this is the only possibility in Polish law to protect the rights of future generations. However, it should be pointed out that the object of the allegation in German Klima-Gezetz case was not a specific legal regulation but, just on the contrary, the lack of an appropriate regulation relating to the rules of reducing CO_2 emissions in the years 2030–2050. In Poland, legislative omissions cannot be challenged before the Constitutional Tribunal. The Tribunal takes the position that its role, as a 'negative legislator', is to review legal norms that have already been enacted in order to indicate their possible unconstitutionality and to eliminate unconstitutional norms from the legal order. Therefore, the constitutional review initiated by a question of law (referred by a court according to Article 193 of the Constitution) or by an application addressed to the Constitutional Tribunal by one of the entities enumerated in Article 191 para 1 p. 1 of the Constitution must always refer to a law that have been already adopted by the parliament.

It must be also noticed, however, that the ongoing challenges facing the Polish judicial system, including Constitutional Tribunal, may complicate the judicial protection of the rights of future generations. According to the Constitution, the Constitutional Tribunal is the main body responsible for constitutional review in Poland, but since 2016 its independence has been seriously questioned, not only by legal circles in Poland but also by European Union bodies or the Venice Commission. The main allegations concern the seating of defectively elected persons in its composition, its politicisation and submission to government influence, leading to concerns not only about the impartiality but also the legality of its decisions. Therefore, the concept of dispersed constitutional review as a potential solution to the above problem has attracted increasing attention in Poland in recent years (Rytel-Warzocha 2022). In view of the paralysis of the exercise of judicial review by the Constitutional Tribunal, it is pointed out that although the Constitution provides for the centralised constitutional review as the basic model, it does not exclude the competences of common courts in this scope. Therefore, it seems that on the grounds of Articles 8, 178 and 193 of the Constitution, common courts can exercise the right to review the constitutionality of law during the process of its application. However, the court's decision on the unconstitutionality of a given provision relates exclusively to a specific case and it only leads to a refusal to apply the law declared by the common or administrative court to be unconstitutional in a particular case. The law is still in force and can serve as a basis for adjudication in other cases. Despite the fact that dispersed constitutional review is now (after several years of debate that resurfaced after 2016) widely accepted by the doctrine of constitutional law, and there are an increasing number of judgments in which courts have already exercised this power, its construction renders it useless in the context of ensuring the protection of the rights of future generations. Therefore, it is of utmost importance to regain an independent Constitutional Tribunal that will carry out an abstract review of the constitutionality of the law in an independent manner. That is important, because in light of the above, the role of the judiciary in protecting the rights of future generations is crucial.

Summing up, it can be pointed out that the need to recognize the rights of future generations was noticed by the drafters of the current Polish Constitution who inserted the relevant provisions into its text. The rights of future generations are related in particular to the preservation of the common heritage and the protection of a clean, healthy and safe environment. Nevertheless, there are no effective mechanisms in Polish law enabling either the enforcement of state obligations in this area or the protection of the interests of future generations. Not only the judicial protection is particularly weak in the latter case, but also extrajudicial protection is lacking. There are no legal mechanisms and institutions for advanced protection of future generations that can be met in other states, such as specialized ombudsman. Although there were some proposals to appoint an ombudsman for future generations who would guard the rights of future generations and represent their interests in matters affecting their future lives, they have not been implemented so far and frankly speaking, this issue is not currently the subject of public debate. That should be changed to follow the global tendency to think in a forward-looking way. By recognising the importance of intergenerational justice, enforcing and promoting the rights of future generations, in particular the judiciary can play an important role in creating a sustainable and just future for all. Therefore, there is still a need for legal instruments to ensure the welfare of future generations.

References

Araújo R, Koessler L (2022) The rise of the constitutional protection of future generations. https://verfassungsblog.de/the-rise-of-the-constitutional-protection-of-future-generations/

Beckman L, Uggla F (2016) An ombudsman for future generations: legitimate and effective? In: González-Ricoy I, Gosseries A (eds) Institutions for future generation. Oxford. https://doi.org/10.1093/acprof:oso/9780198746959.003.0007

Camenzuli L, Neuman M, Green J (2022) Sharma appeal decision: end of the road for novel duty of care? https://www.corrs.com.au/insights/sharma-appeal-decision-end-of-the-road-for-novel-duty-of-care

Dąbrowski M, Jackiewicz A (2023) Komentarz do Konstytucji RP: Art. 74, 86. Delfi, Warszawa

Garofalo C (2022) As the lungs of the earth dry out, climate litigation heats up. https://verfassungsblog.de/as-the-lung-of-the-earth-dries-out-climate-litigation-heats-up/

Gatmaytan-Magno D (2007) Artificial judicial environmental activism: Oposa v. Factoran as aberration. Indiana Int Comp Law Rev 17:1

Jackiewicz A, Rytel-Warzocha A (2022) Natural environment as a fundamental right of future generations in the light of the Constitutional of the Republic of Poland. In: Arnold R (ed) Comparative law studies. The protection of the environment and constitutional law, vol 15

Rytel-Warzocha A (2022) Jak nie Trybunał Konstytucyjny to co? O rozproszonej kontroli konstytucyjności prawa w Polsce. Przegląd Prawa Konstytucyjnego 3(67):25–37

Schramm F (2022) Judges as narrators of the climate crisis? An illustrative analysis of the decision of the German Constitutional Court from 24 March 2021. Eur Pap 7(1):361–378

Stocker S, Hublet A (2022) Sharma v Minister for the Environment: A setback for climate change claimants as landmark decision is overturned on appeal. https://www.whitecase.com/insight-alert/sharma-v-minister-environment-setback-climate-change-claimants-landmark-decision

Theil S (2022) Cautious scrutiny: the federal climate change act case in the German constitutional court. Mod Law Rev 86(1):263–275

Vincent A (2012) Ombudspersons for Future Generations: Bringing Intergenerational Justice into the Heart of Policymaking. The Future We Want? 1 & 2 (XLIX). https://www.un.org/en/chronicle/article/ombudspersons-future-generations-bringing-intergenerational-justice-heart-policymaking

Constitutional Conversations with the Past, Present, and Future

Amanda L. Tyler

Abstract The increasingly dominant approach to constitutional interpretation embraced by the Supreme Court of the United States is known as "originalism." This approach, witnessed in recent decisions regarding gun rights and abortion, is fixated in unearthing the meaning of constitutional provisions based on how they were understood when ratified. Not only is such an approach not concerned with the future, its backward-looking fixation means that it is not even connected to present day.

When I was asked to join in a comparative discussion of the obligation of constitutions with respect to the future, I was very excited about the proposition. Very quickly, however, my excitement turned to distress. I will here explain why.

Let me begin by saying that one of the ways in which many constitutions have planned for the future is by assuming that societies will evolve over time. And one of the ways in which constitutions do this is by including broad language setting out general principles that can be applied to the challenges and changing world that confront each new generation. An example that I will draw upon here is the United States' Constitution's Fourteenth Amendment, which promises all "persons" equal protection under the law.[1] This particular amendment to our Constitution was ratified just following the United States Civil War and was driven by a desire to give the newly freed enslaved persons a shot at true freedom as we emerged from the horrors of slavery. But the Amendment's language is not limited solely to outlawing discrimination based on race—it provides more generally that all "persons" are equal before the law.

Why is this important? Because, as one of our earliest and most influential Chief Justices, John Marshall once said, constitutions are "designed to be permanent."[2]

[1] U.S. Const. amend. XIV, § 1.

[2] *Marbury v. Madison*, 1 Cranch (5 U.S.) 137, 176 (1803).

A. L. Tyler (✉)
Berkeley School of Law, University of California, Berkeley, USA
e-mail: atyler@law.berkeley.edu

R. Arnold and T. Fickentscher (eds.), *The Responsibility of a Constitution for the Future*, https://doi.org/10.1007/978-3-031-65296-7_7

And when you have one, like ours, that is quite short in length and likewise short on details—and when it is very hard to amend, as ours is—the only way such a constitution can endure is for it to provide for its adaptation over time. Indeed, it was this very understanding that explains why, in the 1970s, the Supreme Court of the United States recognized—at the urging of an advocate named Ruth Bader Ginsburg—that the Equal Protection Clause also promises women equality before the law.[3] The decisions recognizing that discrimination based on gender undermines constitutional equality have a sound basis in the text of our Constitution. Recall its high level of generality in providing for equal protection for all "persons." Further, the gender equality decisions of the 1970s marry well with the general idea that a constitution should be, again to borrow from Chief Justice Marshall, "expounded" over time and permitted to evolve as society evolves alongside it. As he phrased it, "we must never forget that it is a constitution we are expounding. "Marshall continued by describing it as" a constitution intended to endure for ages to come, and consequently, to be adapted to the various crises of human affairs."[4] As Marshall also wrote, a constitution should not be the equivalent of a detailed legal code, but it should only offer "great outlines..., its important objects designated, and the minor ingredients which compose those objects, be deduced from the nature of the objects themselves."[5]

Now, with that background in place, let me discuss my current state of distress. Not only are we not even talking about the future in my country when it comes to constitutional law, we aren't even in conversation with the present day. This is because in the last few decades—and particularly in the last handful of years—the increasingly dominant approach to constitutional interpretation in the United States is one called originalism.

Originalism is the exact opposite of the approach to constitutional interpretation that I have just sketched. Instead of reading broad constitutional terms as leaving room for expansion and evolution over time, and instead of understanding our Constitution to be an ongoing inter-generational conversation, originalists wish only to look backward and to freeze the meaning of the Constitution as it was understood at the time a relevant provision was ratified. So, for the body of the original United States Constitution, the key date is the year 1789 when it became operable. And for the Reconstruction Amendments that followed our Civil War, such as the Fourteenth Amendment and its Equal Protection Clause, that date is 1868. As one Supreme Court Justice, Neil Gorsuch, has said: "[J]udges should... strive... to apply the law as it is, focusing backward, not forward, and looking to text, structure, and history to decide what a reasonable reader at the time of the events in question would have understood the law to be."[6]

---

[3] See, *e.g.*, *Reed v. Reed*, 404 U.S. 71 (1971); *Frontiero v. Richardson*, 411 U.S. 677 (1973).

[4] *M'Culloch v Maryland*, 17 U.S. 316, 407, 415 (1819).

[5] *Id.* at 407. The Supreme Court of the United States features these Marshall quotations prominently on its public-facing website. See "The Court and Constitutional Interpretation," https://www.supremecourt.gov/about/constitutional.aspx (last visited Dec. 15, 2022).

[6] Gorsuch (2016), pp. 905–906.

Only a few decades ago, originalism as an approach to constitutional interpretation had little foothold at our Supreme Court. Then, a justice named Antonin Scalia joined the Court and slowly but surely as he promoted the idea, it became more and more popular, even as critics highlighted a host of problems with the approach.[7] Over time, originalism has now come to wield exceptional influence over constitutional interpretation in our country.

Two recent high-profile decisions of the Supreme Court underscore just how dominant an approach originalism has become. The first is a decision from 2022 called *New York State Rifle & Pistol Association v. Bruen.*[8] The case concerned whether an over-one-hundred-year-old New York State law that required a showing of "special cause" for a private citizen to obtain a permit allowing possession in public of a concealed weapon—to be specific, a gun—violated the Second Amendment to the United States Constitution. That amendment guarantees in certain circumstance a right to bear arms.[9] The plaintiffs in the case sought to obtain permits for self-defense. Following earlier Supreme Court decisions in *District of Columbia v. Heller*,[10] and *McDonald v. City of Chicago*,[11] which together recognized an individual right to bear arms as protected by the Second Amendment, it was easy to predict that the Court would strike down the law at issue in *Bruen.* Its holding was not at all surprising in that regard. It is *how* it reached its decision that it noteworthy.

Writing for the Court in a 6–3 decision, Justice Clarence Thomas posited that the right to carry a firearm in public for self-defense is deeply rooted in the history of the United States. And, he emphasized, Court precedent does not require a showing of "special need" to exercise any other constitutional right; it followed, on his view, that neither should this one.

In so declaring, Justice Thomas announced a new test to govern the determination of what the Second Amendment to the United States Constitution, ratified in 1791, means. In his words, "To justify its regulation, the government may not simply posit that the regulation promotes an important interest. Rather, the government must demonstrate that the regulation is consistent with this Nation's *historical tradition* of firearm regulation."[12] In keeping with this idea, Justice Thomas subscribes to the view that the meaning of the Constitution is controlled by the understandings of those who ratified it.[13]

---

[7] See Scalia (1997) (setting forth Justice Scalia's approach to constitutional interpretation and including responses to Scalia's approach).

[8] 142 S.Ct. 2111 (2022).

[9] See U.S. Const. amend. II ("A well regulated Militia, being necessary to the security of a free State, the right of the people to keep and bear Arms, shall not be infringed.").

[10] 554 U.S. 570 (2008).

[11] 561 U.S. 742 (2010).

[12] *Id.* at 2126 (emphasis added).

[13] *Id.* at 2137 (positing that "post-ratification adoption or acceptable of laws that are *inconsistent* with the original meaning of the constitutional text obviously cannot overcome or alter that text"). Justice Thomas did not call into question *Heller*'s observation that some laws banning guns in "sensitive" places are constitutional because of the history of such regulations. See *id.* at 2133-34.

And so, in the wake of this decision, lower courts are now looking at regulations of weapons by asking if there were similar regulations in 1791. There is no discussion of how society has evolved and changed—for originalists, such developments are simply irrelevant. And so, following *Bruen*, a lower court recently struck down a law limiting individuals subject to protective orders from possessing firearms because there were no analogous laws at the time of the Founding; a case over which the Supreme Court of the United States granted review.[14] Well, of course, there were no such laws at the time. At the Founding, there were virtually no laws to address domestic violence—women had virtually no rights back then—so it would be surprising to find related firearms regulations then in existence targeting the specific problem of domestic violence.

The second recent decision out of the United States Supreme Court underscoring the rise of originalism is one with which even a foreign audience is likely familiar. It is the Court's recent decision in *Dobbs v. Jackson Women's Health Organization*,[15] in which the Court overruled *Roe v. Wade*[16] and *Planned Parenthood of Southeastern Pennsylvania v. Casey,*[17] while holding that there is no specific right to obtain an abortion recognized in the United States Constitution.[18] It followed, on the majority's view, that any law regulating abortion need only be "rational" to be upheld, a test that almost all, if not all, regulations governing abortion are likely to satisfy.[19]

Specifically, the majority opinion, written by Justice Samuel Alito, posited that:

> The Constitution makes no reference to abortion, and no such right is implicitly protected by any constitutional provision, including the one on which the defenders of *Roe* and *Casey* now chiefly rely—the Due Process Clause of the Fourteenth Amendment. That provision has been held to guarantee some rights that are not mentioned in the Constitution, but any such right must be "deeply rooted in this Nation's history and tradition" and "implicit in the concept of ordered liberty."[20]

Thus, Justice Alito approached the entire constitutional inquiry by looking backward to define what "liberty" is protected in the Fourteenth Amendment. To answer the question, just as Justice Thomas did in *Bruen*, Justice Alito asked whether a right to obtain an abortion is "fundamental," and more specifically, whether such a right is "deeply rooted in... history and tradition".[21] Here, once again, the Court looked backward, focusing on the laws in place during and immediately following the Reconstruction period that came after the Civil War during which time the Fourteenth Amendment went into effect.

---

[14] See *United States v. Rahimi*, 61 F.4th 443 (5th Cir. 2023); rev'd, 144 S.Ct. 1889 (2024) (reversing the Fifth Circuit and upholding the federal law at issue based on more general laws in existence at the Founding that limited firearm possession by dangerous persons).

[15] 142 S.Ct. 2228 (2022).

[16] 410 U.S. 113 (1973).

[17] 505 U.S. 833 (1992).

[18] *Dobbs*, 142 S.Ct. at 2283.

[19] *Id.*

[20] *Id.* at 2242 (quoting *Washington v. Glucksberg*, 521 U.S. 702, 721 (1997)).

[21] *Id.*

The Court's inquiry started and ended there. As Justice Alito viewed things, "Until the latter part of the twentieth century, there was no support in American law for a constitutional right to obtain an abortion."[22] For good measure, he added, most states criminalized abortion at the time of ratification of the Fourteenth Amendment.[23] (Here, I should note that the dissent made a strong case that the historical record was not nearly so clear as Justice Alito made it out to be.[24])

Now, pause for a moment and consider the ramifications of this decision. Although some of the Justices took pains to emphasize that they were only deciding whether abortion was a constitutional right, it is nonetheless the case that by framing the inquiry over whether a right not expressly enumerated in the United States Constitution exists as turning on whether it had a deep historical tradition, a very broad swathe of constitutional protections we now take for granted in the United States are vulnerable. These include the right to same-sex marriage, the right to interracial marriage, the right to engage in consensual sexual activity, the right to control how your children are raised, and the right to use contraceptives. Indeed, Justice Thomas wrote a concurring opinion in the case expressly calling for the Court to overrule some of its key precedents protecting such rights.[25]

One could speak at considerable length as to the shortcomings of this approach to constitutional interpretation. And indeed, many books have been written on the subject and more surely will come.[26] I have written some on the topic, giving special attention to how history is messy and underscoring how looking for one singular "settled" understanding of the Constitution at the time of its Ratification often will lead to indeterminate results, notwithstanding what many originalists claim.[27] To take but one prominent example, the Congress that ratified the Fourteenth Amendment created the Freedman's Bureau to give special aid to the newly freed enslaved persons, but that same Congress also voted to segregate Washington, DC, schools. What should modern constitutional interpreters do with these historical data points in defining where the constitutional boundaries lie with respect to racial classifications?

With space limited, let me highlight one of the biggest problems with the originalist approach to constitutional interpretation, particularly as it relates to questions about how constitutions engage with the future.

---

[22] *Id.* at 2235.

[23] See *id.* at 2236.

[24] See *id.* at 2323-24 (Breyer, Sotomayor, and Kagan, JJ., dissenting).

[25] See *id.* at 2301 (Thomas, J., concurring) ("[I]n future cases, we should reconsider all of this Court's substantive due process precedents, including *Griswold*, *Lawrence*, and *Obergefell*.").

[26] This footnote would be very long if I listed everything. One good place to start is Strauss (2012), p. 1161.

[27] See Tyler (2015), p. 1739. Justice Thomas conceded in *Bruen* that historical analysis can sometimes be difficult and nuanced, but, he argued, reliance on history to inform the meaning of constitutional text is more legitimate, and more administrable, than asking judges to "make difficult empirical judgments" about "the costs and benefits of firearms restrictions," especially given their "lack [of] expertise" in the field. See *Bruen*, 142 S.Ct. at 2130 (internal quotation marks and citations omitted).

As the three dissenters in *Dobbs* highlighted, it is more than a little odd—indeed, one could say perverse—to interpret the meaning of the United States Constitution as having been effectively frozen for all time during periods in which substantial portions of the population—including those whose rights were at stake in *Dobbs*—had zero opportunity to engage in public debate over what the fundamental rights recognized in the Constitution should be. Women would not win the right to vote in the United States until the Nineteenth Amendment went into effect in 1920.[28] In short, when the reproductive rights of women were "settled" under the approach that dominated the Court majority's thinking in *Dobbs*, women did not have a seat at the table.

Put another way, as the dissenters in *Dobbs* who wrote and signed their opinion jointly, powerfully explained:

> The majority's core legal postulate, then, is that we in the 21st century must read the Fourteenth Amendment just as its ratifiers did. And that is indeed what the majority emphasizes over and over again. . . . If the ratifiers did not understand something as central to freedom, then neither can we. Or said more particularly: If those people did not understand reproductive rights as part of the guarantee of liberty conferred in the Fourteenth Amendment, then those rights do not exist.[29]

The dissent continued:

> As an initial matter, note a mistake in the just preceding sentence. We referred there to the "people" who ratified the Fourteenth Amendment: What rights did those "people" have in their heads at the time? But, of course, "people" did not ratify the Fourteenth Amendment. Men did. So it is perhaps not so surprising that the ratifiers were not perfectly attuned to the importance of reproductive rights for women's liberty, or for their capacity to participate as equal members of our Nation. Indeed, the ratifiers—both in 1868 and when the original Constitution was approved in 1788— did not understand women as full members of the community embraced by the phrase "We the People." In 1868, the first wave of American feminists were explicitly told—of course by men—that it was not their time to seek constitutional protections. (Women would not get even the vote for another half-century.) To be sure, most women in 1868 also had a foreshortened view of their rights: If most men could not then imagine giving women control over their bodies, most women could not imagine having that kind of autonomy. But that takes away nothing from the core point. Those responsible for the original Constitution, including the Fourteenth Amendment, did not perceive women as equals, and did not recognize women's rights. When the majority says that we must read our foundational charter as viewed at the time of ratification (except that we may also check it against the Dark Ages), it consigns women to second-class citizenship.[30]

As you can see, the dissent did not hold back in its criticism.

Now, there is indeed much more to say about these recent decisions and where their logic extends but let me return to the example I gave at the outset—namely, the decisions in the 1970s in which our Supreme Court interpreted the Equal Protection Clause of the Fourteenth Amendment to prohibit gender discrimination—to underscore one major takeaway of the approach of the majority opinions in *Dobbs* and

---

[28] U.S. Const. amend. XIX.

[29] *Dobbs*, 142 S.Ct. at 2324.

[30] *Id.* at 2324-25.

Bruen to constitutional interpretation. Under its many decisions promoting gender equality in the 1970s, the Supreme Court of the United States now applies heightened scrutiny to any law that classifies based on gender, leading almost always to the law being held inoperative due to its unconstitutionality.[31] As I read the majority opinion in *Dobbs*, those decisions, too, are now in jeopardy, because they fail under the approach employed by the majority that is fixated on 1868 and how those then in power in American society viewed things. In other words, if we are indeed fixing the gaze of the United States Constitution on the past when women had no rights or voice in society, that same logic suggests that nothing should be different today.

So, now, perhaps one can understand my distress as an American when it comes to approaching any discussion about the obligation of constitutions to address the future. Under the now dominant approach to constitutional interpretation in the United States, our eyes are firmly trained on the past.

And this means that not only are we not talking about the future—we are not even living in the present.

References

Gorsuch N (2016) Of Lions and Bears, Judges and Legislators, and the Legacy of Justice Scalia. Case Wes Res L Rev 66:905–906

Scalia A (1997) A matter of interpretation: federal courts and the law. Princeton University Press, Princeton

Strauss D (2012) Can originalism be saved? Boston U L Rev 92:1161

Tyler A (2015) Assessing the role of history in the federal courts canon: a word of caution Notre Dame L Rev 90:1739

[31] Specifically, as elaborated in *United States v. Virginia*, 518 U.S. 515 (1996), the Court requires an "exceedingly persuasive justification" for any law that draws classifications based on gender. *Id.* at 533.

Constitutions' Responsibility for the Future: Present Practices and Perspectives, with Particular Reference to the Romanian Constitution

Tudorel Toader and Marieta Safta

Abstract One feature that is a strong argument in favour of written Constitutions is their stability. As long as they are the basis of the legal system and the foundation of a State's government, Constitutions must enjoy stability. However, this feature should not be confused with rigidity. A constitution must prove resilience, adapt to the inherent transformations that society is going through, and identify the path that will prevent it, over time, from becoming anachronistic or incapable of fulfilling the role for which it was established. A constitution must be an open window to the wisdom or perhaps to tomorrow's madness to ensure that it can benefit from that wisdom or temper that madness. How these requirements materialize in the regulations contained in the Romanian Constitution is the main question that we intend to answer to below. By conducting our analysis in a context of comparative law that concerns, above all, the constitutional space of the European Union, we will try to identify challenges, experiences, and, hence, regulatory perspectives aimed at strengthening the role of the Constitution in an increasingly dynamic society. Finally, a topic of reflection that we propose herein is the lifespan of a constitution, how and if we need to prolong it by achieving the right balance between the flexible regulation of the rules that it contains and the rigidity of the conditions for its revision.

1 Introduction

As already noted, by their very nature, constitutions are intergenerational documents, "because they intend to place certain questions beyond the reach of simple majorities, the components of which change frequently".[1] Through the principles and standards

[1] Tremmel (2019).

T. Toader
Alexandru Ioan Cuza University, Iași, Romania

M. Safta (✉)
Titu Maiorescu University, Bucharest, Romania
e-mail: marieta.safta@prof.utm.ro

R. Arnold and T. Fickentscher (eds.), *The Responsibility of a Constitution for the Future*, https://doi.org/10.1007/978-3-031-65296-7_8

of the Basic Law, the framers project a framework intended to meet the needs of several generations; on their shoulders rests not only a responsibility for the present, but also for the future, a responsibility towards the generations to come. Although characterized by the greatest stability in the regulatory system of a State, a constitution is not eternal; it lasts as long as it suits and can be adapted to the political, economic and social developments and transformations of the respective State. The interpretation of a constitution (especially by the courts specifically created to guarantee the supremacy of the constitution) obviously plays an essential role here, in the sense of ensuring this adaptation. But how long and how can a constitution withstand the test of time, so as not to become itself an obstacle to the protection that it should provide?

Some specialized studies express concerns in this regard due to the generally rigid nature of constitutions, which would make the necessary adaptations difficult to achieve. It is deemed that this rigidity "is not only a problem for the citizens that live under the jurisdiction of such constitutions, but for the world at large", if we consider the deepening of a series of problems such as, for example, "environmental problems, notably climate change, which is a global problems."[2] On the other hand, the danger of frequent changes is also highlighted, by indicating that there "is a need to strike a balance between the excesses of constant changes and inflexibility, both extremes, sunset constitutions and perpetual constitutions can be regarded as indefensible."[3] At the same time, recent studies show that modern constitutions include more and more references to the future, a tendency meant to strengthen the role and safeguards provided for by constitutions as intergenerational documents. It was thus noted that "Constitutions worldwide have seen the rise of future generations. Considering the 193 UN member states, Kosovo, Palestine, and Taiwan, 41% (81 out of 196) of constitutions explicitly referenced future generations as of 2021. (…) This trend started in the early 1990s, lagging behind environmental constitutionalism by two decades."[4]; "future generations are a significant part of a modern, universalist language of constitution-making. More and more constitutions recognize them as holders of legal interests."[5]

Based on these benchmarks and given the importance of this topic in a society faced with increasingly complex problems, at global level, we will now refer to this "responsibility for the future" reflected in the Constitution of Romania, following three main coordinates: the rigidity/stability of the Constitution, the regulatory content of the Constitution and the constitutional review, all from the perspective of their role as guarantees for the State's commitments towards the next generations. Instead of conclusions, this study prompts reflection on the acceptable "lifespan" of a constitution, so that it does not become obsolete or overly restrictive.

---

[2] Ibidem.

[3] Ibidem.

[4] Araújo and Koessler (2022).

[5] Ibidem.

2 The Romanian Constitution, a Constitution that is Difficult to Amend. The Identity Core

The specialized literature has repeatedly pointed out to the stability of the current Constitution of Romania, which was adopted in 1991, after the fall of the communist regime. It was thus highlighted that the current Constitution is the second longest-lasting one in the history of Romanian constitutions, after that of 1866[6] (the first Romanian Constitution).

Thus, although during these 31 years since the adoption of the Constitution **10 revision initiatives** have been promoted, of which: 5 belonging to MPs [1996, 2003, 2014, 2019 (2 initiatives)], 4 belonging to citizens (2000, 2007), 2016, 2019) and one belonging to the President of Romania, upon proposal by the Government (2011), *only one initiative has completed the full process, leading to the 2003 revision of the Constitution.*[7] The driving force for the revision was the so-called Europe clause,[8] i.e., the need to fulfil the constitutional requirements for Romania's integration into the EU and for its accession to the North Atlantic Treaty.[9]

The revision certainly marked the opening of a path for future generations, given that the constitutional requirements for Romania's accession and integration to the EU were thus met, and so, a future attached to a new constitutional structure, in the making. Article 148 of the Constitution set the obligations of the public authorities arising from the act of the accession and ensured the "connection" to the EU legal system, regulating the priority of the EU Treaties and other binding European acts over any contrary provision in the domestic laws.[10] At the same time, *Title II—Fundamental rights, freedoms and duties* of the Constitution was enriched, through the introduction of new fundamental rights (e.g. the right to a healthy environment, access to culture) or safeguards thereof (e.g. the right to a fair trial, arrest/search ordered only by the judge), most of which as a result of capitalizing on the Convention for the Protection of Human Rights and Fundamental Freedoms, to which Romania became a party in 1994,[11] and on the case-law of the European Court of Human Rights. On the same occasion, provisions contained in all the other titles of the Constitution were amended (79 revision points, which affected to approximately half of the constitutional texts), and institutions such as the Advocate of the People and the Constitutional Court, with an essential role in the protection of fundamental rights, were strengthened.

---

[6] Stoica (2021), pp. 33–34.

[7] CCR Decision No 148/2003 (Official Gazette No 317/12 May 2000).

[8] For a distinction concerning the reasons for the revision, see Maus (2020).

[9] See also Toader and Safta *Development of constitutionalism in Romania* in *Revista de drept constituţional nr. 1/2015*, http://www.revistadedreptconstitutional.ro/wp-content/uploads/nr_revista/2015_1/Revista-de-Drept-Constitutional-nr-1-2015.pdf.

[10] According to the reasoning of the CCR in Decision No 148/2003 (Official Gazette No 317/12 May 2000).

[11] Law No 30/1994 (Official Gazette No 135/31 May 1994).

As for the failed revision initiatives, their causes can surely be examined in detail, including the unconstitutionality of some of them. However, beyond specific reasons, the complex procedure for revising the Constitution has certainly been a shield or an obstacle (depending on the perspective and the arguments) against frequent changes to the Romanian Basic Law. Thus, according to the provisions contained in Articles 150 to 152 of the Constitution, the revision of the Constitution involves going through several stages; the initiative, which belongs to a series of specific subjects (the President, upon the Government's proposal, at least one fourth of the number of Deputies and Senators, at least 500,000 citizens with the right to vote coming from at least half of the country's counties), the review of the initiative by the Constitutional Court of Romania, the debate and adoption of the revision law by Parliament, the constitutional review of the revision law and its approval by referendum organized within 30 days, at the most, from the adoption of the law. Also, the Constitution expressly establishes the substantive limits of the revision (the sacrosanct core of the Constitution), in Article 152 (1) and (2), worded as follows: "*(1) The provisions of this Constitution with regard to the national, independent, unitary and indivisible character of the Romanian State, the Republican form of government, territorial integrity, independence of justice, political pluralism and official language shall not be subject to revision. (2) Moreover, no revision shall be made if it results in the suppression of the citizens' fundamental rights and freedoms, or of the safeguards thereof.*"

From the perspective of the topic subject to analysis herein, we consider that *the limits of the revision of the Constitution* are particularly important, as they can be interpreted, indeed, as limiting the right of disposal of future generations, but, more importantly, as a *shield, a protection thereof against frequent or abusive constitutional changes that might affect democratic values and fundamental rights.* In other words, "this boundary nature is not a hindrance, but rather a helpful reference point for all generations in the organisation of society and the state".[12] This last role was perhaps best expressed by the German Federal Constitutional Court, in the doctrine regarding the "eternity clause".[13] In the same vein, the Constitutional Court of Romania has recently characterized, in an otherwise controversial decision,[14] the constitutional values and principles enshrined in Article 152 as representing "the fundamental identity core of the Romanian Constitution". It is true that the concept of "national identity" appears in the case-law of the Constitutional Court of Romania in other contexts as well, for example in a decision in which it ruled that "the invocation of the national history and values represent elements of a people's identity", and that "Parliament has intervened on numerous occasions and established, by law, days marking the significance of certain events for the national identity", from which it follows that the Romanian constitutional identity has a broader content. However, the protection provided by preserving a sacrosanct, intangible core gives consistency to the concept of constitutional/national identity.

---

[12] Gárdos–Orosz (2017).

[13] Polzin (2016), pp. 411–438. https://doi.org/10.1093/icon/mow035.

[14] CCR Decision No 390/2021 (Official Gazette No 612 of 22 June 2021).

Aware of the many debates surrounding the concept of constitutional/national identity at European level, at the confluence of national and EU law, we believe that, in fact, this concept is a guarantee for future generations and a key to integration, with a respect for diversity. Just as the common values unite us in the European area, each State has a uniqueness that gives, in the end, the beauty of the idea of European Union, a construction with a structure different from the traditional State structures. This uniqueness must be protected, and we believe that it must be seen as a guarantee for the future, and not as an obstacle to a deeper integration under the sign of the values that characterize the EU as a whole. On the contrary, this identity, put forward by each State, must support the dialogue, an expression of their mutual respect. The European Union is not a "third party" in this equation, but actually the Member States, a whole of what they, we, the Europeans, have agreed to put together, while keeping each its own identity.

Browsing through the Constitutions of other Member States as well, we notice this intertwining between provisions aimed at preserving diversity and provisions aimed at developing our European unity. For example, the preamble of the *Constitution of the Czech Republic* mentions the status of "member of the family of European and World democracies", while indicating the resolution to protect and develop together "their natural, cultural, material and spiritual heritage" and the commitment to observe human rights: "*An integral component of the constitutional system of the Czech Republic is the Charter of Fundamental Rights and Freedoms*"[15] (Article 3). The preamble of the *Latvian Constitution* indicates, among others, the following: "*Since ancient times, the identity of Latvia in the European cultural space has been shaped by Latvian and Liv traditions, Latvian folk wisdom, the Latvian language, universal human and Christian values. Loyalty to Latvia, the Latvian language as the only official language, freedom, equality, solidarity, justice, honesty, work ethic and family are the foundations of a cohesive society. Each individual takes care of oneself, one's relatives and the common good of society by acting responsibly toward other people, future generations, the environment and nature. While acknowledging its equal status in the international community, Latvia protects its national interests and promotes sustainable and democratic development of a united Europe and the world.*"[16] *The Constitution of the Portuguese Republic* declares Portugal's sovereignty and its fundamental values in Article 1, while, in Article 7, it talks about the European identity and the obligations deriving from the status of EU Member State, as follows: "5. *Portugal shall make every effort to reinforce the European identity and to strengthen the European States' actions in favour of democracy, peace, economic progress and justice in the relations between peoples.*"

The topic is, of course, much broader, and can be subject to extensive analysis, but, in this context, we want to highlight that the stability of the Constitution and the preservation of values deemed intangible are, in themselves, an expression of responsibility towards future generations. The preservation of a State's identity elements (understanding here, in a broad sense, traditions, culture as well), as a legacy for

[15] Codex Constituțional (2015), p. 265.

[16] Ibidem, vol. 2, pp. 17–18.

future generations, is, moreover, a topic of concern reflected in many Constitutions, being usually mentioned in their very preamble.[17]

3 The Constitutional Provisions—Windows Open Towards Future Generations

General Aspects

As already stated in the introduction, modern Constitutions show an increased concern for the protection of those who will come after us, some of them containing express provisions in this regard. As noted, after 1990, the wordings of the constitutional provisions include a much more concrete/specific language, likely to express the responsibilities of the State and authorities in this regard. "From 1990 onwards, newly included constitutional provisions contain more concrete words. First, they clearly establish 'future generations' as holders of legal interest, as words such as 'right,' 'benefit,' and 'needs', as well as 'preserve,' 'protect,' 'measures,' and 'responsibility' increase in frequency."[18]

Concerning the Romanian Constitution, we identify, first of all, a general framework of "connection" to the international sources of protection of the fundamental rights, likely to compensate for the rigidity of the Constitution and allow its permanent and comprehensive adaptation to the highest standards of protection of human rights. Secondly, we note the introduction, following the 2003 revision of the Constitution, of new rights that express intergenerational solidarity, such as, in particular, the right to a healthy environment and access to culture. In the following, we shall refer distinctly to the two highlighted dimensions.

Connection to the International Sources of Protection of Human Rights

In the European legal landscape, the Constitution of Romania is among the constitutions that include a well-defined architecture of the relationships between national, European and international law and a clear affirmation of the international openness as concerns the fundamental rights and freedoms,[19] expressly regulated through the

[17] Maybe the most substantive and representative preamble, of the EU Member States' Constitutions, is that of the Hungarian Constitution.

[18] Araújo and Koessler, *cited work.*

[19] Part of point II in this paper is taken from Stanciu and Safta (2021).

provisions of Article 11—*International law and domestic law*, Article 20—*International treaties on human rights*, and Article 148—*Integration into the European Union.*

Thus, according to Article 11 of the Constitution, the treaties ratified by Parliament are part of the domestic law. They acquire, in domestic law, the legal force and the position in the hierarchy of regulatory acts given by the act of ratification, with the corresponding consequences.

Regarding the general system of protection of the fundamental rights and freedoms, during the debates that accompanied the adoption of the texts in Title II of the Constitution, the idea of a permanent evolution of this institution stood out and, "from the multitude of individual rights, those that seem to be essential, as the authors of public law say, for the life, freedom and free development of the human personality were selected for the Constitution, and this value selection was made by examining international declarations, covenants and conventions, the democratic Constitutions in Romania, similar provisions in the Constitutions of certain States with an indisputable democratic tradition, the realities and, especially, the perspectives of human rights at domestic and international level."[20] At the same time, it was emphasized that *"the topic of human rights has long gone beyond national borders, becoming a world problem, a common language of people everywhere, hence the need for a correlation between domestic law and international law."*[21]

Consequently, the general framework for the protection of human rights was regulated in accordance with these wishes, Article 20 of the Romanian Constitution (as it was even better outlined in 2003) establishing in this regard that the treaties in the field of human rights that Romania is a party to become a part of the "block of constitutionality", having constitutional interpretative value (in the sense that the provisions of the Constitution must be interpreted and applied in accordance with the provisions of international treaties on human rights that Romania is a party to) and priority of application in case of inconsistency with the domestic laws, except where the Constitution or the domestic laws contain more favourable provisions. Article 20 of the Constitution thus provides the legal basis for the direct invocation of the international human rights treaties both before the Constitutional Court and the courts of law, as well as of the case-law of the European Court of Human Rights.

We stated that this regulation, which allows for a permanent constitutional oxygenation, compensated for the rigidity of the Constitution, allowing it to be easily adapted to the developments of the protection of fundamental rights and freedoms and permanently aligned with the highest standards of protection in the matter.

---

[20] Iorgovan (1998), p. 182.

[21] Ibidem.

New Rights and Safeguards. Access to Culture and the Right to a Healthy Environment

We have indicated that the entire fundamental rights catalogue regulated by the Romanian Constitution adopted in 1991 was enriched during the revision, in that new rights or safeguards have been introduced, partly as a result of the consideration of the case-law of the European Court of Human Rights. *State-of-the-art rights have been regulated as fundamental rights, relevant for the topic addressed here*, such as *Access to culture* (Article 33) and the *Right to a healthy environment* (Article 35). Also, the Romanian Constitution provides the obligation of the State to secure"*environmental protection and recovery, as well as preservation of the ecological balance"* (article 135-*Economy and public finance*).

Thus, with regard to *access to culture*, the Romanian framers guaranteed, in Article 33, that "*the freedom to develop one's spirituality and to have access to the values of national and universal culture*" could not be restricted (paragraph 2) and stated the State's obligation to ensure "*the preservation of spiritual identity, the support of national culture, the fostering of arts, the protection and preservation of the cultural legacy, the development of contemporary creativity, the promotion of Romania's cultural and artistic values in the world*" (paragraph 3). A comment on this article[22] noted that "the development of contemporary creativity, the promotion of Romania's cultural and artistic values are also important requirements of a genuine accessibility of the cultural values, ensuring the 'focus on the future' of the right subject to analysis. An accessible culture is also a 'living' culture, encouraged to develop itself, including through protection and stimulation measures from the State. Another facet of this obligation of the State is the promotion of cultural identity abroad".

Also, the Romanian Basic Law regulates, in Article 35, *the right to a healthy environment*, recognizing "*the right of every person to a healthy and ecologically balanced environment*" (paragraph 1), the State's obligation to ensure "*the legislative framework for the exercise of such right*" (paragraph 2), but also the duty of natural and legal persons "*to protect and improve the environment*". These safeguards have allowed the Constitutional Court to rule in a series of case-files with consequences for the future as well, as we will highlight below.

Noting the modernity of the Romanian Constitution from the perspective of an express consecration of the right to a healthy environment, the need to supplement the safeguards established by the constitutional text was also implicitly emphasized, by evoking the 2014 revision initiative, which established that: "*In Article 35, after paragraph (2), two new paragraphs are added, paragraphs (2^1) and (3^1), worded as follows: '(2^1) The State shall ensure the protection, sustainable use and restoration of the natural heritage. (3^1) All forms of abuse against animals, as defined by law, are prohibited'.*"[23] It was thus considered that "this would have been a more accurate description of the specific obligations of the State not only for ensuring

[22] Selejan Guțan (2022), p. 278.

[23] Ibidem, p. 292.

the fundamental right to a healthy environment, but actually for the effective legal protection of the ecological balances and even for obliging the State to restore the environmental conditions so that they can be enjoyed by future generations as well, knowing that *intergenerational solidarity is one of the strongest arguments in favour of the legalization of environmental protection*[24]". Even if the respective initiative failed, this proposal can be taken up in a future revision initiative.

4 The Constitutional Review, a Safeguard of the State's Commitments Towards Future Generations

Legal pluralism in the field of fundamental rights and freedoms, as regulated by the Romanian Constitution, has facilitated the dialogue between courts of law at national/international/supranational level, which resulted in the redefinition and raising of the standards of protection in this field in the Romanian legal system. The institutionalization of the European model of constitutional review in Romania also contributed to the achievement of this objective, through the establishment of the Constitutional Court, which has recently celebrated its 30th anniversary (it started operating in 1992). Even if, at the time of adoption of the Constitution, several options were discussed in the Constituent Assembly, the European model of constitutional review won, a review conducted by a unique, special, specialized court of law, an option in line with the existing developments at European level.[25]

Perhaps it is the merit of the Constitutional Court, rather than of the courts of law in the traditional justice system, of being the "gateway" through which the case-law of international courts entered the Romanian legal system, especially that of the European Court of Human Rights. According to a study carried out in 2005, in the period up to the revision of the Constitution, the Constitutional Court based around 380 of its decisions (out of the almost 3 000 decisions delivered during this period) on the texts of the Convention for the Protection of Human Rights and Fundamental Freedoms and on the case-law of the European Court of Human Rights. This proves the setting of the bases for and the development of the dialogue with the European Court of Human Rights, a dialogue that has led to a common language and to common standards for achieving the safeguarding of human rights and fundamental freedoms. The Romanian constitutional judge has undertaken the role and authority to ensure the consideration of the Convention and of the practice of the European court, with effects both for the regulation of the issue of fundamental rights and freedoms (as it shall be shown below, including at constitutional level), as well as for the implementation of these regulations by national courts.[26]

As more recent developments, we note the capitalization on this jurisdictional dialogue (especially with the European Court of Human Rights, but also with the

[24] Ibidem.

[25] Broadly, Toader and Safta, *cited work*.

[26] Ibidem.

Court of Justice of the European Union and with other European constitutional courts) including in the interpretation and enforcement of the rules that form the "sacrosanct core" of the Constitution, i.e., of those intangible values, which are defining for the very essence of the Romanian State, regulated by Article 152 of the Constitution. We have in mind, in particular, the definition retained by the Constitutional Court of Romania, from the perspective of international and supranational catalogues, for human dignity.[27] According to the Constitutional Court of Romania, "the fundamental rights and freedoms of citizens and their safeguards cannot be considered a diffuse set of elements without any connection between them, as they make up a coherent and unitary system of values, based on human dignity. In addition to the fact that the fundamental rights and freedoms qualified as such in the Constitution are based on human dignity (Decision No 1.109 of 8 September 2009), this being a supreme value of the Romanian State, human dignity does not have only a declarative value and is not emptied of regulatory content, but, on the contrary, it has a regulatory value and can be qualified as a fundamental right with a distinct content, which calls into question the human nature and condition of the individual. [...]". Therefore, "*human dignity is the essence of fundamental rights and freedoms and represents in itself a limit of the revision of the Constitution.*"[28] We note the convergence, within the same considerations that highlight a new approach to human dignity as an intangible constitutional principle, the interweaving of the case-law of the European Court of Human Rights, the Court of Justice of the European Union, as well as of the constitutional courts of other Member States of the European Union, which proves that the "sacrosanct core" of the Romanian Constitution *includes universal and timeless fundamental values.*

We also identify, in the case-law of the Constitutional Court of Romania, express references to the legislator's responsibility towards current and future generations, in contexts aimed at:

- capitalising on the constitutional right to a healthy environment:

By examining the exception of unconstitutionality of the provisions of Government Ordinance No 96/1998 regarding the regulation of the forestry regime and the administration of the national forestry fund that prohibit the reduction of the area covered by forests in the national forestry fund and the exceptions allowed by law, the Constitutional Court of Romania held, among other things, that it was "*the exclusive attribute of the State to establish a strategy for the economic, social and environmental promotion of the forests, regardless of the owner of the property right over them. In such a circumstance, Romanian forests are managed and administered in a unitary system, aiming at the continuous capitalisation, for the benefit of current and future generations, on their environmental and socio-economic functions. As a*

[27] Stanciu and Safta (2021), The report of the Constitutional Court of Romania. General part: Human rights and fundamental freedoms catalogues, Congress of the Conference of European Constitutional Courts, Prague, 2021 https://www.cecc2017-2020.org/fileadmin/Dokumenty/Pdf/Questionnaire/National_Reports/National/Romania_-_Questionnaire_XVIII_Congress_of_CECC.pdf.

[28] CCR Decision No 464/2019 (Official Gazette No 646 of 5 August 2019.).

guarantee of this declared purpose, the provisions of Article 24 (1) expressly provide for the prohibition of the reduction of the area covered by forests in the national forestry fund."[29];

- sanctioning the measures based on uncertain financial sources; the medium and long-term impact on the economic development

There is a substantial and constant case-law of the Court in this vein, which sanctions the lack of a financial statement when adopting laws with budgetary impact. The Constitutional Court of Romania noted in this regard that "*The efficient management of public finances, so as to serve the public interest in the long term, is one of the objectives of Law No 69/2010 on fiscal-budgetary accountability. According to Law No 69/2010, the fiscal-budgetary policy must also observe the principle of stability, so as to ensure its predictability in the medium term, in order to maintain macroeconomic stability, but also the principle of equity, which takes into account the potential financial impact on future generations, as well as the impact on the economic development in the medium and long term.*"[30]

- the private pension schemes; financial support for future generations

The Constitutional Court of Romania has held in a case-file that, regarding the private pensions regulated by Law No 411/2004, the relationship between participants and the private pension funds was not a simple private law relationship concluded between a natural person and an insurance company, in which the State played the role of arbitrator, ensuring that, to the extent that it has was concluded under the conditions set by law, it would be observed (*pacta sunt servanda*). On the contrary, the State plays a crucial role in the actual birth and development of this legal relationship. One of the goals pursued by the legislator when adopting Law No 411/2004 and which can be identified by examining its content was that the State wanted to offer future generations the possibility to increase the amount of their pensions, by involving a series of subjects of private law, namely the pension schemes, which administer a part of the financial resources that the State collects from the legal subjects.[31]

- location of the infrastructure elements and requirements related to environment and health protection

Ruling on the pleas lodged by the Advocate of the People on the regulations concerning the placing of the physical infrastructure elements necessary to support the electronic communications networks on the green spaces within city built-up areas, the Constitutional Court of Romania found them to be unconstitutional. As grounds for the solution delivered, the Constitutional Court of Romania noted, among other things, that "the provisions of Article 35 of the Basic Law establish the positive obligation of the State to ensure a legislative framework for the exercise of the right of every person to a healthy and ecologically balanced environment. In the

[29] CCR Decision No 1200/2007 (Official Gazette No 60 of 25 January 2008).

[30] CCR Decision No 874/2020 (Official Gazette No 44 of 14 January 2021).

[31] CCR Decision No 200/2021 (Official Gazette No 653 of 1 July 2021).

specialized literature, it was noted that the phrase ‘healthy environment’ referred to a certain quality of the environment, and the preservation of a healthy environment meant, in reality, the preservation and improvement of the living conditions, the maintenance of the ecological balance, of the ecosystems that the human being is a part of. By analogy with this right, it was necessary to have a public recognition of the right to information on the state of the environment and access to justice in case of violation of the right to a healthy environment, as well as of the rights of future generations, starting from the idea of preserving the natural heritage for the present and future. A healthy environment ensures the framework for the harmonious development of individuals and the possibility of a full exercise of other rights, such as the right to health protection. The State’s obligation to ensure the restoration and protection of the environment, as well as to maintain the ecological balance, is also emphasized in Article 135 (2) (e) of the Constitution regarding the economy, as a sign of the special importance that the framers have placed on preserving the quality of the environment. Therefore, even when the legislator adopts legislative measures in favour of certain economic interests, it is bound to do so while considering the prevalence of environment protection and of maintaining the ecological balance.”[32]

5 Conclusions

We believe that the stability of the Romanian Constitution can be considered, in itself, an expression of the responsibility towards future generations. Likewise, the manner in which the framers have envisioned the permanent “refreshing” of the Constitution through close connection to the international framework for the protection of fundamental rights, as well as new rights introduced serve the same purpose. The constitutional review is a support and drive for the permanent adaptation of the Constitution.

This does not mean, however, that there is no place or need for changes. On the contrary, the last few years have been marked by debates, in Romania, regarding the need to revise the Constitution.

This topic was also discussed at the recent 30th anniversary since the establishment of the Constitutional Court, celebrated this year. Besides the anniversary messages and the overview of these 30 years of activity, the idea of a broad constitutional reform was once again proposed by the representatives of the political authorities participating in the event. In the same context, the representatives of the judiciary mentioned the tensions in the European constitutional justice system, emphasizing the need for dialogue between courts of all degrees and levels.

[32] CCR Decision No 295/2022 (Official Gazette No 568 of 10 June 2022).

Also, a recent volume[33] dedicated to the anniversary of 30 years since the adoption of the Constitution gathered together the opinions expressed by university professors, current and former constitutional judges regarding the topic of the revision. The careful reading of the doctrinal and practical material thus prepared can help the reader draw a real "list" of reasons for the revision, the ideas ranging from a minimalist approach to the revision,[34] such as "fine adjustments in the way the State operates, based on previous experiences and taking into account the behaviour of State institutions",[35] up to extensive reforms, approached[36] from at least three perspectives: technical (removing from the text of the Constitution certain phrases that have lost the constitutional significance that they had 30 years ago); of political option (in the sense of reconfiguring certain constitutional institutions and procedures); *innovative (in the sense of introducing new elements determined by social and even scientific evolutions).*

As far as we are concerned, we believe that, while only fine adjustments are really needed with regard to the way in which public authorities are organized and function, a more extensive reform would be needed for the innovative component, so that the Constitution, thus consolidated, responded to the increasingly dynamic changes in society and needs for as long as possible.

Perhaps any initiative to revise the Constitution should begin with the question "what are our responsibilities towards the future generations?" Intergenerational solidarity and the effectiveness of the safeguards established in this regard should be one of the headlines of the revision. As stated, it "is needed to ensure that the constitutional recognition of future generations as holders of legal interests becomes effective."[37] We consider that a dimension of this effectiveness refers to the strengthening of the constitutional review as constitutional texts, together with their interpretations by judges, play a significant role in determining the meaning of the constitution: "*the understanding of constitutional provisions might change according to the requirements of time and space, while preserving prior knowledge.* […] The normative approach requires, in accordance with the rule of law, that the decisions, justified on the basis of the constitution, be reasonably justified to the generation in which the case actually emerges. That enables the constitution, with its unamendable provisions, to provide a stable framework that is capable of adapting in order to serve

[33] *Caiet Constituțional 1991–2021, 30 de ani de la adoptarea Constituției* (2021) Cazanciuc R.M, Pârvulescu C (coord), Monitorul Oficial Publishing House, Bucharest.

[34] V. Stoica, *cited work*: "the imperfections in the wording of the Basic Law and the dysfunctionalities identified in the functioning of the authorities that exercise the three State powers can be corrected and have been corrected partly through the set of constitutional customs and through the case-law of the constitutional court"; "the adoption of a new Constitution or the frequent revision of the current one would endanger the results of the three-decade effort to create the premises of a national constitutional tradition.".

[35] Deaconu, *Importanța Constituției pentru cetățeni (The importance of the Constitution for the citizens—T.N* in *Caiet Constituțional 1991–2021, 30 de ani de la adoptarea Constituției*, Cazanciuc RM, Pârvulescu C (coord), Monitorul Oficial Publishing House, Bucharest, p. 57.

[36] Cazanciuc (2021), p. 7.

[37] Araújo and Koessler, *cited work*.

the needs of future societies."[38] Therefore, we need strong constitutional courts with a high level of credibility, we need independent and highly professional judges to be the voice, the support and maybe even the example needed for the harmonious development of future generations.[39]

References

Araújo R, Koessler L (2022) The Rise of the Constitutional Protection of Future Generations. https://verfassungsblog.de/the-rise-of-the-constitutional-protection-of-future-generations/

Cazanciuc RM (2021) Argument constitutional (Constitutional argument—T.N.), in *Caiet Constituțional 1991–2021, 30 de ani de la adoptarea Constituției*, Cazanciuc RM, Pârvulescu C (coord), Monitorul Oficial Publishing House, Bucharest

Codex Constituțional (2015) vol I, II Deaconu Ș (coord) Monitorul Oficial Publishing House, Bucharest

Deaconu Ș, *Importanța Constituției pentru cetățeni (The importance of the Constitution for the citizens—T.N* in *Caiet Constituțional 1991–2021, 30 de ani de la adoptarea Constituției*, Cazanciuc RM, Pârvulescu C (coord), Monitorul Oficial Publishing House, Bucharest

CCR Decision No 1200/2007 (Official Gazette No 60 of 25 January 2008)

CCR Decision No 148/2003 (Official Gazette No 317/12 May 2000)

CCR Decision No 200/2021 (Official Gazette No 653 of 1 July 2021)

CCR Decision No 295/2022 (Official Gazette No 568 of 10 June 2022)

CCR Decision No 464/2019 (Official Gazette No 646 of 5 August 2019)

CCR Decision No 874/2020 (Official Gazette No 44 of 14 January 2021)

Gárdos–Orosz F (2017) The stability of constitutions and their role in promoting intergenerational justice. https://hrcak.srce.hr/file/286131

Iorgovan A (1998) *Odiseea elaborării Constituției (The odyssey of the drafting of the Constitution—T.N.)*. Uniunea Vatra Românească Publishing House, p 182

Maus D (2020) *Revizuirea constituțională în țările Uniunii Europene (Constitutional Revision in the European Union Countries—T.N.)*. http://www.icj.ro/Materiale_7martie.pdf

Polzin M (2016) Constitutional identity, unconstitutional amendments and the idea of constituent power: the development of the doctrine of constitutional identity in German constitutional law. Int J Const Law 14/2:411–438. https://doi.org/10.1093/icon/mow035

Safta M (2021) Courts vs. Courts? Or a way together? The evolution of constitutional review in the EU and worldwide. Revista de drept constitutional/Constitutional Law Review. https://doi.org/10.47743/rdc-2022-1-0006

Selejan Guțan B (2022) *Constituția României. Comentariu pe articole (The Romanian Constitution. Articles commented—T.N.)*, 3rd ed. CH Beck Publishing House, Bucharest

Stanciu LD, Safta M (2021) The report of the Constitutional Court of Romania. General part: human rights and fundamental freedoms catalogues, Congress of the European Constitutional Courts, Prague. https://www.cecc2017-2020.org/fileadmin/Dokumenty/Pdf/Questionnaire/National_Reports/National/Romania_-_Questionnaire_XVIII_Congress_of_CECC.pdf, which dealt extensively with the topic of human rights and fundamental freedoms catalogues

Stoica V (2021) *Păstrarea actualei forme de guvernământ (Maintaining the current form of government—T.N.)*, in *Caiet Constituțional 1991–2021, 30 de ani de la adoptarea Constituției*, Cazanciuc RM, Pârvulescu C (coord), Monitorul Oficial Publishing House, Bucharest, pp 33–34

[38] Gárdos–Orosz, *cited work*.

[39] See also Safta (2021).

Toader T, Safta M (2015) Development of constitutionalism in Romania in *Revista de drept constituțional nr. 1/2015*. http://www.revistadedreptconstitutional.ro/wp-content/uploads/nr_revista/2015_1/Revista-de-Drept-Constitutional-nr-1-2015.pdf
Tremmel J (2019) Environment & sustainability. https://www.ippi.org.il/constitutions-for-future-generations/

Specific Studies

Evolution of Constitutional Justice in Georgia as an Effective Remedy for the Protection of Fundamental Rights

Merab Turava and George Lomtadze

Abstract The Constitution of Georgia is founded on the key principles of democracy, the rule of law, the separation of powers and the respect for human rights. The realisation of these inherent principles is vested in both the Constitutional Court and common courts that make up the judicial system in Georgia. This renders the institutional cooperation between the two courts necessary for the whole system to be effective. Since the Constitutional Court is not authorised to review the constitutionality of judgments of ordinary courts, it has developed an interpretative approach, whereby the Constitutional Court accepts the meaning of an impugned legal norm as given by the courts of general jurisdiction, provided the common courts are consistent and uniform in their interpretation of the law. This approach has helped the constitutional jurisprudence to become more effective in real cases and also, furthered the application of the Constitution by ordinary courts. Although challenges remain in terms of understanding and applying the constitutional jurisprudence by judges of the common courts, the tendency towards utilising the mentioned mechanism by the ordinary courts is on the rise driven by solid and persuasive case-law of the Constitutional Court.

1 Introduction

The Constitution, as a foundational legal document, has to ensure the stability and longevity of the existing model of governance predicated upon the Rule of Law, whereas constitutional review bodies are inherently bound to maintain the foregoing constitutional imperative by their duty to set forth clear, consistent and uniform constitutional standards that are legitimately reasoned and fit for the time. With its

M. Turava (✉) · G. Lomtadze
Constitutional Court of Georgia, Batumi, Georgia
e-mail: m.turava@constcourt.ge

G. Lomtadze
e-mail: g.lomtadze@constcourt.ge

R. Arnold and T. Fickentscher (eds.), *The Responsibility of a Constitution for the Future*, https://doi.org/10.1007/978-3-031-65296-7_9

evolutive case law the Constitutional Court of Georgia guarantees the effectiveness of constitutional jurisprudence in real cases and thus helps the aforementioned objective.

The present paper is divided into three main parts. Initially, brief overview of the governance model of the Constitution and the description of the judicial system of power is presented The paper then moves on to discuss the evolution of constitutional jurisprudence and its impact on the effectiveness of constitutional justice in Georgia. As an illustration of the latter point of view, the paper present specific aspect of constitutional the case law regarding the constitutionality of criminalisation of drug-related offences.

2 Model of Judiciary and Constitutional Review

Being a civil law country, in Georgia, most of the rules utilised in the course of constitutional adjudication are formalised either in the legislation on the Constitutional Court ("Organic Law on the Constitutional Court of Georgia" 2016) or by the Rules of Procedure of the Court (Rules of the Constitutional Court of Georgia 2024). Nevertheless, there are practices developed by the Constitutional Court with respect to the preliminary reference procedure that has not been formalised so far in the legislative provisions.

Namely, the original system of constitutional proceedings in Georgia does not allow for a case that is initiated by the reference from an ordinary court to be considered in *curia*—in an open court. Furthermore, the law does not even provide for an adversarial procedure in this regard. There was no possibility (until 2020 when the Court institutionalised the practice in its Rules) envisaged in legislation for a respondent—e.g. the Parliament of Government—to state their case before the Constitutional Court. The Constitutional Court started to inform and request the respective authority—depending on the adopting authority of a disputed legal act—to submit their position officially to the Constitutional Court.

Furthermore, whilst deciding on one of the preliminary references, (Judgment of the Constitutional Court of Georgia on the Constitutional Submission of the Supreme Court of Georgia, 2015) the Constitutional Court expounded on the inquisitorial nature of constitutional proceedings and determined that it would not refuse a preliminary reference filed by an ordinary court on the grounds of inadmissibility when the problem indicated in the submission is incorrectly identified *vis-à-vis* a stated constitutional provision. In other words, if a common court judge mistakenly believes that the scope of a given constitutional norm, wrongly identified by him/her, covers the problematic aspect of an applicable law in a given case, the Constitutional Court will still consider the case on the merits. It will assess the claims of unconstitutionality by an ordinary court in relation to another, more relevant constitutional provision, as defined by the constitutional case law. This important aspect of decision-making was in fact invented by the Constitutional Court, which placed a separate interpretation on admissibility grounds of petitions, which interestingly are common to both direct and indirect constitutional proceedings, and helped to expand the scope of application of preliminary references by ordinary courts.

Since the establishment of the Constitutional Court in 1996 in Georgia up until now less than 5% of cases decided by the Court were instigated by the submissions from ordinary courts. It should be noted that in the past 9 years, compared to an earlier period, the number of constitutional submissions by the common courts has increased. In particular, in 2014 5 constitutional submissions were registered in the Constitutional Court, in 2015—10 submissions, in 2016—44 submissions, in 2017—3 submissions, in 2018—2 submissions, in 2019—2 submissions, in 2020—3 submissions, in 2021—5 submissions, and in 2022—2 submissions were initiated.

As to the legal acts that govern for the preliminary reference procedure, the Organic Law on the Constitutional Court (and also the Organic Law on Common Courts (Organic Law of Georgia on General Courts 2019)) stipulates that when a judge, while deciding a case at hand, suspects that an applicable law could be in contradiction with the constitution, he/she shall suspend a case and refer it to the Constitutional Court (). A consideration of a case will continue once the Constitutional Court renders a final judgement on the matter. In addition, the law—the Organic Law on Common Courts—provide that "[i]f the court of trial finds that a normative act, the examination of which does not fall within the scope of authority of the Constitutional Court, is incompatible with the Constitution of Georgia, the court shall deliver a decision according to the Constitution of Georgia".[1] The wording of this provision can be argued to distort the idea of a concentrated constitutional review model in a way that it allows for the judges of ordinary courts to make an evaluation of a subject matter, which in essence may in all likelihood fall within the powers of the Constitutional Court. I would say this rule in Georgia has acted, among other things including lack of relevant expertise among ordinary judges to digest the nature of the constitutional proceedings as well as its final effects on ordinary litigation, to discourage judges of ordinary judiciary to refer cases to the Constitutional Court.[2]

The idea behind such a procedure, as argued elsewhere (p. 17 in The Venice Commission 'Study on Individual Access to Constitutional Justice' (2010)), is that ordinary courts are believed to be well informed and capable of making valid requests. Therefore, ordinary courts serve as an initial filter and can help minimise the number of vexatious or repetitive requests. Furthermore, preliminary ruling procedures complement the abstract consideration of any provision, as they facilitate review arising from concrete situations in which a provision is applied or should be applied. Alternately, it is argued that in some judicial systems, this procedure

[1] Articles 7.3 and 7.4. Interestingly though, the legislation provides for the possibility by the ordinary courts to directly invoke constitutional provision if they deem there is no constitutional jurisdiction in place and there is a clear conflict of laws. Similarly to Georgia, in Germany, Italy, Spain, the right to address to Constitutional Court has been given to each judge, in other countries (e.g. Austria) this right is enjoyed by Supreme Courts and courts of second instance only.

[2] Interestingly, the Constitutional Court of the Republic of Moldova has significantly broadened the access to constitutional justice by allowing all ordinary courts to raise the issue of exception of unconstitutionality. Please further see: http://www.bbcj.eu/profound-changes-legal-system-constitutional-court-republic-moldova-made-possible-every-litigant-raise-exception-unconstitutionality/.

may have certain drawbacks. It is important to note that in Georgia the effect of a final judgement of the Constitutional Court, unlike many systems in Europe, is of a general nature—*erga omnes*. More specifically, irrespective of individual petitions or referrals from ordinary courts, the Constitutional Court, pursuant to its constitutional mandate, assesses the constitutionality of legal norm(s), and its final ruling of unconstitutionality extends towards every subject in jurisdiction and not only in relation to the parties.

From the Georgian experience, it can be said that the effectiveness of preliminary ruling procedures heavily relies on the capacity and willingness of ordinary judges to identify potentially unconstitutional normative acts and submit preliminary questions to the Constitutional Court, which over the years has not been applied constantly.

It could still be said that the respective legal framework in Georgia provides the basis for an institutionalised dialogue between the common courts and the Constitutional Court. Namely, the Constitution (Article 60.4(c)) sets up a mechanism of constitutional submission, whereby common courts may refer a case to the Constitutional Court if they deem that the law, which they are about to apply, contradicts the Constitution. This allows the judiciary, namely, common courts, with participation of the Constitutional Court, to discard unconstitutional laws, thus ensure supremacy of the Constitution and direct applicability of fundamental rights in actual cases. In one of the cases emanated from the referral of the Supreme Court, (Judgment of the Constitutional Court of Georgia on the Constitutional Submission of the Supreme Court of Georgia 2015) the Constitutional Court indicated:

> "[...] constitutional submission represents an essential guarantee for the constitutional supremacy in the state, which allows common courts to avoid application of allegedly unconstitutional normative acts... [It] also gives vigour to constitutional values in practice..."

It is worth noting in this regard that in the process of constitutional decision-making Constitutional Court influences not only parliamentary laws, but also affects regular courts' adjudicative mandate. Because of individual complaint mechanism, the Constitutional Court of Georgia has the power to take actual cases and assess the impugned law *in abstracto*. Therefore, constitutional proceedings may become increasingly fact-driven on the basis of real disputes between parties, much like to ordinary judicial decision-making. Such a development, under the concentrated review model, makes institutional cooperation between regular courts and the constitutional court essential to ensure consistency and effectiveness of the entire legal system.

Over the years the Constitutional Court of Georgia has made a considerable effort to revamp its norm-interpretative technique in order to help effectuate its decisions in ordinary cases. The Constitutional Court, when construing a norm and identifying its substantive meaning, has changed its practice to give the common courts' interpretation an utmost account. As of now, while deciding on constitutionality of a legal provision, the Constitutional Court, in principle, gives the greatest importance to evaluation made by the ordinary courts, because the ordinary courts are institutionally in a better position to determine substance (meaning) of the legal norm. This meaning then ought to be assessed by the Constitutional Court, as it no longer needs to go on with its own interpretation. In case it did so, this might have caused the Constitutional Court to interpret a law differently from the ordinary judiciary and adopt a decision, which could hardly be enforceable in practice. As individuals petitioning the Constitutional Court are directly interested in getting an effective remedy out of their claim, ignorance of common courts' interpretative practice would have likely made the constitutional justice, and especially its individual complaint mechanism, inapt and futile.

Needless to say that it is practically important for the constitutional review to be closer to specific problems outlined by the complainant. Due to its abstract character, normative act involves a number of precepts, rules of conduct that are difficult to identify and consider on merits. It thus seems reasonable for the Constitutional Court to evaluate particular normative meaning of the law that is disputed by the complainant. The Court has to determine normative content of the disputed law in order to judge upon the level of interaction between the identified legal norm and the relevant constitutional provision. This technique becomes greatly pertinent in Georgia, where the ordinary judiciary does not purport a legal obligation to take into account the interpretations of the constitutional court (that go beyond the operative part of the latter judgements) and it may result in actual divergence between the two court systems regarding the meaning (content) of law.

3 Concept of 'Normative Content' and Interrelation with the Ordinary Courts

Per its case law, the Constitutional Court of Georgia recognises the significance of effective application of constitutional standards established by the Court's case law in individual cases. The provision(s) declared unconstitutional by the Constitutional Court lose legal force once the Court officially publishes the decision. However, since the Constitutional Court of Georgia has the authority to rule on constitutionality of the normative act only, the judgment may not have instant result on individual cases. The Constitutional Court serves as a negative legislator; it invalidates unconstitutional normative acts; however, the application of a changed normative reality in individual cases is up to the general courts. Thereby, the latter serves as the enforcer of the constitutional case law in practice. The general courts are guarantors for the effectiveness of constitutional jurisprudence; therefore, a clear understanding and a workable institutional dialogue between these courts are imperative for the effectiveness of constitutional control in the Georgian legal system.

It is noteworthy in this respect that the Constitutional Court of Georgia has developed the notion of "normative content" of the provision. After developing the mentioned notion, the Constitutional Court can evaluate constitutionality of only the normative meaning of the provision that is problematic to the complainant. The idea of "normative content" is based on a simple assumption that the provision is not merely the text written on a paper but its substance, actual regulation (a set of rules) established thereof. It thus follows that formally, single text of a legal provision could have several normative meanings; it might regulate different relations, out of which only some would be challenged. Therefore, the Court has developed the case law to the point where it is now authorised to separate different normative meanings from the same text and provided only some are problematic, declare those unconstitutional without invalidating remaining normative substance of the provision.

By introducing the mentioned notion, the Constitutional Court is enabled to rule on more specific issues, making it easier to settle an actual problem identified by the complainant. It has proved to be one of the most effective ways to evaluate constitutionality of the interpretation of the law made by the general courts within the competence of normative control. Thus, evaluating the constitutionality of the problematic normative meaning of the provision has allowed the Constitutional Court of Georgia to make efforts towards becoming almost as effective as the Constitutional Courts, which have the competence to review constitutionality of the judgment of the general courts.

The execution of standards of the Constitutional Court in actual cases, as noted above, is up to the common courts. The general courts interpret and apply the laws adopted by lawmakers, whereas the Constitutional Court rules on compatibility of the law with the Constitution. However, the division of competences, in practice, may not be always simple; in order to check constitutionality of a provision, the Constitutional Court is in need to interpret the disputed law, determine their meaning and then, by elaborating on the latter, evaluate its constitutionality. The issue becomes complicated in cases when the interpretation of a disputed vague legal provision made by the Constitutional Court does not correspond to the reading by the general courts. In such cases, the Constitutional Court faces a dilemma of whether it should interpret the law as it deems to be correct, or to follow the interpretation made by general courts as a guiding source of finding a true meaning behind the legal provisions.

The approach of the Constitutional Court has changed gradually. The change was formally declared by the Constitutional Court in its Judgment N1/2/552 of 4 March 2015, when the Constitutional Court indicated that:

> "…the general courts, within the scope of their competence, deliver a final decision on normative content of the law, on its practical application and therefore on its enforcement. Consequently, the interpretation of the legal norms made by the general courts has huge importance for determining real content of the law. As a general rule, the Constitutional Court considers and assesses a legal provision with the same normative content as it was applied by a general court" (II-16).

By this statement, the Constitutional Court underlined that, in principle, it will deem the meaning of a legal provision as is interpreted by the general courts. However, in the same judgment the Constitutional Court indicated that in exceptional cases, it shall not follow the general courts' interpretation. For example, when the Constitutional Court is certain that the interpretation of the law made by the common courts are contradictory. Besides, in exceptional cases, the Constitutional Court shall also disregard the interpretation of the provision made by the general court if it is clearly unreasonable.

The mentioned approach is an important step forward for increasing effectiveness of constitutional review enabling the Constitutional Court to have effect on individual cases decided by the general court via evaluating the constitutionality of the law as it is applied in practice. Furthermore, it helps to define a clear line between the competencies of two separate systems within the judiciary, by declaring that the interpretation of laws and determining its content is the mandate of the general courts, and the Supreme Court of Georgia has a final say on that issue, whereas the Constitutional Court rules on the compatibility of such normative content with the Constitution.

The correct comprehension of the constitutional standards by interested parties is also crucial for effective protection of human rights. Misinterpretation of a court judgment might lead to ambiguity and harmful application of the case law, as well as damage to the authority of the Court. Therefore, the representatives of the Constitutional Court of Georgia participate in public discussions on a regular basis to increase comprehensibility of constitutional jurisprudence. The Constitutional Court often meets with representatives from non-governmental organisations and the media to discuss new developments in the case law. The work of the Court as well as the development of legal culture and education in Georgia has led to the considerable increase of interest toward the Court. The number of Constitutional complaints as well as judgments delivered by the Court increases annually, evidencing the need and benefits of further dialogue with the stakeholders.

4 Jurisprudence Regarding the Constitutionality of Criminalisation (and the Proportionality of Sanctions) of the Consumption of Drugs

The foregoing problem of understanding the standards by the courts of general jurisdiction as laid down by the Constitutional Court became vivid in the number of cases that concerned, initially, the constitutionality of criminal sanctions for the consumption of marijuana and in the subsequent case-law, to the criminalisation of consumption of marijuana (and other ‘soft’ drugs). Namely, in the original case (Judgment of the Constitutional Court of Georgia 2015) regarding this matter, the Constitutional Court declared unconstitutional Article 260.2 of the Criminal Code, which provided imprisonment from 7 to 14 years for purchasing and owning up to 70 g of dried leaves of cannabis for personal use, with regard to the constitutional guarantee against inhuman and cruel punishment. The Constitutional Court noted that, in determining criminal sanction policies, the state has a broad margin of appreciation, i.e. when deciding what acts to criminalise and the respective punishment thereof. However, such discretion is not unlimited: the state must select the level of amenability before the law, which is adequate and effective to neutralise risks coming from the action in question. Furthermore, “the state cannot interfere in human freedoms (and rights) more than is objectively required”.

The Court also pointed out that the existence of punishment is only justified when it is an adequate means to achieve the aims of punishment. Otherwise, the punishment becomes an end in itself, which is not compatible with the idea of state based of the rule of law. The Court elaborated upon the aims of punishment: restoration of justice, re-socialisation, private (of crime committed by the same person) and general prevention (of a crime committed by other person). It determined that the goals of the punishment must be reached in tandem. General prevention solely is not enough to impose punishment. According to the Court, punishing an individual only for the purpose of preventing others from the same crime turns a person into a tool to fight crime, which is not justifiable in itself and thus, renders punishment grossly disproportionate.

In the given case, the subject of dispute was not testing the constitutionality of disallowing cannabis from lawful circulation (de-criminalisation), but disputing the constitutionality of the proportionality of the punishment for purchasing and storing large quantities of cannabis (50–500 g). To determine the proportionality of the punishment, the Court discussed the nature of the act itself and the risks associated with the action in question. The legitimate aim of criminalising the act of purchasing and storing cannabis was to prevent the distribution of cannabis and this way, to ensure public order, safety and the health of human beings. The Court determined that the "assessment of constitutionality of the disputed norm is determined in conjunction with the very legitimate aims the norm itself lists, and with taking into consideration the possibilities to achieve these aims with the norm in question".

The Court concluded that when the threats of selling the disputed amount of cannabis and damaging the health of others are hypothetical, restriction of freedom for an act that only damages the health of a person committing the act is disproportionate and inadequate punishment, which violates the Constitution (the right to dignity and the prohibition of inhuman and degrading punishment).

This case has become the reason of misunderstanding by the courts of general jurisdiction as judges struggled to comprehend how to directly apply the ruling of the Constitutional Court in a numerous drug-related pending cases, where the subject matter varied from different amounts of possessed cannabis and ranging to the substance of a drug in question (moist or dried up cannabis). In the legal sense, these different scenarios give different normative meaning to the disputed legal act, thereby, posing an important question to the common court judges—whether to directly apply the constitutional standard as determined by the Constitutional Court and resolve the pending cases or to suspend the proceedings and refer the case at hand to the Constitutional Court.

In majority of instances, the judges chose the latter option. Hence, the Constitutional Court had at a certain point in time become overwhelmed with referrals from the common courts regarding the drug-related cases. It is worth noting that in its subsequent case law, and in the absence of legislative reform in the field of criminal justice in respect of drug-related offences, the Constitutional Court broadened the approach it had taken in the original judgment. Namely, the Constitutional Court declared unconstitutional various provisions of the Administrative Offences Code that imposed administrative responsibility for the non-prescribed use of marijuana.

The Court emphasised that the role of an individual user in the distribution of marijuana and the threats emanating from individual use are very minimal. Therefore, the blanket restriction on the use of marijuana is not proportionate (Judgment №1/3/1282 of July 30 2018).

The Constitutional Court further noted that sanctions relating to the use of marijuana is in line with the Constitution where, under specific circumstances, individual use of marijuana poses a threat to third persons, for example, in educational establishments, on public transport or in the presence of adolescents.

In its later judgment upon this subject, the Constitutional Court has expounded a more general constitutional standard that the harm emanating from drugs that do not cause individuals to become addicted quickly and/or cause aggressive behaviour when used was not sufficient to justify the imposition of a sentence of imprisonment. Imprisonment represents a disproportionate response to the level of harm they posed (in particular, the Constitutional Court declared the imposition of sentences of imprisonment unconstitutional on individuals for the production, purchase, and storage of drugs in amounts sufficient for no more than single use) (Judgment №1/6/770 of August 2 2019).

The Constitutional Court assessed two varying set of circumstances: first, the punishment for the production, purchase, and storage of a narcotic drug, its analogue or precursor for what was clearly personal use and in an amount that would permit no more than a single use; and, secondly, the production, purchase and storage thereof that exceeds the amount of a single-use. It noted that drug users create demand and that that encourages the illegal turnover of drugs. Accordingly, restricting the use of drugs serves the purpose of protecting drug users, as well as protecting public health generally.

Nevertheless, the Constitutional Court stressed that the criminalisation of drug use that does not result in the development of addiction in a short period of time and/or does not cause an aggressive behaviour fall short of ensuring the protection of public order and security. Therefore, criminalisation of the use of narcotic substances was limited to situations where it protected public health, whereas the production, purchase, storage of a narcotic drug for personal or single-use, however, only poses minimal, hypothetical risk. For these reasons, the Constitutional Court concluded that the imposition of prison sentence thereto amounted to disproportionate sanction.

Separately, the Constitutional Court addressed the approach taken to highly addictive drugs and those that cause their users to engage in aggressive behaviour in their user. The Court noted that in respect of highly addictive drugs, single-use, as well as their production, purchase, storage for personal use, constitutes a threat to public order and security. In such circumstances, imprisonment was justified as a preventative measure. Furthermore, it held that that the imposition of prison sentences for the production, purchase, storage of drugs that exceed an amount sufficient for single-use is constitutional. The Constitutional Court indicated that, as a general rule, in similar circumstances, the risks of individual participation in the illegal turnover and distribution of narcotic substances, and also of inflicting harm to other individuals' health equally justified the imposition of criminal sanctions.

Consequently, the Constitutional Court declared the normative content of the disputed provisions, which provided for the imposition of administrative detention and the sentence of imprisonment for the production, purchase, storage of drugs, their analogues or precursors where such is solely sufficient for single-use, to be unconstitutional.

5 Conclusion

In conclusion, it is submitted that the Constitutional Court's interpretative approach helps to ensure the Constitutional Court judgments in Georgia are effectively enforceable in practice, and individuals affected are better equipped to get a proper redress in ordinary courts. Although questions may still persist in relation to the comprehension of constitutional standards by the common courts and also, due to inconsistent approach as to when to directly apply the Constitution and when to resort to the constitutional submission mechanism (exception of unconstitutionality), Constitutional Court's position in the context of making constitutional standards more applicable in real cases has been solidified. This is the illustration of the evolution of constitutional case law in Georgia in a way as to provide viable normative framework for interaction between the Constitutional Court and ordinary judiciary in order to bring the constitutional provisions closer to actual cases, as well as increase effectiveness and consistency within national legal order.

References

Judgment №1/3/1282 of July 30, 2018, "Citizens of Georgia—Zurab Japaridze and Vakhtang Megrelishvili v. Parliament of Georgia". Available in Georgian at: https://constcourt.ge/ka/judicial-acts?legal=1949

Judgment №1/6/770 of August 2, 2019, "Public Defender of Georgia v. the Parliament of Georgia". Available in Georgian at: https://constcourt.ge/ka/judicial-acts?legal=1148

Judgment of the Constitutional Court of Georgia "Beka Tsikarishvili vs. Parliament of Georgia" N1/5/592 as of October 24, 2015. Available in English at: http://www.codices.coe.int/NXT/gateway.dll/CODICES/Full/EUR/GEO/ENG/GEO-2016-2-009?f=templates$fn=document-frameset.htm$q=$uq=$x=$up=1#0-0-0-29005

Judgment of the Constitutional Court of Georgia on the Constitutional Submission of the Supreme Court of Georgia, № 3/1/608,609, 05/10/2015

"Organic Law of Georgia on General Courts". Available at: https://matsne.gov.ge/en/document/view/90676?publication=34

"Organic Law of Georgia on the Constitutional Court of Georgia". Available at: https://matsne.gov.ge/en/document/view/32944?publication=25&scroll=0

Rules of the Constitutional Court of Georgia. Available in Georgian at: https://constcourt.ge/ka/court/legislation/rules-of-the-court

The Venice Commission 'Study on Individual Access to Constitutional Justice', p 17. Available at: https://www.venice.coe.int/WebForms/documents/default.aspx?pdffile=CDL-AD(2010)039rev-e

Historical Aspects of Formation and Development of Constitutional Law in the Kyrgyz Republic

Meergul Bobukeeva

Abstract The article examines a comprehensive overview of the evolution of constitutional justice in the Kyrgyz Republic, spanning from the country's early steps towards independence to recent constitutional reforms. It highlights the pivotal role of the Constitution in shaping the nation's legal and political landscape. In the initial stages, the establishment of the Constitutional Oversight Committee in 1989 marked the beginning of the country's institutional mechanism for protecting the Constitution. This evolved into the formation of the Constitutional Court in 1990, signaling a significant step towards democratization amidst the dissolution of the USSR. The adoption of the 1993 Constitution ushered in systemic changes, including the establishment of the Constitutional Court of the Kyrgyz Republic, aimed at ensuring the balance of state authorities. However, subsequent constitutional reforms, particularly after the events of April 7, 2010, led to the disbandment of the Constitutional Court, raising concerns about power usurpation. Despite criticisms, the establishment of the Constitutional Chamber of the Supreme Court of the Kyrgyz Republic provided a new avenue for constitutional control. This transition continued with the adoption of a new Constitution in 2021, which transformed the Constitutional Chamber into the Constitutional Court, granting it expanded powers to safeguard constitutional legality. The article delve into specific legal cases, such as the review of laws related to electoral norms and constitutional amendments, underscoring the Constitutional Court's role in upholding democratic processes and the rule of law. They emphasize the importance of citizen participation in lawmaking processes and highlight the necessity of expedited legislative action in exceptional circumstances, such as during the COVID-19 pandemic and socio-political crises. Overall, the article illustrate the ongoing evolution of constitutional justice in Kyrgyz Republic, reflecting both achievements and challenges in the country's democratic development and commitment to the rule of law.

M. Bobukeeva (✉)
Constitutional Court of the Kyrgyz Republic, Bishkek City, Kyrgyz Republic
e-mail: mbobukeeva@constsot.kg

R. Arnold and T. Fickentscher (eds.), *The Responsibility of a Constitution for the Future*, https://doi.org/10.1007/978-3-031-65296-7_10

The history of the development of the body of constitutional justice in the country closely linked to the history of the formation of an independent state of Kyrgyzstan.

The first steps to create an institutional mechanism for protecting the Constitution were made during the years of reforms, even before the collapse of the USSR and Kyrgyzstan's independence.

The Constitutional Oversight Committee of the Kyrgyz SSR was established on September 23, 1989. This Committee was the first stage in the emergence and formation of the constitutional control body. This body was non-judicial, exercised preliminary and subsequent constitutional oversight over legal acts of various levels.

In the process of amending the Constitution of the Kyrgyz SSR on December 14, 1990, Kyrgyzstan was the first of all the states that were part of the USSR to liquidate the Constitutional Oversight Committee and form the Constitutional Court.

The Constitutional Court of the Kyrgyz SSR during the period of its existence, that is until May 5, 1993, was not completely formed and did not adopt any act.

It is clear that during the existence of the Soviet state, the creation of an independent body of constitutional justice—the Constitutional Court—did not fit into the existing concept of state structure.

From 1990 to 1993, the country was in severe political crisis—the decline of Soviet power and the Communist Party, a declaration of independence of the country was adopted. Against the background of these events, a new Constitution was being developed, which was adopted by the Parliament on May 5, 1993. An interesting fact is that the Parliament, which at that time was formed back in 1990 at the junction of the transition from a communist regime to a democratic one, adopted a new Constitution despite the fact that it was developed in a fierce struggle of various social and political forces over the choice of the country's further development path.

The Constitution of the Kyrgyz Republic of 1993 made a transition from a totalitarian regime to a democratic one, establishing modern foundations of society and the state, its values and ideas. Accordingly, with its adoption in Kyrgyzstan, both the law and, as a result, the legal culture has undergone changes.

Thus, with independence in the Kyrgyz Republic not only the model of socio-economic development, forms of government, but also a fundamentally new hierarchy of social values has radically changed. In this regard, it seems important to emphasize that the Constitution is the basis for the formation and development of legal culture in general.

We believe that the Constitution of May 5, 1993 became the Basic Law of social harmony and played an important role in stabilizing the political situation at the beginning of forming a sovereign independent state. From this moment begins a new stage in the development of Kyrgyzstan as an independent democratic, legal state.

The new Constitution introduced significant systemic changes and an important component in the formation of institutions of power was the creation of the Constitutional Court of the Kyrgyz Republic, which had fairly broad powers, such as: recognition as unconstitutional of laws and other normative legal acts in case of their divergence from the Constitution; resolution of a dispute related to the operation, application and interpretation of the Constitution; giving an opinion on the legitimacy of elections of the President of the Kyrgyz Republic; giving an opinion on the issue of removal of the President of the Kyrgyz Republic from office as well as removal of judges of the Constitutional Court, the Supreme Court, the Supreme Arbitration Court of the Kyrgyz Republic; giving consent for bringing judges of local courts to criminal liability; giving opinions on amendments and additions to the Constitution of the Kyrgyz Republic; canceling decisions of local self-government bodies that contradict the Constitution of the Kyrgyz Republic; deciding on the constitutionality of law enforcement practices that affect the constitutional rights of citizens.

It was clearly stated in the Constitution that the decision of the Constitutional Court of the Kyrgyz Republic is final and not subject to appeal. It was pointed out that the recognition of any act by the Constitutional Court as unconstitutional cancels its effect in the territory of the Kyrgyz Republic, as well as cancels the effect of other, based on it, legal and other acts.

The 1993 Constitution was the first to establish the principle of separation of powers, and the Constitutional Court, in turn, was called upon to ensure the balance of the system of state authorities.

Over the past 20 years, however, constitutional reforms have followed that have subjected the body of constitutional justice to functional and institutional changes. It underwent the most painful changes after the events of April 7, 2010. As a result of these events there were changes in the socio-political and legal spheres of the country, which led to reorganization of the system of state authorities, including the termination of the Constitutional Court as a body that contributed to usurpation of power in the country (Decree №2 of April 7, 2010 the Constitutional Court of the KR was disbanded until a special decision).

Analyzing the draft Constitution of the Kyrgyz Republic after these events, the Venice Commission of the Council of Europe noted in its Opinion that the draft Constitution deserves high praise, especially in terms of human rights, strengthening of legislative power and distribution of powers between the legislative, executive and president. But the decision to dissolve the Constitutional Court was particularly criticized. The Constitution of June 27, 2010 nevertheless provided for the formation of the Constitutional Chamber of the Supreme Court of the Kyrgyz Republic, which was a judicial body of constitutional control, independently exercising judicial power through constitutional legal proceedings.

However, this example from our recent history of the development of constitutionalism shows the clear influence of the concept of constitutional fears when the Constitutional Court was disbanded and the Constitutional Chamber of the Supreme Court was established in its place. As noted above, the reason for the institutional "demotion" of the constitutional justice body was the fear of a repeat of the "legitimization of usurpation of power" by this body. But, as the saying goes: "It does not matter if a cat is black or white, as long as it catches mice", that is, whatever the body, it is important on its part to perform its function in good faith, which in the future the Constitutional Chamber showed its effectiveness in ensuring constitutional legality.

On October 6, 2020, there was popular unrest after elections scheduled for October 4, 2020. This was followed by constitutional reform, which resulted in a new Constitution coming into force on May 5, 2021. Under the new Constitution, Kyrgyzstan changed from a parliamentary-presidential republic to a presidential republic and remained committed to building a democratic and rule of law state.

As the Constitutional Chamber of the Supreme Court of the Kyrgyz Republic lasted until the adoption of the new Constitution on May 5, 2021, it was transformed into the Constitutional Court of the Kyrgyz Republic and given new powers. Along with the powers exercised by the Constitutional Chamber, such as: resolving cases on conformity of laws and other normative legal acts of the Kyrgyz Republic to the Constitution, giving opinions on the constitutionality of international treaties that have not entered into force, to which the Kyrgyz Republic is a party, as well as giving opinions to the draft laws on amendments and additions to the Constitution, the Constitutional Court will exercise the following: giving official interpretation of the Constitution, resolving disputes on competence between the branches of state power, giving an opinion on compliance with the established procedure for bringing charges against the President.

According to experts, the most positive aspect of the new Constitution is the transformation of the Constitutional Chamber into the Constitutional Court and giving it additional powers.

In the context of the theme of the conference session, I would like to give an example from the practice of the constitutional review body of Kyrgyzstan.

When verifying the constitutionality of the norm of the Constitutional Law of the Kyrgyz Republic "On Suspension of Some Norms of the Constitutional Law of the Kyrgyz Republic "On Election of the President of the Kyrgyz Republic and Deputies of Jogorku Kenesh of the Kyrgyz Republic", the Constitutional Court, in its decision of December 2, 2020, took into account the conceptual meaning of the mission of ensuring peace and stability in the country after the popular unrest in the country, which occurred after the elections scheduled for October 4, 2020.

Thus, after the announcement of the preliminary results of the elections to Jogorku Kenesh (Parliament) on October 4, 2020, a number of political parties appealed to the Central Commission on Elections and Referendums to cancel its results.

The complaints of these political parties stated that the elections were held with gross violations, mass vote buying, threats and pressure on voters, as well as irregularities in the counting of votes. The public dissatisfaction with the results of elections accompanied by mass disturbances resulted in the political instability in the Republic; in this connection the Central Commission on Elections and Referendums has recognized the results of elections of deputies to Jogorku Kenesh of Kyrgyz Republic to be invalid.

The contested constitutional law was adopted at a time of difficult political and economic situation, after popular unrest and the events of October 5–6, 2020. The stability of both law and the security of citizens throughout the republic, as well as the prevention of any civil clashes in the country, depended on the decision of the constitutional justice body.

In this case, the applicant claimed that the contested law was adopted by the Jogorku Kenesh of the Kyrgyz Republic to serve the interests of certain political groups and individuals with gross violations of the procedure for adopting laws stipulated by the laws of the Kyrgyz Republic "On the Regulations of the Jogorku

Kenesh of the Kyrgyz Republic" and "On Normative Legal Acts of the Kyrgyz Republic". The complainant concludes that an important principle of exercising state power—the principle of openness and accountability of state bodies to the people and the exercise of their powers in the interests of the people—has been violated. By suspending the operation of the norms governing the procedure for holding repeated elections to the Jogorku Kenesh, thereby paralyzed the operation of the Constitution, which contains the constitutional foundations for holding elections of deputies of the Jogorku Kenesh.

According to the applicant, if the elections are declared invalid and failed, by virtue of the Constitutional Law on Elections, repeat elections are appointed within one month by the Central Election Commission. The repeat elections and the main elections are inseparable cycles of a single process, and the repeat elections are an organic continuation of the main elections.

The subject of the appeal noted that since the elections had been declared invalid due to massive violations of the electoral legislation, which had significantly affected the free expression of the will of the voter and distorted the principle of universal equal suffrage, repeat elections are an important legal means of restoring the violated right to elect and be elected, guaranteed by the Constitution.

By suspending the norms on elections, the state ends its commitment to ensure the supremacy of the power of the people, represented and ensured by the popularly elected Jogorku Kenesh. Suspension of the law affecting the fundamental political rights and freedoms of citizens is a restriction of these rights within arbitrarily established time limits.

The subject of the appeal questioned the legitimacy of the proposed constitutional amendments due to the participation in the constitutional reform of the Jogorku Kenesh, whose term of office had already ended.

The Constitutional Court, arguing its legal position, noted that the Kyrgyz Republic is a legal, democratic state, which means the rule of law in all spheres of public, political and state life, the subordination of all subjects of legal relations (man and citizen, public associations, state and municipal bodies) to the Constitution and laws.

The defining quality of a law as the only possible regulator of social relations in a state governed by the rule of law is its procedural legality, that is, its compliance with the constitutional and legislative prescriptions on rule-making rules and procedures for its adoption and publication.

The Constitution of the Kyrgyz Republic contains fundamental requirements for the procedure for the adoption, signing, publication, and enactment by the Jogorku Kenesh of the Kyrgyz Republic of constitutional laws, and guarantees the right of citizens to participate in the discussion and adoption of laws and decisions of national and local importance.

It is no coincidence that the Basic Law attaches particular importance to the participation of citizens in the discussion and adoption of laws, having enshrined in an imperative order the obligation of the state to ensure the implementation of this right. This is due to the inseparable connection of this constitutional provision with the principle of people's power. The Constitution proclaims the people of Kyrgyzstan as the bearer of sovereignty and the only source of state power in the Kyrgyz Republic, the people of Kyrgyzstan exercise their power directly at elections and referendums, as well as through the system of state bodies and local authorities on the basis of the Constitution and laws.

This principle is the fundamental beginning of the organization of the life of the state and society as a whole. In this sense, the law-making activity of the state, through which its legal system is formed, cannot be an exception. As a totality of interrelated, coordinated and interacting legal means, developed in specific laws and other normative legal acts, the legal system establishes the regularity of events occurring in society and the level of legal development of the country. In this regard, ignoring the role of society as a primary source of power in the law-making activity of the state is not acceptable.

The Constitutional Court also noted the position of the Venice Commission of the Council of Europe, cited in Opinion CDL-PL(2020) 015 of November 17, 2020, where it was noted that the rule of law implies, with regard to lawmaking procedures, the right of citizens to participate in public affairs and requires that the public has access to draft laws and the opportunity to contribute.

At the same time, the constitutional review body, agreeing with the statement that in the life of the state there may be circumstances requiring immediate legislative measures, considers it acceptable to refer to the legislator's discretion the establishment of exceptional cases where the law-making process can be carried out in an expedited mode. It should be taken into account that all exceptions, although they contain regulators other than the basic rule, remain an integral part of it and do not violate its true content, but only detail it due to the impossibility of resolving the issue in a general manner for obvious and objective reasons. Of course, these reasons must be substantial and comply with the principle of exceptional necessity.

Thus, since in special cases the enactment of bills on an expedited mode is possible, public debate, as an integral part of the legislative process, also cannot hinder the swift manifestation of legislative power. In such cases, the consent of the electorate to the legitimacy of this form of normative activity is reflected in the fact that the legislative power itself is exercised by its representatives, elected directly in periodic, free and democratic elections. In other words, not every action can be approved by the electorate, since in democracies its consent is expressed primarily through representation.

The urgency of legislative decisions in special cases should not be impeded by other procedural issues that take up a time lag that can negate the point of a quick legislative response.

It is well known that due to the declaration by the World Health Organization of a pandemic of a new coronavirus infection COVID-I9 and identification of mass cases in the territory of the Kyrgyz Republic in accordance with the Law of the Kyrgyz Republic "On Civil Protection" by order of the Government of the Kyrgyz Republic on March 22, 2020 № 93 an emergency regime was introduced, which was in effect during the period of consideration of this case by the Constitutional Court. In addition, the events that took place on October 5–6, 2020 in the city of Bishkek, caused by public dissatisfaction with the results of the elections of deputies to the

Jogorku Kenesh of the Kyrgyz Republic, accompanied by mass disobedience and riots, had all the signs of social instability.

Destabilization (instability) is defined as the process of disruption and disorganization of the methods of political and legal regulation of public life that have developed in society. A political crisis leads to a undermining of the foundations of the existence and functioning of the political and legal system and to a change in the methods of resolving political conflicts.

Under conditions of political crisis, threats to both internal and external security of the country inevitably increase. Accordingly, it may fall within the discretion of the legislator to determine the accompanying social phenomena, provided that it is associated with the need to stabilize the social, economic situation, issues of law and order and security, due to the introduction of a state of emergency, an emergency situation or force majeure circumstances.

The principles of periodicity and mandatory elections are the guarantors of a fair democratic structure of the state, meaning that the origin of power with the constitutional duration of the mandate of the outgoing parliament, and, consequently, the prorogation of its powers, must be supported by special justifications and extraordinary circumstances.

According to the Venice Commission of the Council of Europe, the suspension of the electoral process affects the civil and political rights of the electorate and can damage democracy, so the postponement of elections for any purpose should be limited to the principles of proportionality and necessity. The assessment of the "legitimate purpose" and "proportionality" of the restriction of voters' rights can be made contextually, taking into account the actual situation in the country. In very exceptional circumstances, authorities may postpone elections in order to ease tensions and allow voters to express their will in a safe and well-organized context. The postponement of parliamentary elections to a later date, determined by the constitutional duration of the mandate of the outgoing parliament and therefore the prorogation of its powers, must be supported by special justifications and extraordinary circumstances.

According to the Convention on the standards of democratic elections, electoral rights and freedoms in the member states of the Commonwealth of Independent States, during a state of emergency or martial law, in order to ensure the safety of citizens and protect the constitutional order in accordance with the Constitution, laws may establish restrictions on rights and freedoms with an indication of their limits and duration, and elections may be postponed. Thus, the postponement of elections, including from the standpoint of international law, is permissible if it is due to an exceptional need caused by global crises that threaten to damage the interests of society as a whole.

Dissatisfaction of significant groups of citizens with the results of the elections of deputies of Jogorku Kenesh of the Kyrgyz Republic, held on October 4, 2020, resulted in their open protest against the state power, which led to disorganization of the political system, devaluation of state power in the eyes of society and the inability of public authorities to perform their functions in a proper manner. In addition, the country has been in a state of emergency since March 22, 2020, due to the pandemic and mass illness of the population with the COVID-19 coronavirus infection.

In these circumstances, it is impossible to deny the obvious fact that the Kyrgyz Republic is in a state of large-scale socio-political crisis. Accordingly, there is no reason to believe that the legislator had no good reason to recognize the circumstances under which the decisions were taken as extraordinary.

According to the aforementioned Opinion of the Venice Commission of the Council of Europe, in order to prevent interruptions in the work of the legislature, the current Parliament should have limited capacity. During the prorogation, which occurs after the expiration of the legislature's term, Parliament is allowed to perform only certain ordinary functions, while it is not allowed to approve emergency measures, including constitutional reforms. During prorogation, the level of legitimacy of legislative decisions is lower.

In this regard, the Constitutional Court emphasized that, while retaining its mandate as a legislative body, nevertheless, during the prorogation period, the Parliament of the Kyrgyz Republic is obliged to demonstrate a high level of political responsibility to society and be guided in its activities by the principle of reasonable restraint. In other words, the Parliament may make decisions caused by an exceptional need and of immediate nature, i.e., aimed at stabilizing the socio-political situation in the country, overcoming various kinds of crises and social tensions, ensuring the rule of law, security of the state and the population, the activities of the Government, as well as maintaining the effective functioning of the principle of separation of powers. In addition, the actions of Parliament related to the adoption of the contested constitutional law cannot be regarded as interference in the activities of the Central Commission for Elections and Referendums in violation of the principle of separation of powers.

The Constitutional Review Body emphasized the particular importance of compliance with the principle of inviolability of the Constitution of the Kyrgyz Republic, however, noted that the challenged constitutional law by its subject matter is not an act of constitutional reform. In other words, the intention of the Jogorku Kenesh of the Kyrgyz Republic set out in Article 1 of the challenged constitutional law cannot be regarded as an independent norm of law, containing a dictate or an authoritative instruction to carry out constitutional reform. That is, the constitutional review body cannot assess the legitimacy of the actions of the Parliament of the Kyrgyz Republic that have not yet been completed in the framework of the case under consideration, since the contested constitutional Law is not a legal basis for the constitutional reform.

Thus, the Constitutional Court recognized the challenged norm as constitutional, minimizing the negative legal consequences, taking into account the current socio-political situation in the country, while fulfilling its mission of ensuring peace and stability in the country.

Playing the "Constitutional Wild Card"—Future-Shaping by Central Banks

Jörn Axel Kämmerer

Abstract Climate change mitigation and adaptation have been entering the agenda of the central banks. While embracing the cause of the Paris Agreement, the self-empowerment for the pursuit of a non-monetary goal in their monetary policy may further exacerbate existing deficits in the democratic control of central banks. Moreover, as regards the European Central Bank (ECB), the principle of conferral in the Treaty on the Functioning of the European Union (TFEU) might set bounds to a "greening" of its monetary policy.

1 The "Constitutional Restraint" Regarding Central Banks

Central banks are the "grey eminences" of constitutional orders. Although the refinancing capacity of both the State and economic actors, the preservation of individual fortunes and—indirectly—social welfare depend, to a considerable extent, on their monetary policy, the role assigned to central banks by constitutional law is, at best, blurry. Many constitutions do not even mention central banks at all: The US Constitution speaks of coining money and public expenditure, but the Federal Reserve does not feature (which leaves originalists with rather little food for thought). The Japanese constitution is also silent on the central bank (and so on monetary policy in general). The (revised) Swiss constitution is very concise in stipulating that the National Bank shall conduct, as an independent central bank, a monetary policy[1] which serves the general interest of the country (Article 99(2)). Among the few constitutions assigning a slightly more elaborate function to the central bank is also the South African one

[1] "Geld- und Währungspolitik"; in French, these terms merge to one notion: «En sa qualité de banque centrale indépendante, la Banque nationale suisse mène une politique monétaire servant les intérêts généraux du pays […]»

J. A. Kämmerer (✉)
Chair for Public Law I, Bucerius Law School, Hamburg, Germany
e-mail: axel.kaemmerer@law-school.de

R. Arnold and T. Fickentscher (eds.), *The Responsibility of a Constitution for the Future*, https://doi.org/10.1007/978-3-031-65296-7_11

(Section 224).[2] Its provisions are very similar to those of the Treaty on the Functioning of the European Union (TFEU),[3] which may also be regarded as a constitution.[4] According to its articles, the ECB and along with the central banks of the Eurozone (that, together with the ECB, constitute the "Eurosystem" (Article 282(1) 2 TFEU), conducts the monetary policy for the euro member States of the Union and is in charge of (permitting) the issuance of banknotes (Article 127(2), 128(1) TFEU). The primary objective of all central banks within the EU (which together form the European System of Central Banks, Article 282(1) 2 TFEU) is monetary stability (Article 282(2) and Article 282(2) 3 TFEU) and the ECB and all central banks of the Member States must be completely independent in the exercise of their respective functions (Articles 130, 131, 282(3) 2 TFEU).

2 Purchase Programs as a Paradigmatic Shift of Powers

Although monetary policy is what the activities of central banks focus upon, few constitutions mention, let alone define, it. This is known to have triggered conflicts between the German Constitutional Court on the one hand and the European Court of Justice, with the ECB behind it, on the other.[5] The trigger of this constitutional conflict was the paradigmatic change in the practice of the ECB, which in the face of the global first financial and then fiscal crisis started setting up giant programs on the purchase of public and/or private bonds and clung to this for a decade and a half.[6] The German Constitutional Court contended that the central bank's activities had surpassed the scope of monetary policy and qualified them as *ultra vires* acts.[7] I resist the temptation to go into whether the Court was right and whether its call for a more comprehensive proportionality assessment by the ECB was in fact suitable to remedy the alleged excess of powers. That the question at to whether the central bank acted within the confines of its mission could be raised at all before a constitutional court was conditioned by the specific constellation of supranationality: It is incumbent on constitutional courts to prevent the erosion of sovereign rights—or "sovereign statehood", as the German Constitutional Court puts it.[8]

---

[2] Which reads: (1) The primary object of the South African Reserve Bank is to protect the value of the currency in the interest of balanced and sustainable economic growth in the Republic.

(2) The South African Reserve Bank, in pursuit of its primary object, must perform its functions independently and without fear, favour or prejudice, but there must be regular consultation between the Bank and the Cabinet member responsible for national financial matter.

[3] OJ C 326, 26.10.2012, p. 47.

[4] See the discussion on EU constitutionalism in Fichera (2018), p. 4 et seq.

[5] See BVerfGE 146, 216 (PSPP order for reference); ECJ C-493/17 (Weiss), EU:C:2018:1000; BVerfGE 154, 17 (PSPP).

[6] See Hettinger (2018), p. 66 et seq.

[7] BVerfGE 154, 17 (95, para 117 et seq.) (PSPP).

[8] BVerfGE 123, 267 (343) (Lisbon).

It must be underpinned that, in the wake of the financial crisis, other major central banks throughout the world adopted policies that were very much akin to that of the ECB. However, this did not prompt debates on whether the central bank was entitled by constitutional law to adopt the respective purchase programs. It seems that the propensity of constitutional systems that retain their monetary powers for making the policy of their respective national central banks the object of constitutional disputes is much lower, regardless of whether the bank and its functions are enshrined in the constitution or not. Even if, from this perspective, the bank overstretches its mission, this still "stays in the family".

3 The (De-)Stabilising Function of Central Banks

Criticism of independent central banks eluding constitutional control is not new. Yet, it is astonishing how little attention constitutional theory has been attaching to these players. Leaving aside doctrinal criticism of the PSPP judgment, the Federal Constitutional Court rightly drew attention to one, sometimes underrated, fact: What central banks do (or fail to do) has fundamental implications for the exercise of individual rights and freedoms.[9] While inflation and the struggle against it and the interest rates fixed to this end have always affected individual rights, this effect has become more and more pronounced since the central banks stepped in as "firefighters" in 2008. With mixed success, which explains the sequence of giant purchase programs. These programs affect the market balance, along with the extremely low interest rates fixed by the central banks until recently, in a similar manner as subsidies. At the same time, owners of savings accounts and all sectors reliant on the generation of interest (such as the insurance sector, pension systems, or trusts) came under considerable pressure.

We may even hold that the policy of central banks is key to the very functioning of the State insofar as much of their activity in recent years seems to have aimed to prevent sovereign default, i.e., a situation which arises from the incapacity of the State to comply with its (financial) duties and which may lead to the legal and factual inability to comply with all its non-financial duties (welfare, human rights, etc.).[10] This may be less obvious in jurisdictions which have retained their sovereignty in monetary matters; moreover, inflation—whose prevention is the primary task of a central bank—helps a State shrink its sovereign debt, so that, at first glance, its risk of default is reduced. However, even on a lower level of indebtedness, a State may face bankruptcy where its yields from taxation shrinks dramatically and/or its potential for refinancing is lost. In the European Union, where the economic policy remains in the hands of the Member States, monetary policy is also a means of cohesion: The Monetary Union must be prevented from breaking apart, which is not unlikely in a sovereign default of a State party. The ECB repeatedly justified its purchases

[9] BVerfGE 154, 17 (106 et seq., para 134 et seq.) (PSPP).

[10] Cf., for example, Kämmerer (2020), mn. 8 et seq.

with the need to mend disrupted financial transaction mechanisms (both within and between Member States).[11] In the case of Outright Monetary Transactions (OMT),[12] only Member States in fiscal distress would have benefitted from the purchases. It is evident that preventing the loss of creditworthiness, and ensuing sovereign default, was an objective of this policy. This was endorsed by the drop of interest rates on the sovereign debt of the affected States after thence ECB President Mario Draghi had made his famous address that "whatever it takes"[13] would be done.

4 New Green Bonds Strategies: Towards an Even Wilder Card?

We may hold that the stabilizing function of central banks has incrementally evolved towards future-shaping, and in an increasingly programmatic manner: Long-term commitments shall ensure that both markets and the State remain operational. However, the central banks are now setting new, and other, yardsticks in their striving for shaping the future—a *green* future, for that matter.

Many central banks have already adopted programs on the acquisition of green bonds, one of them being the People's Bank of China.[14] In the case of the ECB, a "green bond strategy" is only in the making; its implementation reportedly has been slowed down because of its features and dimension still being controversial among the bank's Board members.[15] The ECB had announced a "Climate Action Plan" in 2021, involving "further incorporating climate change considerations into its monetary policy framework",[16] which was specified to become the "ECB climate agenda 2022" in July 2022.[17] These goals appear to be perfectly in line with the programs and strategies adopted both internationally and within the EU to enhance, as an element of the European Green Deal, the sustainability of financial markets. Article 2(1) of the 2015 Paris Agreement[18] aims "to strengthen the global response to the challenge of climate change, in the context of sustainable development and efforts to eradicate poverty" and, to this end, make "finance flows consistent with a pathway towards low greenhouse gas emissions and climate-resilient development". Although "green bonds" had been invented before the agreement was concluded and had been standardized by the International Capital Markets Association (ICMA),[19]

---

[11] See ECJ, C-62/14 (Gauweiler), ECLI:EU:C:2015:400 para 55; see also ECJ, C-493/17 (Weiss), ECLI:EU:C:2018:1000 para 41.

[12] ECB (2012); the program was never implemented.

[13] The Guardian (2012).

[14] See Macaire and Naef (2021); Mauderer (2021).

[15] Siedenbiedel (2023).

[16] ECB (2021).

[17] ECB (2022).

[18] United Nations, Treaty Series, vol. 3156.

[19] See ICMA (2015).

an NGO dominated by financial market players, the concept has gained considerable momentum thanks to "Paris". Meanwhile, the EU has also adopted, within the context of its Green Deal, its proper European Green Bond Standard (EUGBS).[20] It must be noted that the categorization of a bond as "green" or "brown" shall not entail restrictions on its marketability, at least not in the near future, but the acquired label is expected to nudge investors into purchasing green rather than other bonds. I should add that "green" is only an element of "sustainable", which combines environmental and social components relevant to future generations. However, an equivalent of the ICMA's "sustainability bonds"[21] and "social bonds"[22] is not in sight in EU law, which focuses on decarbonization.

The ECB has already intimated that it would take the EGBS as an inspiration but not as a yardstick and that it is determined to develop its own standards.[23] Details have not been disclosed so far. There has not been much debate among legal scholars on whether the TFEU permits the ECB the adoption of a "green purchase strategy", but it may gain momentum once the strategy will have become clearer. Since some of the legal questions are intrinsic to the EU, I will not elaborate on details but just present key questions that have been raised in this context:

(1) Can "green purchases" still qualify as monetary policy? The ECB holds that non-sustainable businesses are prone to disruptive events (for example, an oil spill) and that privileging them may therefore be in the interest of investors.[24] However, climate change is creeping rather than disruptive and not every non-green business may be held to be accident-prone. While the limits of monetary policy are not clearly defined, they will probably be surpassed where carbon neutrality becomes the true objective of the bank's policy.
(2) May considerations of sustainability be factored into the purchase policy at all? The ECB argues that Article 11 TFEU, which requires the Union to integrate environmental protection with all its policies, is also binding on the ECB.[25] Some scholars object that the Treaty provisions specifically dealing with the ECB require it to support the economic policy in the Union where this does not undermine its primary duties, leaving other—environmental or social—goals unmentioned.[26] Both positions are well-founded and need to be harmonized.[27]

[20] Regulation (EU) 2023/2631 of 22.11.2023, OJ L of 30.11.2023

[21] ICMA (2021b).

[22] ICMA (2021a).

[23] See Panetta (2021): "In addition, to ensure that it remains financially sound, the ECB has to protect its balance sheet from the financial risks caused by climate change that are not correctly priced by the markets. By performing its own analysis of these risks on the basis of rigorous methodologies, the ECB can contribute to the accurate valuation of these climate-related risks and promote awareness among investors, thereby helping to combat climate change." (fn. omitted).

[24] ECB (2021a) p. 13.

[25] See Schnabel (2021); Lagarde (2021), p. 11. Solana (2021) argues that Article 11 TFEU obliges the ECB to take "into account environmental protection requirements in the design and implementation of its monetary policy".

[26] Nees (2021), p. 127 et seq.

[27] For a similar approach, Calliess and Tuncel (2022) p. 25 et seq.

We may hold that the bank has a right to adopt a "green strategy" on condition that the policy thus supported remains predominantly economic (and not environmental in the first place) and that the ECB does not conduct its proper environmental policy.[28] A "green tinge" in its lending may therefore be permitted, a "green reshuffle" of all its activities rather not.

(3) Market neutrality, imposed by the Treaty, could also become an obstacle.[29] The ECB has not disclosed to what extent it aims to prioritise green over non-sustainable bonds. A fair balance must be achieved between this requirement and Article 11 TFEU. A complete ban on "brown purchases" would therefore not be in line with these provisions, but there is room for some form of preferential treatment.

These legal objections are unlikely to halt the zeal of the ECB, neither is the ECJ very likely to get in its way. The constitutional control of other central banks outside the EU is even laxer. The central banks might defer the implementation of their plans because tackling inflation, which is the primary duty of central banks within the EU according to the Treaty (Articles 19(2), 127(1) 1, 282(3) 2 TFEU), suddenly became the major, and most pressing, challenge as well. Yet, but sooner or later the green bond strategy is expected to regain momentum. The ECB's current focus on price stability might defer but not stop it. Despite some warnings of "greenflation", there is little evidence of green investment significantly triggering the depreciation of currencies.[30]

5 Criticism and Conclusions

In sum, the "wild card" that was always assigned to the central banks is incrementally getting "wilder" and more diverse, as it extends to non-economic and non-fiscal considerations. Does this entail bliss or doom for the constitutional order? Many qualify global warming as an "existential threat" and efforts of the international community to stop it unsatisfactory. The constitutional orders assign the primary responsibility for monetary stability on the central banks on the assumption that governments tend to have a sloppy attitude towards it. So why not entrust the independent and flexible central banks with decarbonization (to the extent their toolkit permits) where governments cannot come to terms with it?

The risk one would run is to substitute efficiency for democratic legitimacy and control and rule-based acting. Central banks—"counter-majoritarian institutions" as US political theory calls them—elude them both in large measure but this is acceptable—as long as they appear as mere guardians of monetary stability. In the last 15 years, the banks have increasingly appeared as political actors and "green lending"

[28] See also Calliess and Tuncel (2022), p. 20 et seq.

[29] See Nees (2021), p. 130; see also *Häde* in: Calliess and Ruffert (2022), Article 127 AEUV at mn. 16.

[30] See Olovson and Vestin (2023); Airaudo et al. (2023); Konradt and Weder di Mauro (2022).

might even enable them to adopt proper environmental and social political strategies the system has not been designed for. This is aggravated by a fact I have not mentioned yet: The vast majority of "green bonds" have so far been emitted not by private companies but governments, State-own and transnational banks, and International Organizations. By defining the criteria for the purchase of bonds, the central banks would be in the position to set the actual political guidelines for decarbonization, to nudge the governments into the projects securitised by the bonds the bank believes to be eligible.

Central banks can make relevant contributions to making the constitutional orders "future-proof", but the danger of sacrificing constitutional mechanisms to constitutional values must be taken seriously. Constitutional and statute law is called upon to contain the "wild card" that has been assigned to central banks.

References

Books and Articles

Airaudo FS, Pappa E, Seoane HD (2023) The green metamorphosis of a small open economy. https://fairaudo.github.io/uploads/AiraudoPappaSeoane_Greenflation.pdf

Calliess C, Ruffert M (2022) EUV/AEUV, commentary, 6th edn. Beck, München

Calliess C, Tuncel E (2022) Greening the Euro? The impact of the environmental integration clause (Article 11 TFEU) on the European Central Bank (ECB) primary and secondary objectives, Berlin e-Working Papers on European Law no. 136, p 25. https://www.jura.fu-berlin.de/forschung/europarecht/bob/berliner_online_beitraege/Paper136-Calliess-Tuncel/BOB136FINAL.pdf

Fichera M (2018) The foundations of the EU as a polity. Edward Elgar, Cheltenham

Hettinger C (2018) Die Rechtskontrolle der Geldpolitik der Europäischen Zentralbank in der Eurokrise. Nomos, Baden-Baden

Kämmerer JA (2020) State bankruptcy. In: Max Planck encyclopedia of public international law (MPEPIL). www.mpepil.com

Konradt M, Weder di Mauro B (2022) Carbon taxation and greenflation: evidence from Europe and Canada. https://papers.ssrn.com/sol3/papers.cfm?abstract_id=3928675

Nees D (2021) Klimaschutz durch die EZB? Europarecht 56:119–136

Olovson C, Vestin D (2023) Greenflation? Sveriges riksbank, working paper series 420. https://www.riksbank.se/globalassets/media/rapporter/working-papers/2023/no.-420-greenflation.pdf

Solana J (2021) Climate change litigation as financial risk: central banks and financial institutions. In: ECB legal working paper series 21, p 51

Other Sources

ECB (2012) Technical features of Outright Monetary Transactions, 6 September 2012. https://www.ecb.europa.eu/press/pr/date/2012/html/pr120906_1.en.html

ECB (2021a) An overview of the ECB's monetary policy strategy, 2021. https://www.ecb.europa.eu/home/search/review/pdf/ecb.strategyreview_monpol_strategy_overview.en.pdf

ECB (2021b) ECB presents action plan to include climate change considerations in its monetary policy strategy, 8 July 2021. https://www.ecb.europa.eu/press/pr/date/2021/html/ecb.pr210708_1%7Ef104919225.en.html. (cited as ECB (2021b))

ECB (2022) ECB climate agenda 2022, 4 July 2022. https://www.ecb.europa.eu/press/pr/date/2022/html/ecb.pr220704_annex~cb39c2dcbb.en.pdf

The Guardian (2012) Euro is irreversible, declares European Central Bank president Mario Draghi, 26 July 2012. https://www.theguardian.com/business/2012/jul/26/euro-irreversible-mario-draghi-ecb

ICMA (2015) International Capital Markets Association, Green Bond Principles. https://www.climatebonds.net/files/files/GBP_2015_27-March.pdf

ICMA (2021a) International Capital Markets Association, Social Bonds Principles https://www.icmagroup.org/assets/documents/Sustainable-finance/2022-updates/Social-Bond-Principles_June-2022v3-020822.pdf

ICMA (2021b) International Capital Markets Association, Sustainability Bond Guidelines. https://www.icmagroup.org/assets/documents/Sustainable-finance/2021-updates/Sustainability-Bond-Guidelines-June-2021-140621.pdf. (cited as ICMA (2021b))

Lagarde C (2021) Climate change and central banking, Keynote speech, 25 January 2021. https://www.ecb.europa.eu/press/key/date/2021/html/ecb.sp210125~f87e826ca5.en.html

Macaire C, Naef A (2021) Greening Monetary Policy: Evidence from the People's Bank of China, Bank for International Settlements. https://www.bis.org/ifc/publ/ifcb56_08.pdf

Mauderer S (2021) Green Finance—die Rolle der Zentralbanken, 13 June 2019. https://www.bundesbank.de/de/presse/reden/green-finance-die-rolle-der-zentralbanken-798824

Panetta F (2021) Sustainable finance: transforming finance to finance the transformation, Keynote speech, 25 January 2021. https://www.ecb.europa.eu/press/key/date/2021/html/ecb.sp210125_1~2d98c11cf8.en.html

Schnabel I (2021) From green neglect to green dominance?, 3 March 2021. https://www.ecb.europa.eu/press/key/date/2021/html/ecb.sp210303_1_annex~3c03f9a09c.en.pdf?fd6ef7f73776990f2921fb3ba7daa785

Siedenbiedel C (2023) Streit um grüne Anleihekäufe, FAZ online, 16 January 2023. https://recherche.faz.net/fazPlus/document/FAZN__20230116_8600612?p._scr=search&p.id=bundesbank+gr%C3%BCne+anleihen&p.pos=0

EU Climate Change and Energy Transition Law

Ekaterini Iliadou

Abstract Climate change mitigation is possible only if the energy sector undergoes a radical restructuring by eliminating emissions from the combustion of fossil fuels and their replacement by new technologies, such as those using renewable energy sources. Aiming at the Green Energy Transition, the European Union is currently undergoing an unprecedented shift in the scale and ambition of climate policy following the announcement of the "European Green Deal" and the enactment of the "European Climate Law". The assessment of the EU policies and legislation in the field of energy and climate shows that even under conditions of increased uncertainty, such as those of the severe energy crisis following the pandemic and the war in Ukraine, the basic option for the decarbonization of the economy and the pursuit of pre-defined climate targets, in line with the EU's international commitments, are not negatively affected, since acceleration as regards the achievement of such goals is repeatedly and steadily confirmed.

1 Introduction

Seeking solutions to mitigate climate change has been at the top of the political agenda since the end of the twentieth century. Undoubtfully, the Paris Conference of Parties at the UN Climate Change Conference (COP21) in 2015[1] succeeded in placing the issue on the policy agenda globally. In addition, the European Union is undergoing an unprecedented shift in the scale and ambition of climate policy

[1] United Nations (2015) COP 21. https://unfccc.int/event/cop-21.

E. Iliadou (✉)
National and Kapodistrian University of Athens Law School, Athens, Greece
e-mail: iliadouk@law.uoa.gr

R. Arnold and T. Fickentscher (eds.), *The Responsibility of a Constitution for the Future*, https://doi.org/10.1007/978-3-031-65296-7_12

following the announcement of the "*European Green Deal*"[2] and the enactment of the "*European Climate Law*".[3]

Climate change mitigation is possible only if the energy sector undergoes a radical restructuring by eliminating emissions from the combustion of fossil fuels and their replacement by new technologies, such as those using renewable energy sources (RES). In addition, reforms are necessary for several sectors, such as agriculture and heavy industry, to eliminate emissions related to the production process. The changes in consumption and production patterns need to propagate over the entire economy, affecting materials and equipment at an unparalleled scale. Moreover, the changes, described as a "*Green Transition*", i.e. a transition towards a low carbon, resource-efficient, and socially-inclusive economy (UNEP 2011), will need several decades to reach a climate-neutral energy and economic system.

The Green Transition cannot succeed by pure market forces. On the contrary, it involves considerable positive and negative market externalities that only the state can resolve through an active policy. Energy, transport and industrial policies are the main domains for which the state has to act and legislate to enable investment, new technology development and a change in behaviours. Furthermore, suppose climate change is out of control. In that case, the widely accepted prediction is that future generations will suffer devastating impacts, such as loss of properties, massive migration, poverty and environmental degradation. Therefore, the energy and climate change policy is multifaceted, exerts broad and large social and economic impacts and could entail considerable costs if failed to avoid the climatic consequences.

The effort to deal with climate change directly affects the legal order, which is changing, supplemented, and modified at the international, European, and national levels. The enaction of new legislation and the evolving interpretation of existing rules imply a challenging complexity. As a result, "*Climate Change Law*" emerges as a new discipline (Peel 2008). For instance, the simple overview of the system of legal rules, as already adopted and regularly updated at the level of EU Law,[4] clearly confirms the development of written legislation in the direction of formulating a "*climate legislation*". Furthermore, the basic choice of the EU for climate neutrality by the year 2050, as reflected in the Communication on the "*European Green Deal*", leads to reshaping the European legal framework governing various manifestations of economic activity in general (see below under IV.B). The change in the interpretation of existing rules appears, on the other hand, particularly eloquently in cases of state aid approval, as, for example, in the case of the approval of operating aid for nuclear power plants, deviating from the basic option for free competition in the electricity market.[5] In parallel, mechanisms of judicial review of legislation are mobilized,

[2] COM (2019) 640 final, 11 December 2019.

[3] Regulation (EU) 2021/1119 of the European Parliament and of the Council of 30 June 2021 establishing the framework for achieving climate neutrality and amending Regulations (EC) No 401/2009 and (EU) 2018/1999, OJ L 243, 9.7.2021, pp. 1–17.

[4] https://ec.europa.eu/clima/eu-action/european-green-deal_en.

[5] See Commission Decision (EU) 2015/658 of 8 October 2014 on the aid measure SA.34947 (2013/C) (ex 2013/N) which the United Kingdom is planning to implement for support to the Hinkley Point C nuclear power station (notified under document C(2014) 7142), OJ L 109, 28.4.2015, pp. 44–116.

including the questioning of the legislator's intervention adequacy. The latter may arise when the legislator remains inactive and does not adopt appropriate measures failing to consider the importance of climate change. Furthermore, the activity of private entities is often subject to judicial review and evaluation, which brings about significant climate consequences, as in the case of the fossil fuel industry. In this way, specialized "*climate jurisprudence*" is gradually evolving globally, to evaluate various aspects of the climate change problematic (Setzer and Higham 2022).

The present paper postulates that due to the particular features of the climate change issue and the broad impacts of the Green Transition, the legal order for climate change is considerably different than legislation for traditional environmental protection. The paper analyses the implications of the climate change specificities for the legal order and emphasizes the European legal order, considering the pioneering climate policy of the EU. Furthermore, the paper also focuses on the energy sector, which is responsible for more than 75% of the total emissions of greenhouse gases (GHG). Therefore, the paper infers that analyzing the energy policy legislation and its supporting role in the Green Transition process is important. Finally, due to the unprecedented threat for future generations entailed by climate change, the paper discusses an approach aiming at the constitutional significance of climate change legislation. An effective legal order is not simply about greenhouse gas emission reduction but, more fundamentally, an institutional change to impose restructuring of the economy for climate change mitigation as a permanent obligation of high priority for society.

Bearing in mind all these parameters, it becomes clear that climate protection and energy legislation are critical issues directly related to the question of the constitutional basis of future generations' protection and intergenerational justice concerns. Thus, the theme of the present paper is directly linked to the subject matter of the Workshop on "the Constitution's inherent responsibility for the Future", which was organized within the framework of the 2022 World Congress of Constitutional Law on "Constitutional Transformations".

2 Specificity of Climate Change

The Systemic Nature of Climate Change

According to the definition of Article 1 para 2 of the United Nations Framework Convention on Climate Change (UNFCCC), the term "climate change" *means "a change of climate which is attributed directly or indirectly to human activity that alters the composition of the global atmosphere and which is in addition to natural climate variability observed over comparable time periods*".[6] The main negative

[6] United Nations (1994) United Nations Framework Convention on Climate Change. https://treaties.un.org/pages/ViewDetailsIII.aspx?src=IND&mtdsg_no=XXVII-7&chapter=27&Temp=mtdsg3&clang=_en.

consequence of climate change is global warming, i.e., the increase in temperature over time and in a stable manner, as observed from the industrial era onwards. The causes of the problem are, to a greater extent (75%), the accumulation of carbon dioxide emissions in the atmosphere due to the burning of fossil fuels (coal, lignite, oil and natural gas), to a lesser extent (15%) methane emissions due to the activities of the animal husbandry and other activities such as heavy industry (production of cement, steel, etc.), loss of forests, etc. Based on such evidence, the problem of climate change is primarily anthropogenic, and it is related to the established concept of economic development and the economic model applied from the end of the eighteenth century onwards.

As the planet functions as an integrated system, climate change brings significant negative consequences, such as the problems of increasing the frequency of extreme weather events, wildfires, floods, melting of ice in the polar regions, rising sea levels, loss of land, degradation of ecosystems, the negative effects on biodiversity, etc. Such situations endanger or even damage human property while simultaneously creating immediate risks to human life, health, and safety now and in the future. Moreover, the estimated damages are of such magnitude that a question of risk arises concerning the ontological conditions for the smooth continuation of life on the planet. In addition, the problems associated with climate change have a direct negative impact on the global economy. In this sense, society has to place climate change as an issue of primordial importance -if not as the main- *systemic* problem of the modern era, i.e. as a problem that has the potential to cause adverse and irreversible economic and social damages with consequences spread as a "*domino effect*," leading to the material impairment of the market (Choudhury 2021).

Specific Characteristics

In addition to its systemic nature, the climate change problem has key features that make it unique compared to classic environmental protection problems:

First, the emissions of gases that cause climate change are directly diffused throughout the planet and are not limited spatially. In this way, the emissions do not burden only those that emit greenhouse gases and not only those who are geographically adjacent to the source of said emissions. The problem is thus inherently a problem of the planet as a whole and does not affect only specific areas, even though certain areas, due to their specific geographical location or economic situation, may be affected more or more intensely, as may be the case of coastal zones or less developed countries of the planet.

As mentioned above, the problem of climate change is anthropogenic and structurally linked to industrial activity. Until recently, the economically developed countries with high industrial activity were the countries that accumulated the emissions of GHG that are mainly responsible for climate change. More recently, in the context of the globalized economy and the international competition that brought about, among other things, the spatial displacement of production activities, the countries that emit GHG, exacerbating the problem of climate change, are the developing ones. From this point of view, the traditional classification of states based on economic indicators loses its importance, among other things, in the search for the attribution of responsibility or the distribution of the costs for climate change mitigation and adaptation.

Precisely because of the spread of pollutants throughout the planet, everyone must reduce emissions, while at the same time, individual action at the local level is not enough to mitigate climate change. After all, if someone takes measures unilaterally, inactive countries also will benefit from such action. But conversely, if everyone remains inactive, climate damages are unavoidable. So, the attitude "the solution to the problem does not depend on me" cannot apply. Climate change exemplifies the "*tragedy of the commons*" (Hardin 1968). The tragedy of the commons describes the dilemma that arises from a situation in which many, acting independently and having the same interests, are led to ultimately destroy a common finite resource, even though it is clear that, in the long run, such a result benefits no one. In such cases, to deal with the problem, it is considered necessary to ensure collective action, which may be considered equivalent to international cooperation in the case of climate policy (Schenck 2008).

Furthermore, in the case of climate change, it is unknown who is harming whom and rather extremely difficult to determine. After all, even if this could be determined, it would have little value since the burden on the climate through emissions burdens the entire planet over time. Even more, no one bears harm at the moment, or such harm is yet not apparent enough, but it is likely to occur in the distant future. In addition, there is no obvious proof of the causality of effects, and it isn't easy to construct an evidentiary process to assign responsibility.

Additionally, the effects of climate change are due to the accumulation of emissions over many decades. However, already in the present time, the problem is posed in terms of urgency as the results of the activity of the preceding decades become evident.[7] After all, the emissions of the current generation, added to the result of the past years, create irreversible effects for future generations. Unlike other environmental damage problems, there is no climate change fix once greenhouse gases in the atmosphere exceed a certain concentration level. In addition, the possible inaction of the current generation considerably reduces the possibilities of the next generation to mitigate the devasting impacts. Therefore, climate change is inherently a problem of intergenerational justice between current and future generations (Brown Weiss 1992).[8]

---

[7] See United Nations (2023) Statement by Simon Stiell, UN Climate Change Executive Secretary, on the IPCC's Synthesis Report of the Sixth Assessment Report. https://unfccc.int/news/statement-by-simon-stiell-un-climate-change-executive-secretary-on-the-ipcc-s-synthesis-report-of.

[8] United Nations (2013), Intergenerational Solidarity and the Needs of Future Generations. https://sustainabledevelopment.un.org/content/documents/2006future.pdf: «*In the context of sustainable development, intergenerational solidarity goes beyond the relations among currently living representatives of different generations and embraces future generations, who do not yet exist. At the 1995 World Social Summit, countries committed themselves to create a framework of action to,*

Finally, the economic costs of adaptation to climate change, such as building new infrastructure and taking action to protect existing assets and activities, are enormous. Climate change adaptation entails enormous costs and investment during the Green Energy Transition. Such Transition presupposes a new technology model for power generation, alternative fuels and energy efficiency at a pace far beyond the usual speed of technological progress. The private sector cannot address the challenges of transformation alone, given the uncertainties and the resources needed for new technologies to mature. Consequently, public policy has to act as the enabler of technological progress and investment (Mazzucato 2014).

3 Climate Change and the Law

Climate Change and Environmental Law

Despite the particularities observed, climate protection does not cease to be part of the broader circle of environmental protection problems. One classic issue that arises is, therefore, the question of whether Environmental Law, as it has developed especially since the 1970s and subsequently as an autonomous branch of the legal discipline, encompasses the set rules aiming at neutralizing the negative consequences of technical and economic progress and at dealing with the ecological problem, also includes the basic values and rules for addressing climate protection.

If it is accepted that the problem of emissions of GHG is only a case of atmospheric pollution, the answer to this question is positive. This was admitted, for example, in the US Supreme Court's landmark decision *Massachusetts v Environmental Protection Agency*,[9] in which it was held that GHG emissions cause environmental pollution that falls within the scope of the Clean Air Act and, by extension, falls under the regulatory competence of the Authority for the Protection of the Environment.

However, within modern theory there is broad agreement to highlight the specific characteristics of climate change and characterize them as primarily different from "*first generation*" problems of environmental damage and pollution (Shellenberger and Nordhaus 2004), i.e. those reflecting "*concerns about human pollution of the environment or the over-exploitation of natural resources*" (Peel 2008, p 970). A key argument for accepting this concept is the finding that in the relationships regulated by Environmental Law, there is clarity as to causality, a fact which allows the application of basic liability mechanisms following the "*polluter pays*" principle. On the contrary, climate change with the characteristics described above is a problem of great ambiguity in terms of the cause-and-effect relationship, and additionally, it generates unmanageable damages and risks, especially regarding the dimension of the necessity to ensure smooth human living conditions in the future.

---

among other things, "fulfil our responsibility for present and future generations by ensuring equity among generations and protecting the integrity and sustainable use of our environment."».

[9] 549 US 583 (2007).

The need to adopt a new vision that will steer towards a clean energy economy, zero pollution, security of supply and the creation of new jobs is thus supported. However, such a perception requires action by the legislator to establish new rules, tools and instruments that will allow for dealing with the problem with proactively and for accountability mechanisms to be activated. In this sense, Environmental Law provides useful tools to address problems that make up the complex problem of climate change, but additional specialized measures are necessary to coordinate climate action in various sectors of the economy and consequently to achieve the main goal of preventing global warming.

Climate Legislation

To effectively mitigate the multidimensional problem of climate change, the legal order is changing so that basic political options are incorporated into the law, leading to the emergence of the so-called "*climate (change) legislation*" (Koehl 2022).

The law changes in principle at the international level as specialized international treaties get concluded aiming directly at climate protection. In particular, the UNFCCC (1992),[10] the Kyoto Protocol (1997)[11] and the Paris Agreement (2015)[12] have been critical milestones in this process. In such context, the EU and the European national governments wishing to be the frontrunners enhanced the legal order by adopting complex mechanisms and policy instruments to address climate change mitigation and adaptation. The so-called "climate laws"[16] recently complemented the legal order as a specialized framework. The basic tools applied within that framework are, on the one hand, the establishment of targets for reducing emissions that cause climate change and, on the other hand, the planning of the activity undertaken to achieve such targets. The framework legislation for climate change usually addresses all aspects of climate policy, but the aim is broader, primarily to establish an institutional basis for climate change policies and introduce a mechanism for accountability.

A framework climate law does not render climate legislation unnecessary. On the contrary, it is still important to maintain and enhance an ensemble of acts, decrees and policy measures to effectively implement climate law imperatives. Moreover, the complexity of climate change, its systemic and multi-sectoral nature, requires special legislation to address specificities of various sectors of economic activity with the aim of climate change mitigation and adaptation. Thus, in a broad sense, a complex set of climate legislation emerges, having a much wider scope than establishing climate goals and directing towards a different model of economic development compared

[10] See above footnote (7).

[11] United Nations (1997) Kyoto Protocol to the United Nations Framework Convention on Climate Change https://unfccc.int/documents/2409.

[12] United Nations Paris Agreement. https://unfccc.int/process/conferences/pastconferences/paris-climate-change-conference-november-2015/paris-agreement.

to the past, as required to serve the goal of transitioning to a zero-carbon economy and ensuring climate resilience.[13] This is particularly evident in the energy field, where the relevant legislation is under considerable enhancement towards achieving the so-called "*energy transition*".

Energy Transition Legislation

Addressing energy and simultaneously environmental issues are of central importance for modern policymaking and, by extension, for the legal order. Firstly, it is a common topic that energy is vital for everyday human life and well-being; thus, energy has a "public good" significance in avoiding disruptions or shortages. Therefore, state intervention aiming at ensuring the security of supply is commonly justifiable. Furthermore, affordable energy bills are essential for households and the competitiveness of the economy in general and thus for the growth of all economic sectors; state intervention to address energy price crises or abnormal price hikes is commonly justifiable. At the same time, energy is an important source of environmental damage, creating problems of local and regional pollution as well as a major source of greenhouse gas emissions from fossil fuels that cause climate change at a global scale, which constitutes an unprecedented threat to humanity; environmental protection and notably climate change mitigation is also a reason to justify state intervention. Based on the above, public intervention in the energy sector traditionally aims at serving the so-called "three energy pillars", i.e., security of supply; economic efficiency; and environmental protection. Often, conflicts between such pillars occur since it is not always self-evident or easy to achieve concurrently and equally all three public interest dimensions. So, as it is impossible to establish any hierarchical order between the competing objectives, balancing the three energy pillars is imperative in policy making. Moreover, the balance between the three pillars may change over time or differ across policy issues. Consequently, policy priorities weighing the importance of conflicting criteria are in consideration in the related legal framework.

During the last decades, energy policy and legislation have changed drastically due to the particular significance of the energy sector for the ever-worsening effects of the climate change problem, often referred to as "*climate crisis*". Considering that climate constitutes an ontological prerequisite for the normal continuation of human life on the planet, the necessity to mitigate the problems associated with the climate crisis also creates critical policy priorities for the energy sector. In that way, environmental and climate protection objectives gain importance and become a top priority; in counterpart, economic affordability and security of supply, i.e., the other two energy policy pillars, unavoidably need to be addressed as subordinated to the high priority of enabling climate change mitigation with policies and measures that are often costly. Nonetheless, since domestic resources, such as renewables, replace

[13] See for example the related website of the Sabin center for Climate Change Law of the Columbia Climate School https://climate.law.columbia.edu/content/energy-law.

imported fossil fuels (oil and gas, for example) in the energy transition context, supply security benefits significantly from climate change mitigation policies. Also, from a long-term perspective, the technological and industrial maturity of green technologies enacted thanks to the long-term green transition provides cost reduction benefits and helps improve the performance of the affordability criterion, which, however, is penalized in the short-term during the green transition. For such purpose, specialized legislation aims to support such goals, as may be observed at the level of the EU legal system.

4 EU Energy Law and Climate Protection

From the last decade of the twentieth century onwards, the development of complex secondary EU Law has mirrored the policy choices regarding the structure and goals of EU Member States' energy sectors. A typical example is the legislation on the liberalization of energy markets, which led to the emergence of the "modern" EU Energy Law, a distinct branch of legal science based on the free competition legal framework of the European energy sector (Talus 2016). Moreover, the Treaty of Lisbon has, among others, facilitated a structural connection of EU Energy Law with climate change policy.

"Modern" EU Energy Law

During the last decade of the twentieth century, the EU's energy legislation focused primarily on achieving market liberalization to enhance economic efficiency by abolishing the monopolistic structures of the past, in line with the general framework of the internal market objective. All three consecutive packages of EU energy legislation adopted from 1996 through 2009 focused on the necessity to set the general context for efficient organization and operation of the liberalized energy markets to achieve market integration.

More specifically, following the enactment of the first Electricity Directive[14] and the first Gas Directive,[15] the EU member states' energy sector underwent significant reforms. Monopoly prerogatives traditionally granted to former vertically integrated public utilities were abolished while, at the same time, free competition rules and the right of consumers to choose their suppliers freely were gradually introduced. Additionally, aiming at the achievement of a "*level playing field*" for all market participants (competitors), the "incumbents", i.e. the former monopolistic public utilities,

[14] Directive 96/92/EC of the European Parliament and of the Council of 19 December 1996 concerning common rules for the internal market in electricity, OJ L 27, 30.01.1997, pp. 20–29.

[15] Directive 98/30/EC of the European Parliament and of the Council of 22 June 1998 concerning common rules for the internal market in natural gas, OJ L 204, 21.07.1998, pp. 1–12.

were obliged to comply with accounting unbundling obligations related to the natural monopoly market segments, i.e. the energy networks, to prevent cross-subsidization and unequal treatment. Furthermore, rules granting all market participants Third Party Access (TPA) rights to the networks were adopted.

The second energy markets liberalization legislation[16] emphasized on improving the deficiencies observed in fully liberalized, well-functioning energy markets. For such purpose, the new legislation provided, among other for the member states' obligation to create sector-specific, independent national regulatory authorities (NRAs) with the main duty to regulate access and use of the energy networks; and for the enhancement of unbundling requirements by adding obligations related to legal and functional unbundling of network activities.

Following the energy sector inquiry report (2007)[17] that identified multiple malfunctions in operating the liberalized European energy markets, the EU legal framework changed significantly. More specifically, the third energy liberalization package enacted in 2009[18] provided for stricter unbundling rules as regards the high voltage system operation, including ownership unbundling requirements; the enhancement of the duties and responsibilities of energy regulators; and the establishment of the Agency for the Cooperation of Energy Regulators (ACER) with specific duties and responsibilities within the framework of the integrated, internal energy market.

The main aim of all the legislation mentioned earlier was to create competitive energy markets to reduce costs and prices. At the same time, the legislation included rules to address the security of supply issues (for example, through investment planning) as well as rules for the establishment of Public Service Obligations (PSOs) not to jeopardize the uninterrupted supply of groups of consumers requiring special care at affordable prices.[19]

---

[16] Regulation (EC) No 1228/2003 of the European Parliament and of the Council of 26 June 2003 on conditions for access to the network for cross-border exchanges in electricity, OJ L 176, 15.07.2003, pp. 1–10; Directive 2003/54/EC concerning common rules for the internal market in electricity and repealing Directive 96/92/EC, OJ L 176, 15.07.2003, pp. 37–56; and Directive 2003/55/EC concerning common rules for the internal market in natural gas, OJ L 176, 15.07.2003, pp. 57–78.

[17] SEC(2006) 1724.

[18] Regulation (EC) No 714/2009 of the European Parliament and of the Council of 13 July 2009 on conditions for access to the network for cross-border exchanges in electricity and repealing Regulation (EC) No 1228/2003, OJ L 211, 14.8.2009, pp. 15–35; Regulation (EC) No 713/2009 of the European Parliament and of the Council of 13 July 2009 establishing an Agency for the Cooperation of Energy Regulators; OJ L 211, 14.8.2009, pp. 1–14; Directive 2009/72/EC of the European Parliament and of the Council of 13 July 2009 concerning common rules for the internal market in electricity and repealing Directive 2003/54/EC, OJ L 211, 14.8.2009, pp. 55–93; Directive 2009/73/EC of the European Parliament and of the Council of 13 July 2009 concerning common rules for the internal market in natural gas and repealing Directive 2003/55/EC, OJ L 211, 14.8.2009, pp. 94–136; Regulation (EC) No 715/2009 of the European Parliament and of the Council of 13 July 2009 on conditions for access to the natural gas transmission networks and repealing Regulation (EC) No 1775/2005, OJ L 211, 14.8.2009, pp. 36–54.

[19] ECJ Judgement of 20 April 2010, *Federutility*, C-265/08, ECLI:EU:C:2010:205, para 22 f.; Judgement of 7 September 2016, *ANODE*, C-121/15, ECLI:EU:C:2016:637, para 38 f.

The special legislation for the liberalization of energy markets led to the emergence of a distinct branch of legal science, namely the EU Energy Law. The object of this branch is the systematization of the rules that govern energy markets and the highlighting of the basic principles that create the internal system of EU Energy Law. This new EU Energy Law can be described as "*modern*" (Iliadou 2021) as it marks a break with the legal framework of the past, which was based on a public monopoly business organization model.

In parallel to the modern EU energy law, the EU adopted specific measures, such as RES specific rules[20] and rules on energy efficiency promotion,[21] using the legal basis of the EU competencies on environmental protection (ex Article 174 TEC). Such a legal basis could justify state aid cases deviating from free competition rules provided that they facilitate investment in environmentally friendly technologies and activities.[22] Within the same framework, the most prominent tool of the European legal order for influencing and guiding private business activity in the energy sector towards environmental and climate objectives has, over time, been the EU ETS system, a system of tradable emissions allowances aiming to reduce GHG emissions through a market mechanism.[23]

Energy Transition Legislation

From 2009 onwards, the EU policy elaborated a structural link between energy and environmental goals, leading to a new architecture of the applicable legislation (Skjaerseth 2016). This has been possible because of introducing the new Article 194 TFEU with the Lisbon Treaty. Article 194 TFEU is an energy-specific provision at the level of primary EU legislation, stating the necessity to coordinate energy and environmental EU policy, together with the explicit recognition of the principle of solidarity for the energy sector. The provisions of Article 194 TFEU define the targets of the EU energy policy, which are related to the establishment of the internal market (free movement rights and free competition rules); to EU security of supply; to the

[20] Directive 2001/77/EC of the European Parliament and of the Council of 27 September 2001 on the promotion of electricity produced from renewable energy sources in the internal electricity market, OJ L 283, 27.10.2001, pp. 33–40.

[21] Directive 2012/27/EU of the European Parliament and of the Council of 25 October 2012 on energy efficiency, amending Directives 2009/125/EC and 2010/30/EU and repealing Directives 2004/8/EC and 2006/32/EC, OJ L 315, 14.11.2012, pp. 1–56.

[22] ECJ Judgement of 1 July 2014, *Ålands Vindkraft,* C-573/12, ECLI:EU:C:2014:2037; Judgement of 28 March 2019, *Deutschland/Kommission,* C-405/16 P, ECLI:EU:C:2019:268.

[23] Directive 2003/87/EC of the European Parliament and of the Council of 13 October 2003 establishing a scheme for greenhouse gas emission allowance trading within the Community and amending Council Directive 96/61/EC, OJ L 275, 25.10.2003, pp. 32–46. For the EU-ETS system see for example ECJ Judgement of 8 March 2017, *ArcelorMittal Rodange,* C-321/15, ECLI:EU:C:2017:179.

promotion of energy efficiency, savings and RES, and the interconnection of energy networks (Calliess and Hey 2013).

The new Treaty and environmental protection provisions created new dynamics by providing the legal basis for the structural interconnection between energy and environmental EU policy (Kulovesi and Oberthur 2020). This became evident with the Commission communication of 2015 on "*A Framework Strategy for a Resilient Energy Union with a Forward-Looking Climate Change Policy*"[24] aiming at achieving a "*transition to a low-carbon, secure and competitive economy*" and later, with the so-called "*Clean Energy for all Europeans package*".[25] The Clean Energy Package was proclaimed in 2016 and adopted during 2018–2019. This 4th legislative package for the energy sector includes a set of interrelated rules that reveal the basic policy objective to coordinate economic efficiency goals with climate policy.[26]

The leading legal instrument within the Clean Energy Package is the Governance Regulation.[27] This Regulation: (a) established a stable governance system comprising planning, monitoring and reporting obligations through integrated national energy and climate plans (NECPs) aiming at the efficient coordination of national and EU policies as regards the achievement of climate targets in line with the Paris Agreement (2015), i.e. the binding target of at least a 40% domestic reduction in economy-wide GHG emissions by 2030 compared to 1990 as was formally approved as the Intended Nationally Determined Contribution of the Union and its Member States to the Paris Agreement at the Environment Council meeting on March 6th 2015)[28]; and (b)

[24] COM/2015/080 final.

[25] European Commission, Clean energy for all Europeans package. https://energy.ec.europa.eu/topics/energy-strategy/clean-energy-all-europeans-package_en.

[26] Directive (EU) 2018/844 of the European Parliament and of the Council of 30 May 2018 amending Directive 2010/31/EU on the energy performance of buildings and Directive 2012/27/EU on energy efficiency, OJ L 156, 19.6.2018, pp. 75–91; Directive (EU) 2018/2001 of the European Parliament and of the Council of 11 December 2018 on the promotion of the use of energy from renewable sources, OJ L 328, 21.12.2018, pp. 82–209; Directive (EU) 2018/2002 of the European Parliament and of the Council of 11 December 2018 amending Directive 2012/27/EU on energy efficiency, OJ L 328, 21.12.2018, pp. 210–230; Regulation (EU) 2019/941 of the European Parliament and of the Council of 5 June 2019 on risk-preparedness in the electricity sector and repealing Directive 2005/89/EC, OJ L 158, 14.6.2019, pp. 1–21; Regulation (EU) 2019/943 of the European Parliament and of the Council of 5 June 2019 on the internal market for electricity, OJ L 158, 14.6.2019, pp. 54–124; Directive (EU) 2019/944 of the European Parliament and of the Council of 5 June 2019 on common rules for the internal market for electricity and amending Directive 2012/27/EU, OJ L 158, 14.6.2019, pp. 125–199; Regulation (EU) 2019/942 of the European Parliament and of the Council of 5 June 2019 establishing a European Union Agency for the Cooperation of Energy Regulators, OJ L 158, 14.6.2019, pp. 22–53.

[27] Regulation (EU) 2018/1999 of the European Parliament and of the Council of 11 December 2018 on the Governance of the Energy Union and Climate Action, amending Regulations (EC) No 663/2009 and (EC) No 715/2009 of the European Parliament and of the Council, Directives 94/22/EC, 98/70/EC, 2009/31/EC, 2009/73/EC, 2010/31/EU, 2012/27/EU and 2013/30/EU of the European Parliament and of the Council, Council Directives 2009/119/EC and (EU) 2015/652 and repealing Regulation (EU) No 525/2013 of the European Parliament and of the Council, OJ L 328, 21.12.2018, pp. 1–77.

[28] Governance Regulation (28), Articles 3–14.

granted competencies to the Commission to assess progress towards the achievement of the aforementioned climate objectives and targets through the application of ex-ante monitoring procedures and to make *recommendations* to the member states to increase their ambition, in case their contributions are deemed insufficient.[29]

Confirmation of the Energy Transition Goal During the Energy Crisis

Following the pandemic and the war conflict in Ukraine following the Russian invasion, new challenges often referred to as an "*energy crisis*" arose. The challenges are related mainly to managing the unprecedented high energy price hikes in Europe and the significant energy security of supply threat following the disruption of the Russian gas supply. According to the Commission, effectively addressing similar problems requires the acceleration of the Green Transition. Accordingly, the Commission proposed a package of measures with increased ambition for the green targets known as the Communication on "*REPowerEU*".

More specifically, in 2019, with its Communication entitled "*The European Green Deal*," the Commission unveiled its plan to meet 55% emission reduction by 2030, a first step toward carbon neutrality until 2050, aiming to make "Europe the first climate-neutral continent". Furthermore, the EU Green Deal set up the blueprint for the green energy transition to create new opportunities for innovation and investment, as well as to create jobs and growth, address energy poverty, reduce external energy dependency and improve the EU citizens' health and well-being.[30]

In July 2021, a new piece of legislation, namely the "European climate law", entered into force.[31] With the provisions of this Regulation, the objective for the Union to reach climate neutrality by 2050 becomes legally binding[32] and an ambitious, legally binding 2030 climate target of at least 55% reduction of net emissions of greenhouse gases as compared to 1990 is endorsed.[33]

As proclaimed, the "*Fit for 55*" package is a set of proposals to revise and update the existing EU legislation and implement new initiatives to ensure that EU policies align with the pre-defined climate goals.[34] The procedure for the adoption of such proposals is still ongoing.[35] For example, on Oct 27th 2022, the Council and the European Parliament reached a provisional political agreement on stricter CO_2

[29] Ibid, Article 31(1).

[30] See above footnote (2).

[31] See above footnote (3).

[32] Ibid, Article 4(1).

[33] Ibid, Article 2(1).

[34] European Coucil, Fit for 55. https://www.consilium.europa.eu/en/policies/green-deal/fit-for-55-the-eu-plan-for-a-green-transition/.

[35] See the related timeline: European Council, Timeline European Green Deal and Fit for 55 https://www.consilium.europa.eu/en/policies/green-deal/timeline-european-green-deal-and-fit-for-55/.

emission performance standards for new cars and vans and, more specifically, on a 55% CO_2 emission reduction target for new cars and 50% for new vans by 2030 compared to 2021 levels and on 100% CO_2 emission reduction target for both new cars and vans by 2035.[36]

As the energy crisis became deeper due to the war continuation, the Commission enhanced the policy proposals as the REPower EU plan increased its ambition. In addition, the plan included measures to rapidly reduce dependence on Russian fossil fuels and accelerate the Energy Transition.[37] According to the Commission, there is a double urgency to transform Europe's energy system: ending the EU's dependence on Russian fossil fuels, which are used as an economic and political weapon and cost European taxpayers nearly €100 billion per year; and in parallel, tackling the climate crisis. For such purposes and aiming at phasing out EU dependency on Russian fossil fuels faster, the REPower EU Plan includes measures for energy savings, diversification of energy supplies, and accelerated roll-out of renewable energy to replace fossil fuels in homes, industry, and power generation.

5 Brief Assessment of the EU Energy Transition Legislation

The assessment of the EU policies in the field of energy and climate shows that even under conditions of increased uncertainty, such as those of the current severe energy crisis, the basic option for the decarbonization of the economy and the pursuit of pre-defined climate targets, in line with the EU's international commitments, are not negatively affected, since acceleration as regards the achievement of such goals is repeatedly and steadily confirmed. To this end, the European Union adopted and established a complex and sophisticated system of legal rules, covering many areas of economic activity. Thus, the EU climate legislation is not limited to setting objectives as reflected in the relevant "European climate law"; moreover, it consists of specific interventions in various sectors of the economy, such as the support of renewable energy sources, the promotion of energy efficiency improvement, the development of alternative green fuels, and, even more importantly, the European ETS System, the scope of which is gradually in the process of extension in all sectors. In parallel, recent developments at the pre-legislative level show the concern to highlight climate protection as an "overriding public interest".The Commission's proposal to systematically promote renewable energy investments even at the expense of spatial planning

[36] European Council (2022) First 'Fit for 55' proposal agreed: the EU strengthens targets for CO2 emissions for new cars and vans. https://www.consilium.europa.eu/en/press/press-releases/2022/10/27/first-fit-for-55-proposal-agreed-the-eu-strengthens-targets-for-co2-emissions-for-new-cars-and-vans/.

[37] COM (2022) 230 final.

restrictions or other environmental protection rules follows this approach.[38] Similarly, Article 3 of the Emergency Regulation laying down a framework to accelerate the deployment of renewable energy[39] reflects the same rationale.

Further to state and EU-driven legislation enabling drastic reduction of greenhouse gas emmissions, it is remarkable that private entities and financial instutions are progressing towards establishing climate protection standards, such as low carbon footprint, as common business practice and a basis of corporate accountability. The Environmental, Social and Governance (ESG) standards serving as a benchmark for assessing risks in raising funding and evaluating investment already apply, and is under further extension (OECD 2022). Climate-related indicators, such as carbon emission thresholds is well placed among the set of criteria assessing sustainability of a business and risk evaluation of loans, bonds, etc. The establishment of climate-related ESG has not been imposed by the state, but it has propagated on a voluntary basis because climate-related risks and threats has driven serious concerns for financial institutions and the business sectors exposed to climate risks (MacNeil and Esser 2022). A high carbon footprint entail business risks due to regulation, while business assets are subject to climate change damaging risks. Thus, climate change protection concerns gains momentum in the business sector and becomes a standard business practice. The ensuing responsibility within business practice obviously goes beyond state policy and mandatory rules while being highly bebeficial for climate change protection.

The example of ESG in establishing high priority of climate protection in common business practice needs to analogously apply in all sectors of the economy and all kinds of behaviours. In this way, climate protection becomes a common practice, acquiring an institutional value, meaning a value of an "*established and embedded social rule*" that "*structures social relations*" (Hodgson 2006). Such institutional significance is undoubtfully of primordial importance to ensure persistence of climate change protection in the long-term independently of political uncertainties. Investing in climate change protection gets relief from regulatory risk and allows positive anticipation of the future market of green technologies. Such an institutional development is of invaluable benefit for the effectiveness of the climate protection efforts.

Moreover, taking into account the special features of the climate crisis, as discussed above, and in particular the risk of irreversible damage that threatens the normal living conditions of future generations, it can be argued that there is a strong need to link climate policy and legislation with the perspective of fundamental rights and therefore with constitutional law, which, by reflecting the basic rules of social coexistence not only for today but also for the far future, may enable effective respect for the climate across society, governance and business. As can be seen in landmark court decisions (Higham et al. 2023), such as the German Federal Constitutional

[38] COM (2022) 222 final.

[39] Council Regulation (EU) 2022/2577 of 22 December 2022 laying down a framework to accelerate the deployment of renewable energy, OJ L 335, 29.12.2022, pp. 36–44.

Court's climate decision,[40] fundamental rights may provide a strong argumentative basis for ensuring climate protection and therefore a safety net against the risks of policy change that could hinder the fight to preserve the climate.

On the other hand, attemps to address climate change problems through the application of existing provisions, such as the constitutional rules for environmental protection or fundamental liberties, may encounter significant difficulties. Due to the specific characteristics of the climate change problem, such as in particular the lack of clear causal relationships or or the fact that the risks faced concern primarily future generations, standing requirements,[41] uncertainties in proof of causation, or even dogmatic uncertainties related to the protective functions of fundamental rights (Sachs 2021, Calliess 2023), may create obstacles with regards to effective climate protection. Therefore, the current debate on climate constitutionalism (Ghaleigh et al. 2022), focuses on the necessity to establish new, specific constitutional norms for climate protection. The basic idea is that such provisions echo fixed constitutional commitments (Levy 2022), ensuring a sound legal basis that can lead to the institutional change considered necessary to establish climate change mitigation as a permanent obligation of high priority guiding towards the restructuring of the economy.

References

Brown Weiss E (1992) In fairness to future generations and sustainable development. Am Univ Int Law Rev 8(1):19–26. https://www.futuregenerations.gi/uploads/docs/Edith%20Brown%20Weiss.pdf

Calliess C (2023) Umweltpolitik im Grundgesetz, Staatsziel des Article 20 a GG und Grundrechte nach dem Klimabeschluss des BVerfG, JuS 2023:1–9

Calliess C, Hey C (2013) Renewable energy policy in the european union: a contribution to meeting international climate protection goals?. In: Ruppel OC, Roschmann C, Ruppel-Schlichting K (eds) Climate change: international law and global governance, volume II: policy, diplomacy and governance in a changing environment, 1st edn. Nomos Verlagsgesellschaft mbH, German, pp 477–528

Choudhury B (2021) Climate change as systemic risk. Berkeley Bus Law J 18(2):52–93

Ghaleigh NS, Setzer J, Welikala A (2022) The complexities of comparative climate constitutionalism. J Environ Law 34(3):517–528

Hardin G (1968) The tragedy of the commons. Sci New Ser 162:1243–1248

Higham C, Setzer J, Narulla H, Bradeen E (Mar 2023) Climate change law in Europe, What do new EU climate laws mean for the courts? Policy report. https://www.lse.ac.uk/granthaminstitute/wp-content/uploads/2023/03/Climate-change-law-in-Europe-what-do-new-EU-climate-laws-mean-for-the-courts.pdf

Hodgson G (2006) What are institutions? J Econ Issues 40(1):1–25

[40] BVerfG, Order of the First Senate of 24 March 2021-1 BvR 2656/18 etc., (ECLI:DE:BVerfG:2021:rs20210324.1bvr265618), available online: https://www.bundesverfassungsgericht.de/SharedDocs/Entscheidungen/EN/2021/03/rs20210324_1bvr265618en.html;jsessionid=A9D79F57F94C9BB270132BF1DC5AD5D0.2_cid354.

[41] ECJ Judgement of 25 March 2021, *Armando Ferrão Carvalho and Others v. The European Parliament and the Council*, C-565/19 P, ECLI:EU:C:2021:252, para 67–72.

Iliadou E (2021) Energy law—current challenges and the role of the State, Nomiki Bibliothiki, Greek, pp 20–24
Koehl A (2022) What is climate change legislation?. Availiable via LSE. https://www.lse.ac.uk/granthaminstitute/explainers/what-is-climate-change-legislation/
Kulovesi K, Oberthur S (2020) Assessing the EU's 2030 climate and energy policy framework: incremental change toward racial transformation? Rev Eur Comp Int Environ Law 29(2):151–166
Levy R (2022) Fixed constitutional commitments: evaluating environmental constitutionalism's 'New Frontier', 46 Melb.U.L. Rev.: 82–122
MacNeil I, Esser IM (2022) From a financial to an entity model of ESG. Eur Bus Org Law Rev 23:9–45
Mazzucato M (2014) The entrepreneurial state: debunking public vs. private sector myths. Anthem Press
OECD (2022) Policy guidance on market practices to strengthen ESG investing and finance a climate transition. OECD Business and Finance Policy Papers, OECD Publishing, Paris. Accessed 09 Apr 2023
Peel J (2008) Climate change law: the emergence of a new legal discipline, 32 Melb.U.L.Rev.: 922–977
Sachs M (JuS 2021) † Grundrechte: Klimawandel, pp 708–711
Setzer J, Higham C (2022) Global trends in climate change litigation: 2022 Snapshot. Grantham Research Institute on Climate Change and the Environment. Available via LSE. https://www.lse.ac.uk/granthaminstitute/publication/global-trends-in-climate-change-litigation-2022
Skjaerseth JB (2016) Linking eu climate and energy policies: policy-making, implementation and reform. Int Environ Agreem: Polit, Law Econ 16(4):509–524
Shellenberger M, Nordhaus T (2004) The death of environmentalism: global warming politics in a post-environmental world. Availiable via JSTOR. https://grist.org/article/doe-reprint/
Schenck LM (2008) Climate change crisis - struggling for worldwide collective action. Colo J Int'l Envtl L & Pol'y 319(19):319–334
Talus K (2016) Introduction to EU energy law. Oxford University Press
United Nations Environment Programme (UNEP) (2011), Setting the stage for a green economy transition. https://wedocs.unep.org/handle/20.500.11822/22005?show=full

The Future Dimension of the German Basic Law—Constitutionally Justifiable Consequences for Social Security Law?

Toni Fickentscher

Abstract The article is devoted to the question of the extent to which the German constitution recognizes an intertemporal safeguarding of freedom which, after closer examination, must be affirmed, particularly with consideration of the "duty to protect"—dimension of the fundamental rights. So, the fundamental rights of the German constitution are always to be understood more and more functionally; a need for protection can therefore also only arise in the future. Based on the famous decision of the Federal Constitutional Court from March 2021 regarding climate change, it will be then especially examined whether any conclusions can be derived in terms of social law with regard to the protection of future generations.

1 Introduction

The question about the responsibility of today's generation for the future generation has gained in importance and sharpness with the arrival of the discussion in the broad society about how to deal with and counteract the consequences of climate change. In addition, the rapidly advancing technological development contributes to this both positively (the determinability of future developments) and negatively (the increased risk potential of new types of technologies), although, admittedly, a changed sense of responsibility in society, at least as broadly communicated, also sharpens the focus on these issues. For some time now, this discussion has no longer been taking place at the political and social level alone, but is increasingly being based on constitutional law, as the German Federal Constitutional Court's decision on climate change[1] illustrates.

[1] Federal Constitutional Court (FCC), decision of 24.3. 2021, 1 BvR 2656/18.

T. Fickentscher (✉)
Amberg, Germany

R. Arnold and T. Fickentscher (eds.), *The Responsibility of a Constitution for the Future*, https://doi.org/10.1007/978-3-031-65296-7_13

2 A First Classification: An Inconsistent Picture

The extent to which a future dimension is inherent in the German Basic Law cannot be answered clearly at first glance; rather, a disparate picture emerges:

On the one hand, the provision in the preamble to the Basic Law already indicates that the state has a responsibility for the future, to be derived from the constitution, by stating the demand for "awareness of its responsibility before God and mankind". Responsibility is taken over for the future; it is confessed over a period of time.[2] So, although the preamble has no direct effect, it can be said that it shows the Constitution reaches beyond the present and has the protection of future generations in mind, thus it contains an orientation toward the future.[3]

Furthermore, Article 20a of the Basic Law explicitly mentions that the state is also responsible for protecting the natural foundations of life and animals for future generations. In other words, this mandate, which is addressed to all three state powers, states in its very wording that the constitution not only recognizes an orientation towards the future, but also urges the state to act responsibly to that end. This provision thus indicates that constitutional protection relates to the present and the future; the interests of future generations must be taken into account today as a yardstick.[4] Against the claim that this provision is not part of the catalog of fundamental rights, nor is it provided for in Article 93 para 1 No. 4a of the Basic Law as a right that can be challenged by constitutional complaint—the provision is purely a state objective—,[5] it can be argued that it is sufficiently effective by its very nature as it does not require an individual link to function.[6]

Besides, the law on public debt (cf. Article 115 of the Basic Law) has the effect of protecting future generations by ensuring a fair distribution of the economic burden.[7]

On the other hand, beyond the present point, unborn human beings are not basically subject of fundamental rights, meaning that they are not protected subjectively by fundamental rights.[8] Without a subject, however, there exists no individual right to be thought of in the future.[9] In addition, the principle of popular sovereignty is laid down in Article 20 para 2 of the Basic Law, which conflicts with a temporal dimension of the Basic Law in such a way that the future generations cannot make sovereign decisions, thus they cannot exert any influence on state power and, therefore, the state power itself can only be thought in present terms.[10]

---

[2] Hofmann, Rechtfragen der atomaren Entsorgung, p. 270 et seqq.

[3] Dreier, in Dreier, Kommentar GG, Präambel recital 42.

[4] Also already for instance: Epiney, in v. Mangoldt/Klein/Starck, GG Kommentar, Article 20a recital 30; Appel, Staatliche Zukunfts-und Entwicklungsvorsorge, pp. 121–122; Kloepfer, Verfassungsrecht, § 4 recital 6.

[5] FCC, decision of 24.3.2021, 1 BvR 2656/18, recital 112.

[6] Appel, Staatliche Zukunfts-und Entwicklungsvorsorge, p. 120.

[7] To this closer for example: Mückl, in Festschrift Isensee, p. 182 et seqq.

[8] FCC, decision of 24.3.2021, 1 BvR 2656/18, recital 109.

[9] Concisely: Murswiek, Die staatliche Verantwortung für die Risiken der Technik, p. 207.

[10] Pointing out this contradiction: Hofmann, ZRP (1986), 87, 88.

Furthermore, as a concrete counterexample, reference could be made to Article 14 para 1 sentence 1 of the Basic Law, according to which the right of inheritance is ensured. Thus, one could read from this guarantee that the Basic Law is based solely on a present understanding and protection of freedom, because the testators have the right to decide on their own quality of life and possibilities, as well as on those of their potential heirs, by deciding on the use of money, which makes freedom possible, without having to keep future aspects in mind.[11]

Apart from that, Article 79 para 1 and 2 of the Basic Law declares precisely the Basic Law to be amendable under certain conditions. In this respect, a temporal limit to its validity can be read into the fact that it can be amended, which in other words would have to lead to a denial of an intertemporal function. However, by way of relativization, it should be pointed out at the same time that Article 79 para 3 of the Basic Law stipulates that an amendment to the Basic Law that affects the principles laid down in Articles 1 or 20 of the Basic Law is inadmissible. This provision is also recognized as a "guarantee of eternity". In this respect, it can be interpreted as meaning that certain principles are considered to be unalterable, which in turn expresses a temporal, future dimension: If something is declared to be unalterable, even eternal, this is to continue to apply forever—i.e. precisely also in the future.[12] By declaring that it is inadmissible to amend the principles listed, they are thus given a significance that goes beyond the status quo and is intended to be valid forever, i.e. also for future generations, even though the established law can only claim validity for as long as the state constituted by this constitution exists (cf. Article 146 of the Basic Law).[13]

3 The Interpretation and Function of Fundamental Rights as an Expression of an Intertemporal Dimension

The Human Rights Content of the Constitution

Pursuant to Article 1 para 2 of the Basic Law, the Constitution recognizes inviolable and inalienable human rights as the foundation of every human community, of peace and of justice in the world, thus placing the fundamental rights of the Basic Law in the context of international human rights guarantees.[14] This underlines, at the same time, the fact that fundamental rights are interpreted in the light of international human

[11] Provocative to this extent: Cf. Mückl, in Festschrift Isensee, p. 184.

[12] Also e.g.: Ibid. p. 203; Hofmann, ZRP (1986), 87, 88.

[13] In this respect, however, it is not convincing to relativize the eternity clause due to the dependence on the constitutional power as a reason for argumentation, but so Hofmann, Rechtsfragen der atomaren Entsorgung, p. 260. Since the present investigation is based precisely on the existence of this one constitution. To put it bluntly: Without the Basic Law, the present question would not arise at all.

[14] FCC, decision of 19.5.2020, 1 BvR 28,535/17 recital 94.

rights guarantees.[15] In this respect, it is also important to use this context when defining the terms inviolability and inalienability, which are not very illuminating per se: The Déclaration des droits de l'homme et du citoyen of 1789 describes human rights as "imprescriptibles, " meaning that they are not subject to a statute of limitations. This is a concrete expression of the temporal dimension of human rights. In other words: The fact that they are not subject to a statute of limitations signifies that they are temporally unlimited in their validity and binding effect. Rather, the argument of a temporal expiry cannot be objected to the freedom expressed in human rights; instead, it is precisely the consideration of freedom interests arising in the future that must be derived from this.[16]

The Protective Effect of Fundamental Rights

The fundamental rights of the German Basic Law are initially to be understood as subjective rights, i.e. as defensive rights of the citizen against the state, which can be asserted individually by constitutional complaint (cf. Article 93 para 1 No. 4a Basic Law). However, according to the prevailing opinion, only living persons have the capacity to exercise fundamental rights, and thus also to lodge a complaint; unborn persons cannot yet assert any possible infringement of their fundamental rights. Consequently, no future relationship of the constitution can be derived from question of the fundamental rights' capacity to be exercised, i.e. the personal side of the fundamental rights.[17]

At the same time, however, the Basic Law is also an objective set of values that influences all areas of the German legal system. The fundamental rights therefore have an objective character, the effect reaching beyond protection in relation to an individual person.[18] From this objective dimension, the Federal Constitutional Court then also derives the constitutional duty of the state to protect the individual from violations of fundamental rights (so-called duty to protect).[19] In this respect, the present question can only be answered correctly if the functions of fundamental rights are precisely separated.[20] This is because the objective protection dimension of fundamental rights is, by its very nature, intrinsically related to the future: it obliges the holder of public authority to avert or mitigate impairments of fundamental rights that may arise in the future. The duty to protect demands positive action on the part

[15] Ibid. recital 95 with further reference to the jurisprudence.

[16] Hofmann, Rechtsfragen der atomaren Entsorgung, p. 267 et seqq.

[17] Cf. FCC, decision of 24.3. 2021, 1 BvR 2656/18, recital 108.

[18] Concisely in: FCC, vol. 7, 198, 205–206. In detail on the character of fundamental rights e.g. Starck, in v. Mangoldt/Klein/Starck, Kommentar GG, Article 1 recitals 157 et seqq.

[19] See for instance: FCC, vol. 39, 1, 41–42; 49, 89, 141–142; 53, 30, 57; 125; 39, 78. Cf. to this perfection of function of fundamental rights as a consequence of norm efficiency: Arnold, in Arnold, The Protection of the Environment and Constitutional Law, p. 90 et seqq.

[20] Already considering this distinction as decisive in the present context: Hofmann, Rechtsfragen der atomaren Entsorgung, S. 261.

of the state, which in this respect can only be genuinely in the future. This is to be distinguished from the case where the already existing impairment, on the other hand, has already solidified into an infringement that affects the content of a fundamental right as a right of defense. The establishment of a set of values, the elevation of certain protected interests to constitutional rank, only makes sense if they apply not only in the present but also in the future.[21]

Future generations receive protection, therefore, because the objective content of fundamental rights already induces the state to take or refrain from taking measures that would lead to an unreasonable impairment of the defensive side of the fundamental rights of future generations. Thus, a look at the objective function of fundamental rights alone shows that the Constitution not only knows about a future orientation, but considers it in essence to be one of its characteristics. The fact that unborn generations lack the capacity to exercise fundamental rights cannot therefore limit the state's responsibility for the future, which can be derived from the constitution.[22] Only with such a view can the constitutional guarantees be adequately respected: For in the case of an active state measure, the group of addressees is not necessarily fixed; in order to maintain the effectiveness of the protection of fundamental rights, it is necessary in this respect to have a functioning approach that is detached from an individually determinable group of persons affected, which consequently also does not have to be temporally delimitable.[23] In this respect, the Federal Constitutional Court itself speaks of an "intergenerational obligation to protect".[24]

Such an understanding of fundamental rights corresponds to the identity and essence of a constitution itself. For, by its very nature, it is not final and fixed, but evolves over time, with the identity growing and changing in the same way. It is a living instrument[25]; it adapts to the realities of the world and to people's ways of life. Thus, the community is to be kept functional via its organizational dimension. In the present context, however, this means at the same time that it only corresponds to this meaning if a future-oriented dimension is also attributed to it. Otherwise, it would only do justice to part of the community if it ignored the future concerns of at least younger generations. In other words: It would contradict its nature and its power of organizational connection if it were to disregard future effects.

In this respect, a constitutional legislator always has in mind that the constitution is designed for continuity, meaning that it is intended for an indefinite period of time. The norms are thereby also designed to steer acceptance. Otherwise, the constitution would not be suitable as a permanent instrument. In other words, it wants to express in a continuous form how society is constituted. If, however, the constitution is reduced

[21] Cf. Appel, Staatliche Zukunfts- und Entwicklungsvorsorge, pp. 117–118.

[22] Concisely: Hofmann, Rechtsfragen der atomaren Entsorgung, pp. 261–262. Like this also for instance: Murswiek, Die staatliche Verantwortung für die Risiken der Technik, p. 207.

[23] Hofmann, ZRP (1986), 87, 88.

[24] FCC, decision of 24.3. 2021, 1 BvR 2656/18 recital 146.

[25] This expression, taken from international jurisprudence (see Grabenwarter/Pabel, Europäische Menschenrechtskonvention, pp. 39–40), can be applied to the Constitution.

to a present perspective, there is a risk that it will increasingly meet with a lack of acceptance—at least in parts of society—and that it will ultimately be abandoned.[26]

The Scope of Protection

The extent to which the existing state action is sufficient to meet the requirements of the (intertemporally effective) duty to protect can in principle only be controlled to a limited degree by the courts.[27] This is because, in contrast to the defensive dimension of fundamental rights, which is linked to a more precisely definable measure in terms of goal and content, the duty to protect is fundamentally indeterminate.[28] Instead, the legislature has a margin of appreciation in setting up and implementing a concept of protection.[29] At the same time, the Federal Constitutional Court also assumes a global dimension to the duty to protect, since its effects cannot be resolved solely at the national level, as it were, but only at the international level.[30]

In any case, the Federal Constitutional Court's determination of a violation of the duty to protect is limited to cases in which the measures taken are evidently unsuitable or completely inadequate to achieve the purpose of protection.[31] Applying this to the present issue, it means that the duty to protect is not subject to a time limit, but to a factual limit—the foreseeability and determinability of the relevant factual bases.[32]

It remains to be emphasized that the duty to protect does not fail even if the danger cannot be averted at all. Rather, the obligation under fundamental rights requires that measures be taken for an appropriate adjustment.[33]

The Principle of Proportionality

The Basic Law requires the equal provision of fundamental rights-protected freedom over time. In other words, this means the proportionate distribution of freedom opportunities across the different generations, i.e. that present generations do not exercise their freedom unduly at the expense of future generations, but that an equal degree of freedom exists in the future.[34]

---

[26] Arnold, in Arnold, The Protection of the Environment and Constitutional Law, p. 93.

[27] FCC, decision of 24.3. 2021, 1 BvR 2656/18, recital 152 with further reference to the jurisprudence.

[28] Ibid. recital 152.

[29] Recently: Ibid. recital 152 with further reference to the jurisprudence.

[30] Ibid recital 149.

[31] Exemplarily: Ibid. recital 152 with further reference to the jurisprudence.

[32] Murswiek, Die staatliche Verantwortung für die Risiken der Technik, p. 207.

[33] FCC, decision of 24.3. 2021, 1 BvR 2656/18, recital 150, 164.

[34] Ibid. recitals 183, 192.

Future conditions develop an "intervention-like pre-effect",[35] which leads to an impairment of "future freedom".[36] In this respect, an intertemporal balancing of the present use of freedom with the interest in freedom in the future must take place, which, incidentally, must correspond to the other basic decisions of the Basic Law,[37] such as with the already mentioned Article 20a Basic Law.[38]

In concrete terms, CO_2 emissions pose a threat to future freedom in the sense that generations in the future may be increasingly forced to restrict emissions, i.e. to restrict individual behavior for this purpose, since such interests are not currently taken into account to the same extent.[39]

In this respect, therefore, future restrictions on freedom have to be anticipated in the present, so that they remain reasonable in the future.[40] In other words: The principle of proportionality thus already requires that an appropriate balance be struck between present and future impairments of liberty between the generations.[41]

4 Conclusions Regarding the Social Insurance Systems

With regard to social security systems, the main question concerning the future is their financial viability, which applies in particular to pension insurance.[42]

The Actual Starting Situation

The pension insurance system is based on the idea of a contract of solidarity between the generations: Current working people provide for the pensions of older, retired people, and thus at the same time acquire a right to their own pensions vis-à-vis subsequent, working people as soon as they themselves retire from working life due to age.

As a result of demographic change and the increased life expectancy of people, leading to more and more pensioners drawing their pensions for longer while at

---

[35] Ibid. recitals 184, 187.

[36] Ibid. recitals 186, 192.

[37] Ibid. recital 188.

[38] Ibid. recital 190.

[39] Ibid. recital 186.

[40] Ibid. recital 192.

[41] Ibid. recital 192. See also: Arnold, in Arnold, The Protection of the Environment and Constitutional Law, p. 93 et seqq.

[42] Thus also rightly situating: Becker, NJW (2022), 1222, 1225.

the same time the number of contributors is declining, the current pension insurance system is reaching its limits.[43] In view of the future dimension of the Basic Law described above, this raises the question of the extent to which a constitutional mandate can already be derived for the benefit of future generations of pensioners—precisely because of the Federal Constitutional Court's climate decision—to the effect that their social insurance protection also remains secure after they leave working life, meaning that the system does not collapse to their detriment.

Intergenerational Justice as an Intertemporal Constitutional Mandate in the Context of Social Insurance

According to the explanations given above, to establish a constitutionally justified claim to the adaptation of social security systems to the problems to be expected, it would in any case be a prerequisite that here, too, time alone would lead to irreversible results or adverse restrictions. The circumstances on the basis of which a relevant impairment of fundamental rights or a violation of the duty to protect are justified must be tangible and not too uncertain in order to be able to derive an intertemporal, temporally anticipatory protection of fundamental rights.[44]

However, this is not the situation here. In the case of the climate protection resolution, the passage of time alone establishes such facts. Although the demographic development itself may be irreversible, this does not yet lead to the irreversibility of the threat to old-age security per se.[45] Rather, it remains open to the state to take new measures at any time. In other words, the occurrence of the impairment (cf. the defensive dimension) or the prevention against the danger (cf. the protective dimension) can be solved—no matter how serious or necessary—by other financial (fiscal) compensations and reallocations, in particular by moving away from pay-as-you-go financing, whereas this is no possible in the same way in the case of climate protection.[46] Here, in other words, the passage of time alone establishes facts that violate fundamental rights.[47]

Another argument in favor of a lack of a comparable situation is that the current system of pension insurance is not constitutional obligatory by its very nature. In other words, there is no constitutional guarantee that social insurance systems in their conventional form are constitutionally guaranteed, especially with regard to their organizational design.[48] Thus, if the choice of the form of coverage cannot

[43] See recent statements by the President of the Federal Social Court: https://www.tagesschau.de/inland/rente-bundessozialgericht-praesident-101.html; last accessed Feb. 10, 2022.

[44] In this context also: Becker, NJW (2022), 1222, 1224.

[45] But like this: Kirchhof, Intertemporale Freiheitssicherung, p. 44 et seqq.

[46] Also: e.g. Faßbender, NJW (2021), 2085, 2089.

[47] Likewise: Becker, NJW (2022), 1222, 1224.

[48] FCC, vol. 39, 302, 314–315.

be derived from the constitution at all, a fortiori no modification in favor of an intertemporal protective effect can be claimed.

The protection of the future in the area of social insurance law has a different connecting factor, which was already constitutionally justified before the climate protection decision[49]: In general, the constitution requires that social security systems operate effectively, meaning if there is already compulsory insurance, then it must also provide essential protection, which was justified both with the defense-law dimension and with the duty-to-protect dimension of fundamental rights. In concrete terms, there is a protection of freedom in the sense that there must be a proportional balance between the contributions of the policyholders and the benefits they can claim.[50]

Applied to the present question, this in turn means that current generations should not have to pay too high contributions, while receiving disproportionately low pensions in old age. In other words: It would be incompatible with the proportional intergenerational distribution of freedom if future generations were burdened with excessive contributions and taxes in order to finance the system, while the current generation had to pay low contributions.[51]

Even the Federal Constitutional Court itself mentioned the word "intergenerational justice" in the context of its decision on pension insurance law regarding the absence of pension increases as an essential criterion to ensure the financial stability of the public pension insurance system in order to protect the intergenerational contract, i.e. for future generations.[52] This is particularly true in light of the fact that in today's society, freedom based on wealth is no longer represented primarily by private real assets, but rather by the solidarity-based security systems. In other words: Entitlements from pension insurance take the place of private provision.[53] In short, it is the idea of the intergenerational contract that establishes a link between the future and the present and thus allows an intertemporal dimension to emerge.[54]

In concrete terms, according to the fundamental decision of the Federal Constitutional Court, acquired pension rights are now regarded as property within the meaning of Article 14 of the Basic Law, whereby the property guarantee in particular is closely linked to personal freedom, which can only be restricted in a proportionate manner, since it enables the subject of the fundamental right to shape his life on his own responsibility by providing security in terms of property law.[55] Accordingly, in view of Article 14 in conjunction with the principle of equality under Article 3 of the Basic Law, the generations now entering the world of work must be entitled to an appropriate countervalue for their payments when they retire, whereby a devaluation of

[49] Concisely highlighted by Becker, NJW (2022), 1222, 1226.

[50] FCC, vol. 115, 25, 42–43.

[51] Schlegel, NJW (2021), 2782, 2788; Kirchhof, Intertemporale Freiheitssicherung, p. 48, 51.

[52] FCC, decision of 3.6.2017, 1 BvR 79/09 recital. 56.

[53] FCC, vol. 53, 257, 290.

[54] Kirchhof, Intertemporale Freiheitssicherung, p. 43.

[55] FCC, vol. 53, 257, 289–290.

their pension entitlements must be prevented,[56] although a proportionate compensation can also be achieved in the future by paying a corresponding financial equivalent to the pension entitlement, while preserving the intertemporal protective effect.[57]

5 Conclusion

The fundamental rights of the Basic Law contain an intertemporal protection concept. The understanding of fundamental rights is thus moving more and more in the direction of a functional approach to protection: Where disproportionate impairment exists or the state has not adequately fulfilled its duty to protect, in other words, a need for protection arises, that is where the values expressed in the fundamental rights come into play. The principle of proportionality, expressed through the fundamental rights of Article 14 in conjunction with Article 3 of the Basic Law, provides adequate protection for future generations of pensioners against an unfair distribution of contributions.

At the same time, a constitution is not designed to solve every single political and social issue itself. Rather, such a task is assigned to the legislature, which has a certain degree of regulatory freedom in this regard. In this context, this is particularly relevant in view of the fact that the future is to a certain extent unpredictable. In concrete terms, the constitutionally justifiable and enforceable intertemporal protection mandate must be handled restrictively. Within the framework of the objective guarantee, this is already recognized by the prohibition of inadequacy. However, when examining the extent to which present and future freedoms can be balanced, the same restraint must be exercised to ensure that legislative freedom is only corrected in the event of complete inadequacy.

References

Appel I (2005) Staatliche Zukunfts- und Entwicklungsvorsorge, Tübingen

Arnold R (2022) Comparative law studies, volume 15, the protection of the environment and constitutional law. Regensburg (cited as: Author, in: Arnold, The Protection of the Environment and Constitutional Law)

Becker U (2022) Der Klimaschutz, das BVerfG und die Zukunft des Sozialstaats. NJW, 1222

Depenheuer O, Heintzen M, Jestaedt M, Axer P (2007) Staat im wort: festschrift für Josef Isensee, Heidelberg (cited as: Author, in Festschrift Isensee)

Dreier H (2013) Grundgesetz kommentar, 3rd ed, Volume 1 Articles 1–19, München (cited as: Author, in Dreier, Kommentar GG)

---

[56] See, for example: Wendt, in v. Mangoldt/Klein/Starck, Article 115 Rn. 12; Mückl, in Festschrift Isensee, pp. 199–200, although the latter assumes a limited impact; Becker, NJW (2022), 1222, 1226 ("equality in time"); Kirchhof, Intertemporale Freiheitssicherung, p. 43.

[57] This is not fully recognized by Kirchhof, Intertemporale Freiheitssicherung, p. 49.

Faßbender K (2021) Der Klima-Beschluss des BverfG—Inhalte, Folgen und offene Fragen. NJW, 2085
Grabenwarter C, Pabel K (2021) Europäische Menschenrechtskonvention, 7th ed, Basel
Hofmann H (1986) Nachweltschutz als Verfassungsfrage. ZRP, 87
Hofmann H (1981) Rechtfragen der atomaren Entsorgung, Stuttgart
Kirchhof G (2022) Intertemporale Freiheitssicherung. Tübingen
Kloepfer M (2011) Verfassungsrecht, Volume I, München
von Mangoldt H, Klein F, Starck C (2018a) Grundgesetz kommentar, 7th ed, Volume 2 Articles 20–82, München (cited as: Author, in v. Mangoldt/Klein/Starck, Kommentar GG)
von Mangoldt H, Klein F, Starck C (2018b) Grundgesetz kommentar, 7th edition, Volume 3 Articles 83–146, München (cited as: Author, in v. Mangoldt/Klein/Starck, Kommentar GG)
Murswiek D (1985) Die staatliche Verantwortung für die Risiken der Technik, Berlin
Schlegel R (2021) Der Sozialstaat in und nach der Covid-19-Pandemie. NJW, 2782

Printed in the USA
CPSIA information can be obtained
at www.ICGtesting.com
CBHW071910061024
15456CB00001B/34

9 783031 652950